IMAGES
of America

BOURNE

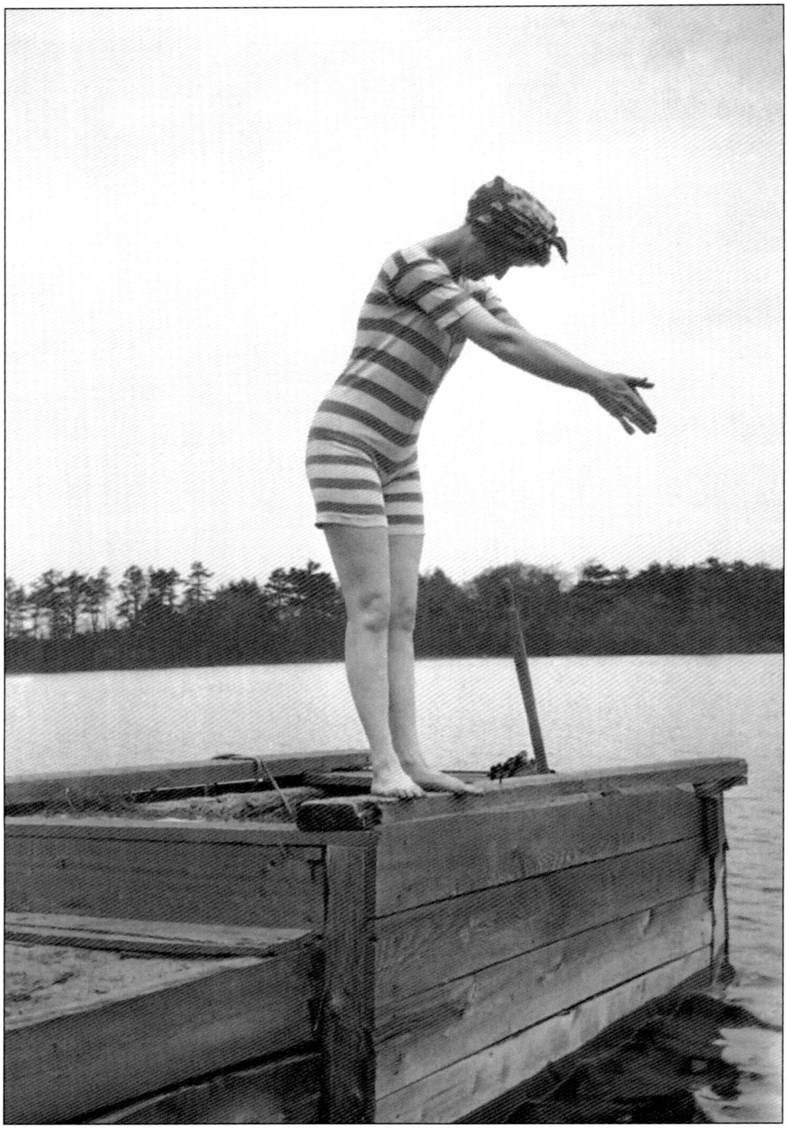

Local photographer Fred Small took this c. 1900 photograph of an unidentified bather in a striped bathing costume preparing to dive into the waters. Small's photographs of the area during the late 1800s and early into the next century document the early years and rugged spirit of Bourne. His photographs of the Cape Cod Canal, from construction to its opening and completion, are iconic. (Courtesy of the Bourne Historical Society and the Bourne Town Archives.)

On the Cover: This c. 1910 photograph shows women and children frolicking in the summertime in the waters of the Cape Cod Canal in Bourne. The family group is part of the growing number of summer visitors that made up the tourist trade, one of the early main industries in the area. While the women and children would come from the cities for the summer, the men of the family would come for the weekends by train, which came to be called the "Dude Train" for its mostly male travelers, and meet their families at the village train stations. (Courtesy of the Bourne Historical Society and the Bourne Town Archives.)

IMAGES of America

BOURNE

Gioia Dimock

ARCADIA PUBLISHING

ISBN 978-1-4671-2198-9

Published by Arcadia Publishing
Charleston, South Carolina

Printed in the United States of America

Library of Congress Control Number: 2013955778

For all general information, please contact Arcadia Publishing:
Telephone 843-853-2070
Fax 843-853-0044
E-mail sales@arcadiapublishing.com
For customer service and orders:
Toll-Free 1-888-313-2665

Visit us on the Internet at www.arcadiapublishing.com

To my granddaughters Skyla, Darby, and Phoebe Hendricks, who mirror the Bourne Historical Society's mission statement for me, "as a bridge from the past to the future." With love.

Contents

ACKNOWLEDGMENTS

The historical community of Bourne includes a multitude of groups and people who have collected and preserved the history of the area from the Native American trails to the Pilgrims, the building of the highway bridges and the Cape Cod Canal, and on into the present day. These groups, including the Bourne Historical Society, the Bourne Town Archives, Bourne Society for Historic Preservation, the Cataumet Schoolhouse Group, and the Pocasset Community Club, have all made this book possible through their hard work.

From the moment I walked into the old Jonathan Bourne Public Library—built by Emily Bourne in 1896 in memory of her father, Jonathan Bourne, for whom the town is named—Bourne Archives director Jean Campbell and Bourne Historical Society executive director Judith McAlister welcomed me and started me on my journey into the history of the town of Bourne, for which I am eternally grateful. I was hooked, and without them this book would not have been possible. I would also like to thank Bourne selectman Donald "Jerry" Ellis and his wife, Beth Ellis, for their confidence in this project and me. Thanks also go to the Ellises for their proofreading skills (Beth) and long memory (Jerry) and to both Judith McAlister and Thelma Rowe Loring for always looking over my shoulder and keeping me on the right historical path. I also want to thank my acquisitions editor at Arcadia Publishing, Caitrin Cunningham, for her guidance and persistence.

I would also like to thank posthumously photographers Fred Small and Ben Harrison. Small took photographs from the late 1800s until approximately the 1920s, and he managed to capture the early life of Bourne and made most of the iconic photographs of the construction of the Cape Cod Canal on eight-inch-by-ten-inch glass plates. Harrison, whose time overlapped with that of Small, documented the town of Bourne through the late 20th century. As a result of the hard work and creativity of these two people, we have an indelible record of what the town was like through the years. Unless otherwise noted, all images in this book are courtesy of the Bourne Historical Society Archives.

INTRODUCTION

In the beginning was the Comassakumcanit tribe whose sachem was Cawnacome. The seat of this tribe was the Herring Pond area, later known as the village of Bournedale, the very heart of the area that would become the town of Bourne. This was the tribe that saved the Pilgrims from starvation in the second year of their sojourn here by providing much-needed corn and other food to keep them through the last of the winter and into spring, when they could plant again. It is where the native trails that crisscross the area converge, namely the Megansett trail that ran south from Plymouth and the Shawme trail that ran from down Cape, north over the Scusset River, and then went towards the west. Although parts of these trails have merged with roads or become overgrown with disuse, they still exist and are in use today (though they look nothing like their ancient counterparts). Thomas Bourne and Richard Tupper also established the first mission to the local people here, and the legendary Bourne Stone was brought to be the doorstep to this mission. Some of the common place-names are in the old language, including Pocasset, the name of the native group that lived in that area, and Aptucxet, which means "little trap in the river" for the system of fishing using fish weirs. Aptucxet is one of the names of the old Dutch Trading Post, which was first established by the Pilgrim colony that was actively trading with the Dutch and the Native Americans by 1627. This trading post, which some call the seat of commerce in the New World, was the place that first used wampum (beads made from purple parts of the quahog shell) as currency between the Dutch, Pilgrims, and native peoples. The tribe, now known simply as the Herring Pond Wampanoag tribe, is part of the current resurgence of native language and customs and maintains its identity to this day.

With European settlement of the area, it became known as Sandwich and South Sandwich and continued to grow for the next 200-plus years.

Fast-forward to 1884, when locals decided that the Sandwich Town Hall was just too far to go for town meetings. They separated from Sandwich, established the town of Bourne, and held their first town meetings in Franklin Hall in Buzzards Bay, then in the Jonathan Bourne Public Library on the south bank of the Monument River. Early industries in the town included the production of salt on Mashnee Island, cranberry growing and harvesting, the production of iron from bog iron found in local ponds, the axe factory in Bournedale, and the Keith Car and Manufacturing Company, which made the first prairie wagons to take pioneers on the westward journey. These wagons made in Bourne took people from the shores of the New World to the far reaches of the continent.

It is a town made up of distinct villages: Bourne, Bournedale, and Buzzards Bay, Cataumet, Pocasset and Monument Beach, and Sagamore and Sagamore Beach. These villages are made up of neighborhoods like Gray Gables, Tahanto, Patuisset, and Mashnee Island, to name just a few. In the early 1900s, these areas all had their own railroad stations, post offices, schoolhouses, and general stores, a convenience for locals and tourists alike. It was a place of larger-than-life people, including US president Grover Cleveland, who spent his summers here; actor Joseph Jefferson, famous for his stage role as Rip Van Winkle; and Jonathan Bourne, who the town is named after, and his daughter Emily Bourne, who built the original library in 1896 to honor him. It is also home to the typical Cape Cod personality—kind of gruff, practical, and down-to-business but generous to a fault. For everyone, there was sand and sun, sailing, boating, and swimming, and abundant seafood, fish, quahogs (thick-shelled clams with purple splotches in the shell), scallops, and lots of lobsters! It has always been and continues to be a place to come when one feels the need to gaze out at the sea, breathe in the salt air, and feel the wonder of life.

One

THE EARLY YEARS

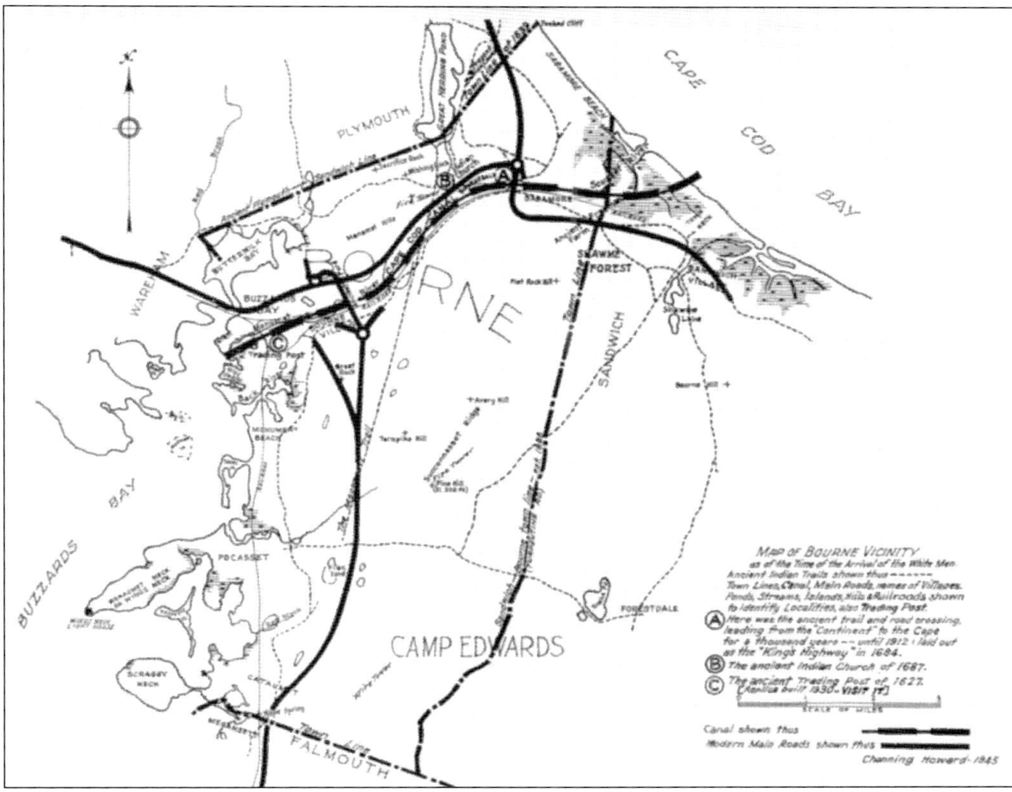

This 1945 map by local author Channing Howard shows the town of Bourne before the building of the Cape Cod Canal and also shows the Native American trails (dotted lines) and ancient sites that ran all through the area before European settlement.

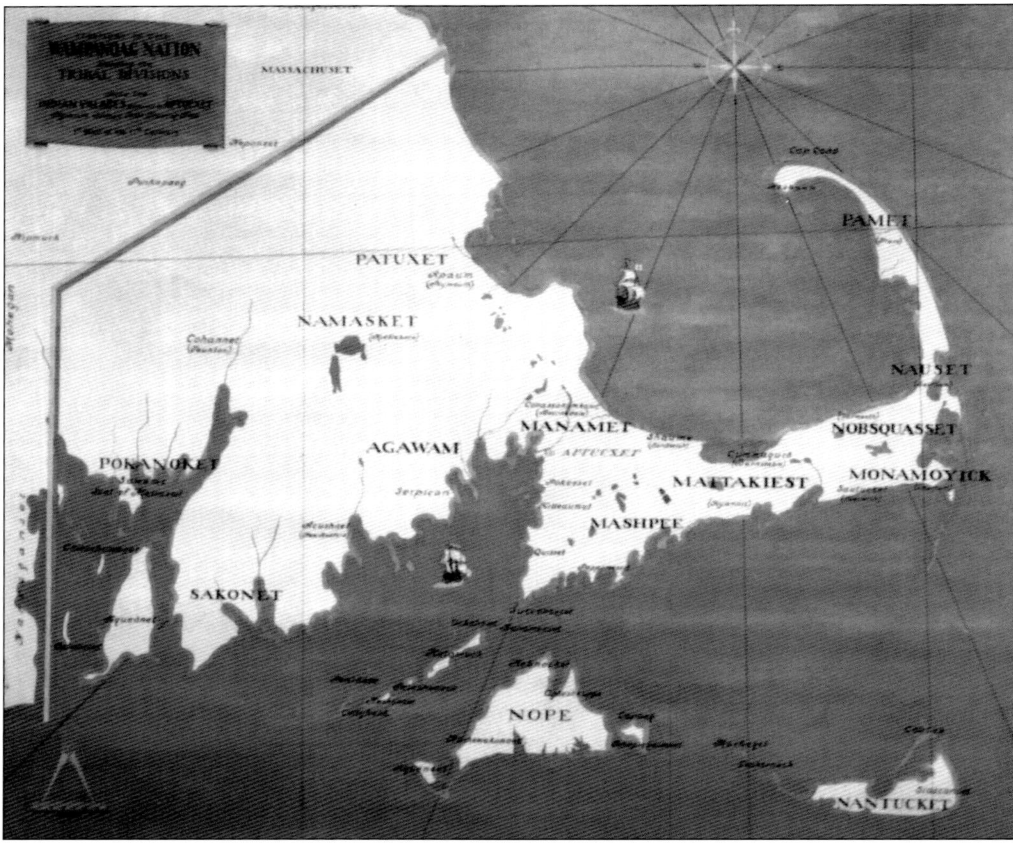

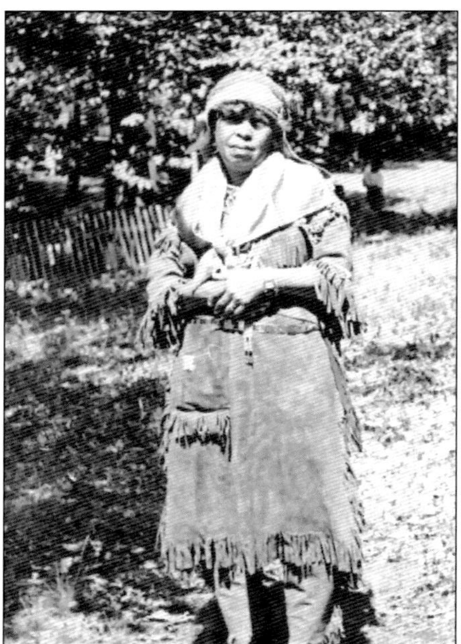

This map shows the Native American tribes that lived in the southeast corner of Massachusetts during the time of the Pilgrims (when the Aptucxet Trading Post was active) and for hundreds, if not thousands, of years before.

Josephine Webquish, Princess Blue Eagle of the Herring Pond Wampanoag tribe, stands in front of Aptucxet Trading Post in Bourne village in her native regalia around 1930.

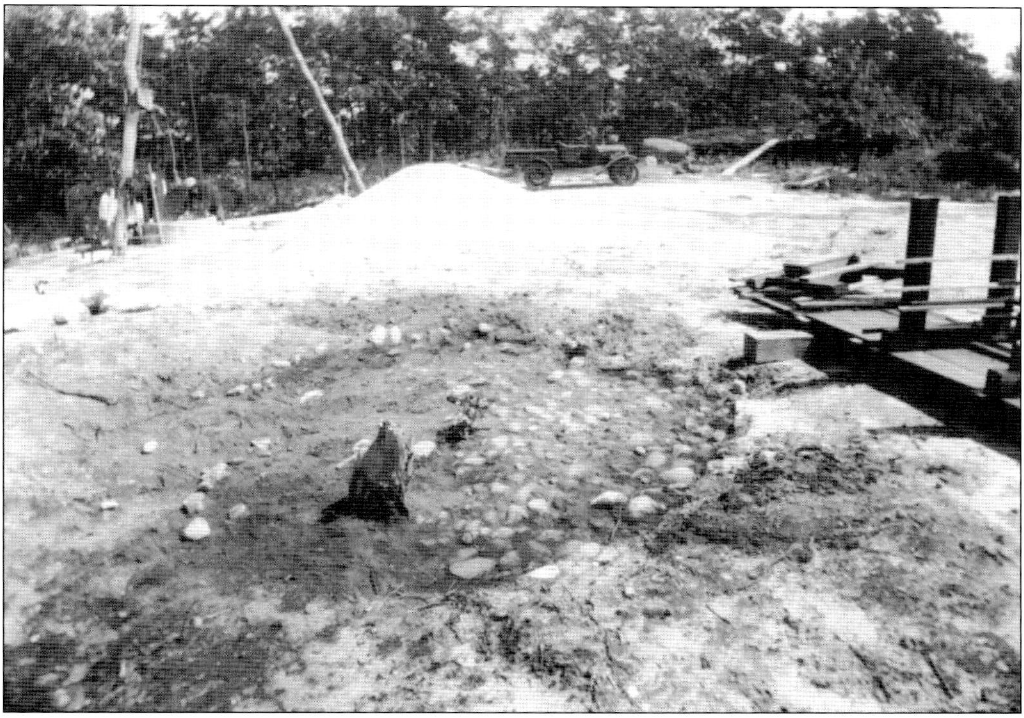

A Native American hearth is discovered during the building of a home for W.H. LaRose in Bourne on August 25, 1931. As European settlement increased in the area, so did the discoveries of the lives of the early inhabitants.

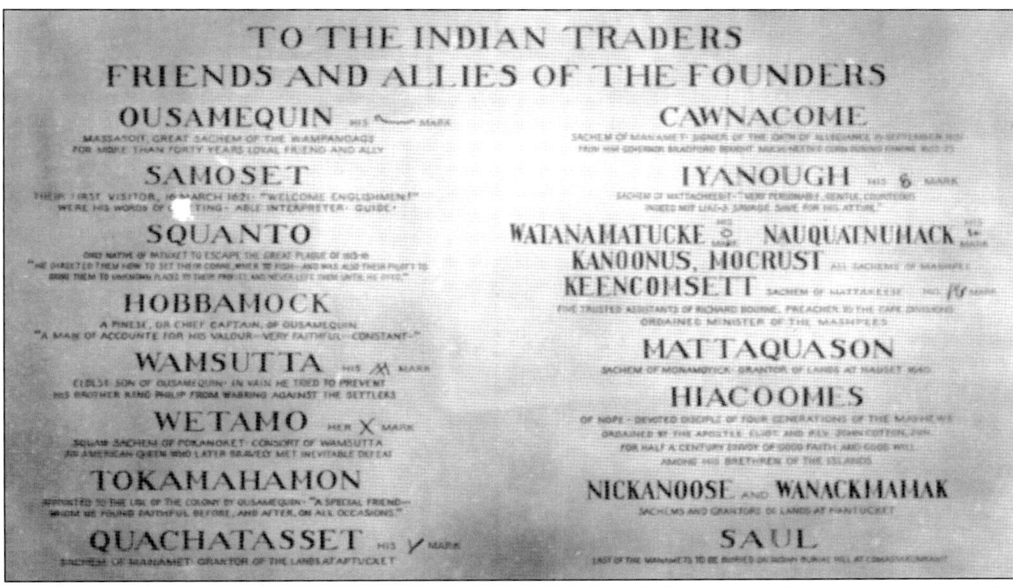

The marks that were the legal signatures used by the early tribal sachems, the native name for the tribes' chiefs, were copied from the book of Indian deeds in the records of the Plymouth Colony, where they were recorded in the early 17th century.

The Bourne Stone, called a rune stone and discovered as the doorstep to the original Bournedale mission to the native peoples, remains a mystery. No one knows who originally brought the stone to the mission, and no one knows what message is hidden in the symbols on it. It has been suggested that it is a Viking rune stone, possibly Phoenician in origin, or a Native American traveling stone.

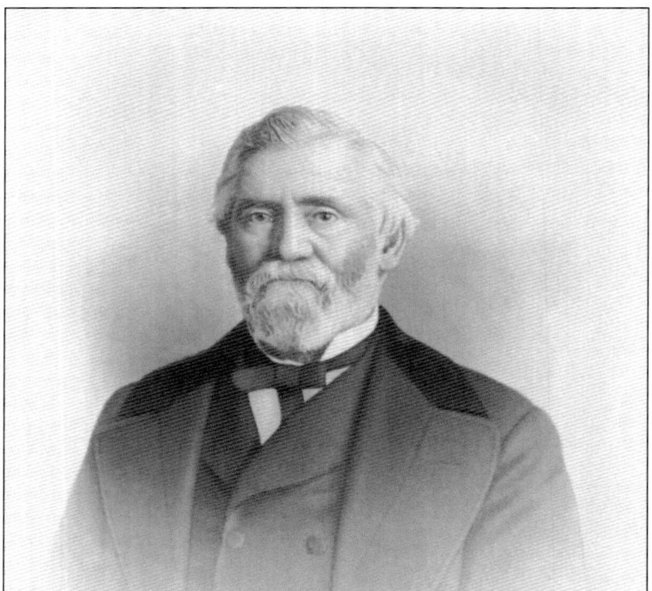

An old woodcut portrait shows Jonathan Bourne (1811–1889), the man for whom the town is named. Bourne donated the bell for the Bourne United Methodist Church but spent most of his time in New Bedford, where he maintained a huge house and was active in the whaling industry. Bourne lived in town until his late teens. His old homestead came down during the building of the Cape Cod Canal.

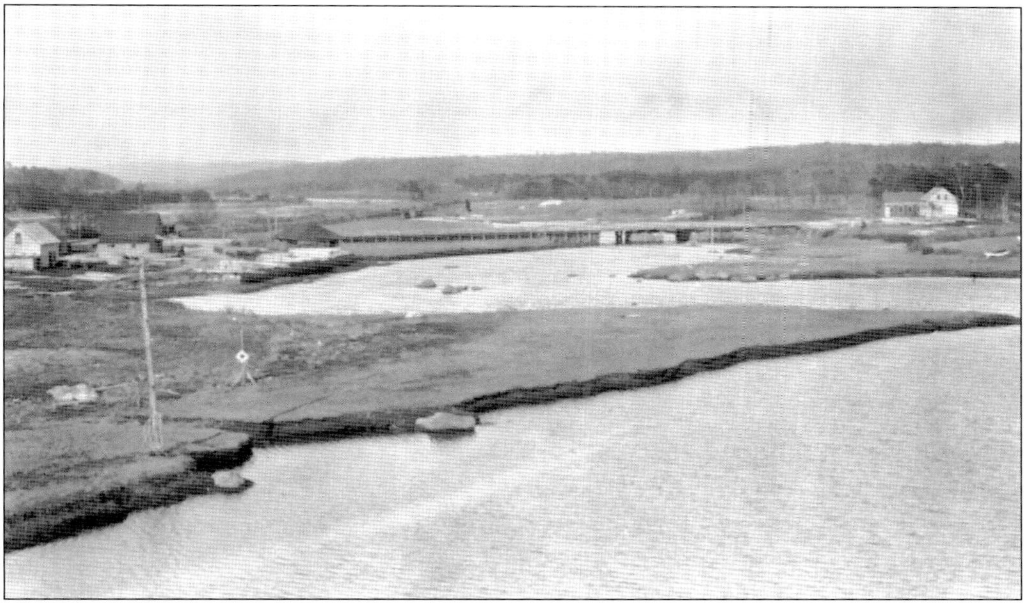

The Monument River winds along from Buzzards Bay and the village of Bourne towards the village of Bournedale and Herring Pond. In this c. 1890 photograph, one can see the original old stone bridge in the center, the welcome center on the right, and Eldridge Lumber on the left bank.

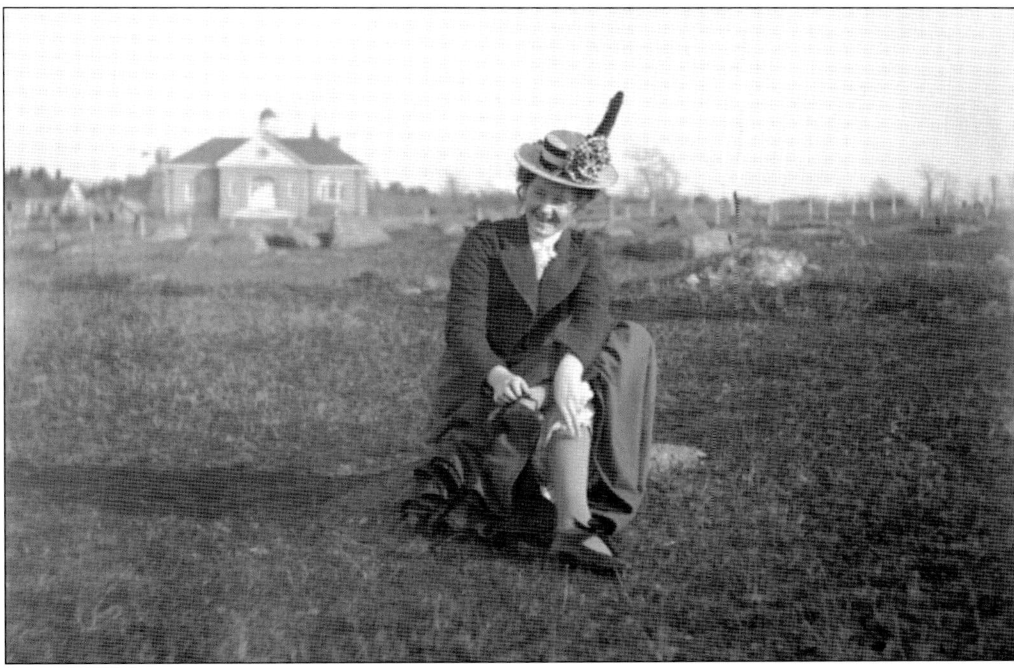

The newly built Jonathan Bourne Public Library makes a lovely backdrop for visitors in this c. 1900 photograph. The library was built by Emily Bourne (1835–1922) as a memorial to her father, Jonathan Bourne. She chose the spot because her father's homestead could be seen across the river, although it came down during the construction of the Cape Cod Canal. It served the town for many years as a library and now houses the Jonathan Bourne Historic Center.

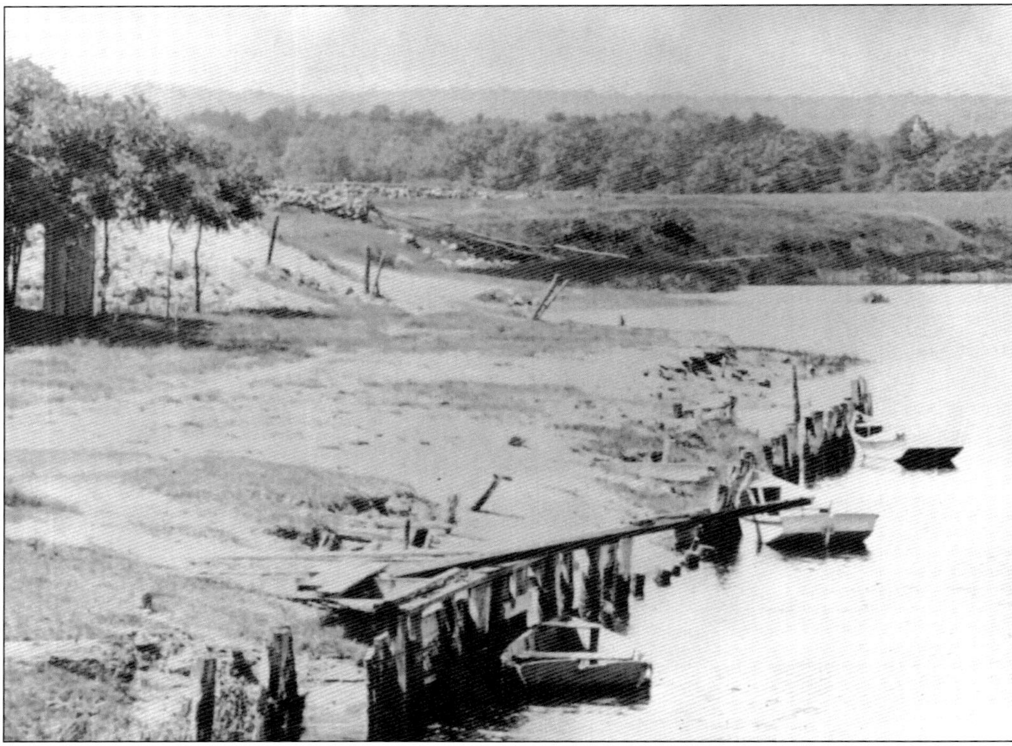

There is a completely different look to Bourne and the Monument River in this photograph of the old town dock from the late 1800s. The area quickly changed with the construction of the Cape Cod Canal and the building boom from Buzzards Bay to Cape Cod Bay that went with it.

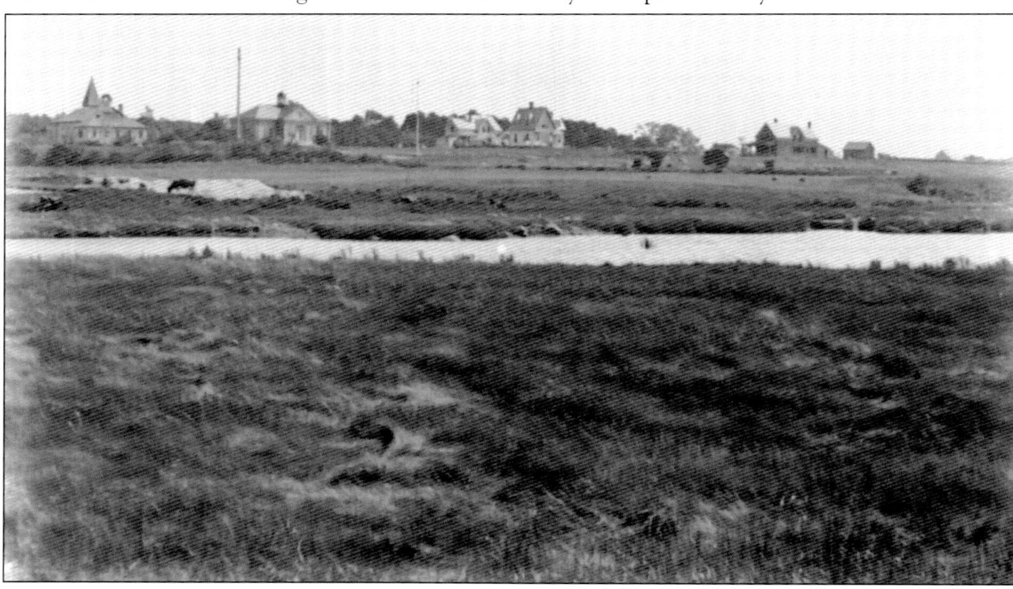

From left to right, the Bourne United Methodist Church, the Jonathan Bourne Public Library, and private homes are viewed from across the Monument River prior to development of the waterway in the late 19th century.

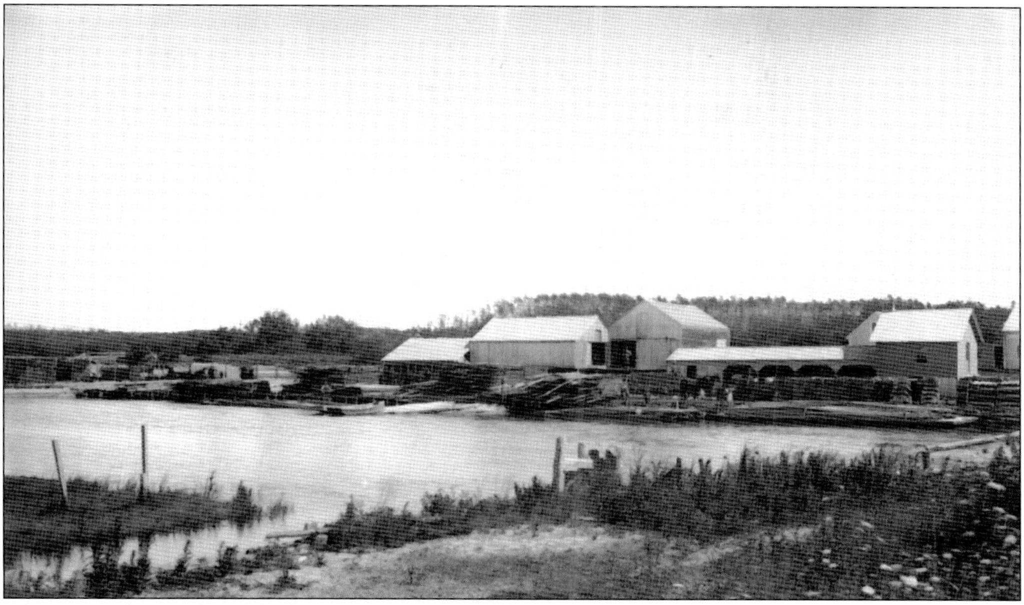

This view shows the Eldridge Lumber Company on the banks of the Monument River when it was still on the south side of the river, prior to 1900. With the building of the Cape Cod Canal, it was moved to the north side.

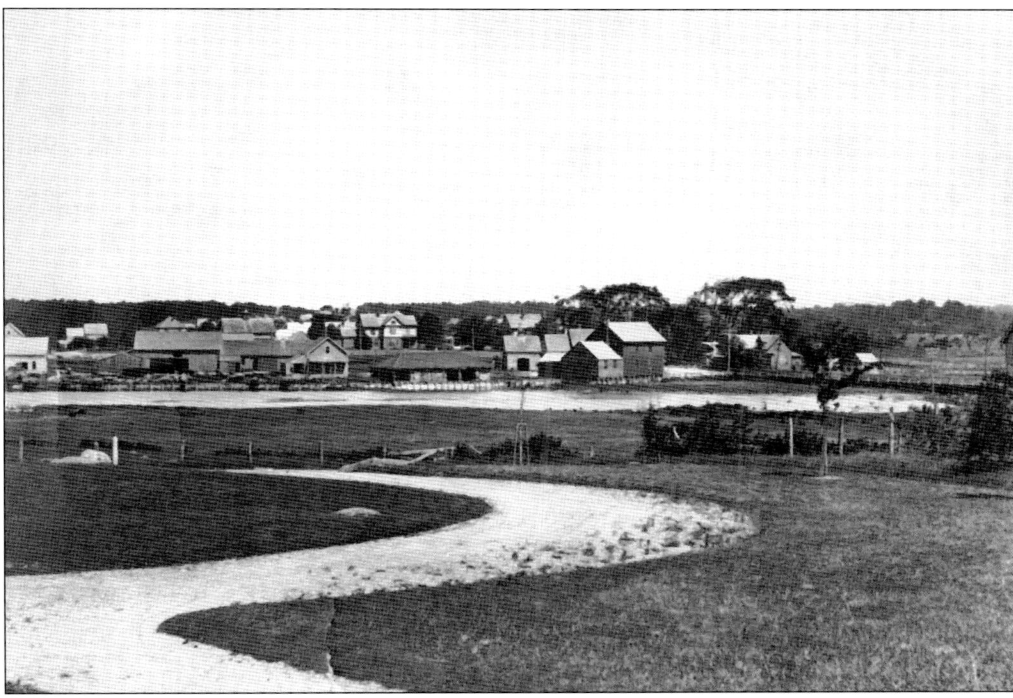

Seen from the front of the Jonathan Bourne Library, the Eldridge Lumber Company is now on the north side of the Monument River around 1913. The company moved to the north side of the river as preparations for the Cape Cod Canal began.

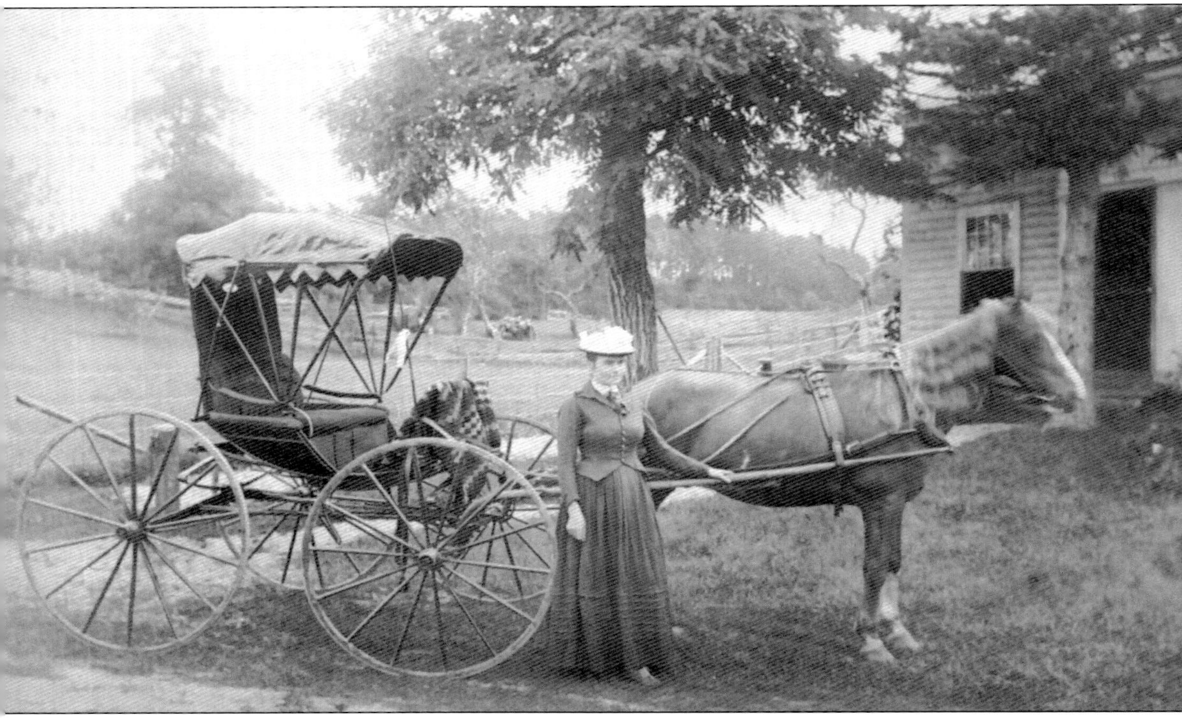

Betsey Keene stands with her horse and buggy in front of the family home on County Road. Keene, a lifelong Bourne resident and well-known woman about town, later wrote *History of Bourne from 1622–1937.*

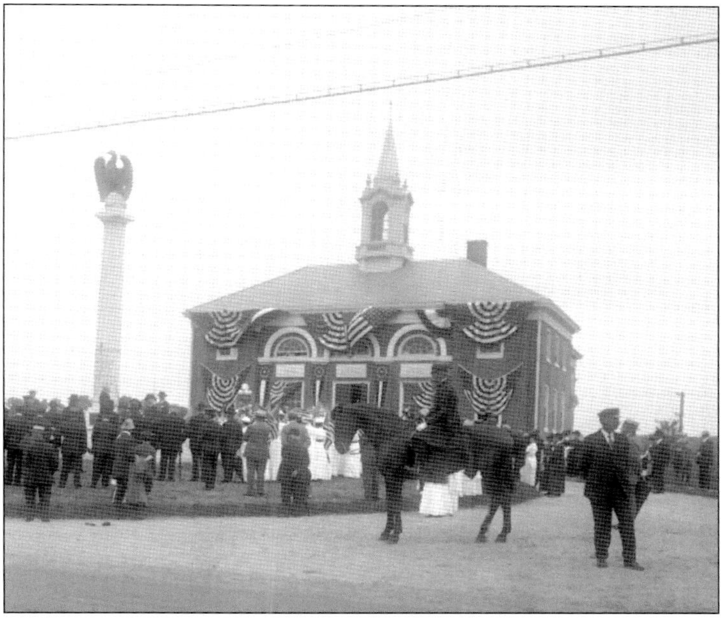

The Bourne Town Hall in Buzzards Bay village is decorated for dedication ceremonies in 1914. The Soldiers and Sailors Monument, dedicated at the same time, is at left. The town hall and monument were made ready to be dedicated during the ceremonies for the opening of the Cape Cod Canal on July 23, 1914.

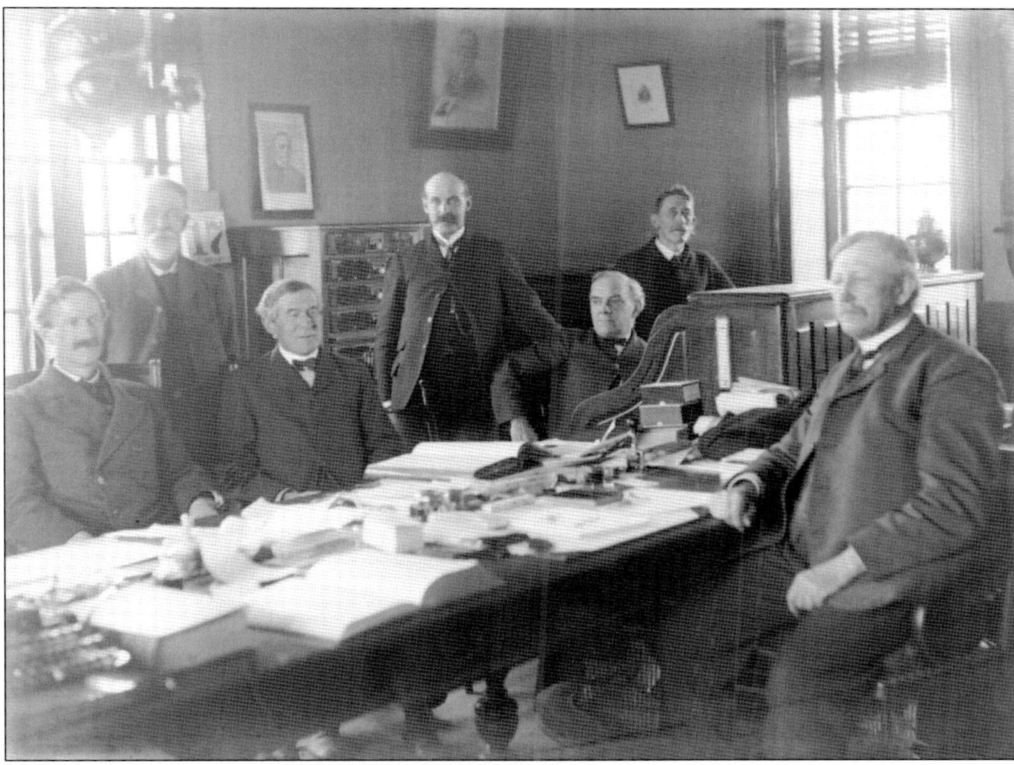

This 1905 photograph shows town officers of Bourne in the Jonathan Bourne Historic Center, where they met before the town hall was built. Pictured are, from left to right, Edward S. Ellis (selectman), Anthony Little (auditor), David D. Nye (selectman), George L. Atherton (selectman), Ordello R. Swift (town clerk and treasurer), Moses W. Daggat (auditor), and George Briggs (selectman).

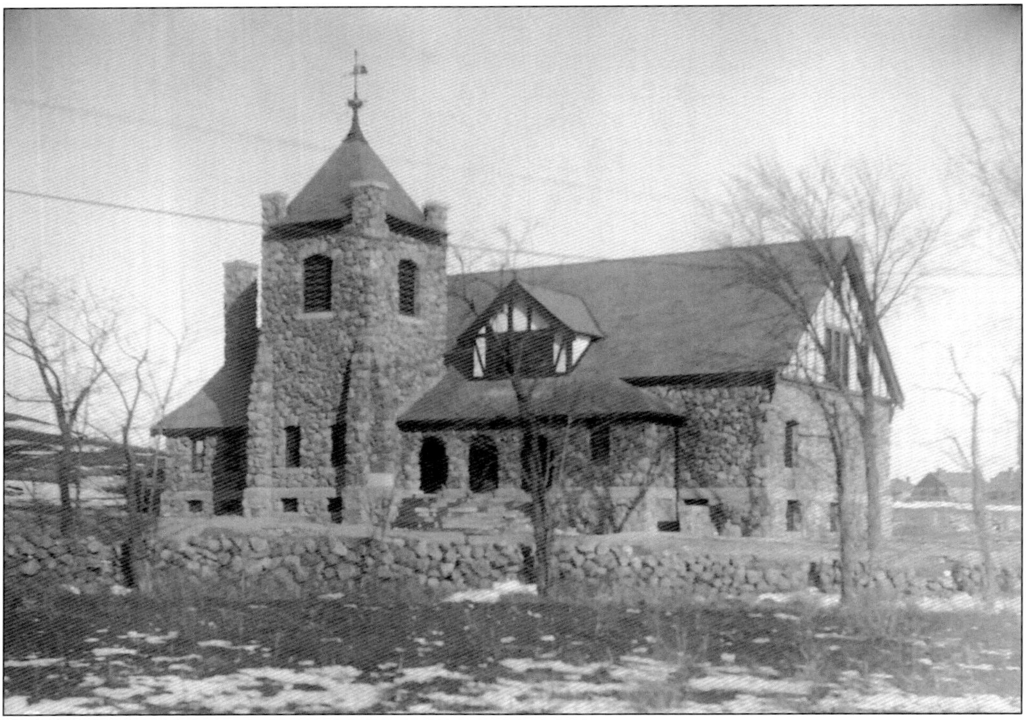

The cornerstone is laid in 1910 for the new Swift Memorial Church in what is now Sagamore Beach. It was named for the Swift brothers, who first drove cattle from the cape to Boston for slaughter and later founded the Swift Beef Company in Chicago. Their donations, in part, funded the stone church that was constructed to replace an earlier incarnation built of wood. The stones used to build the church were taken from the Cape Cod Canal as it was being dug.

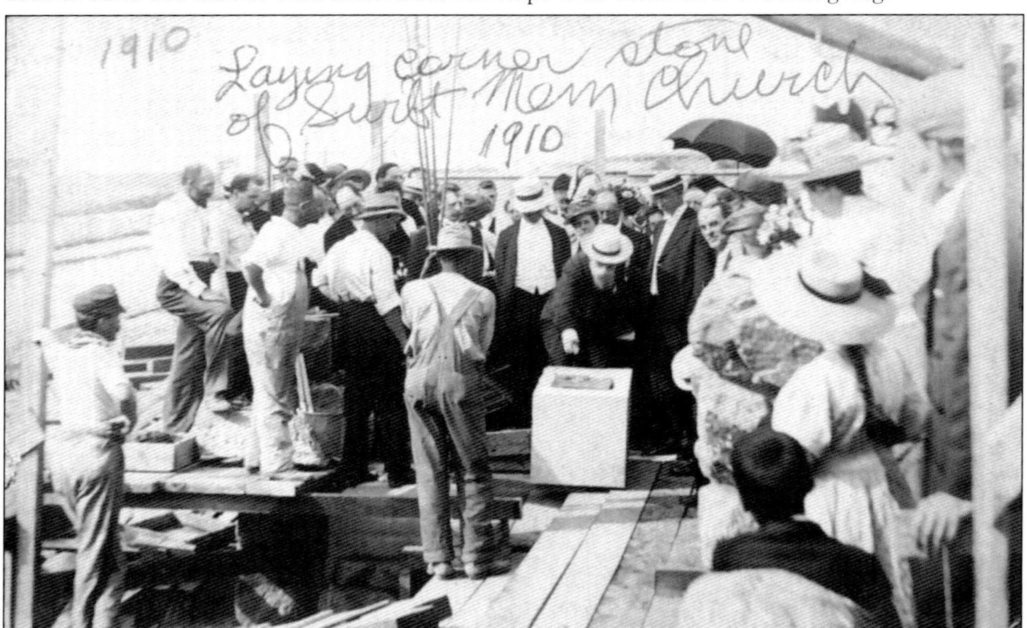

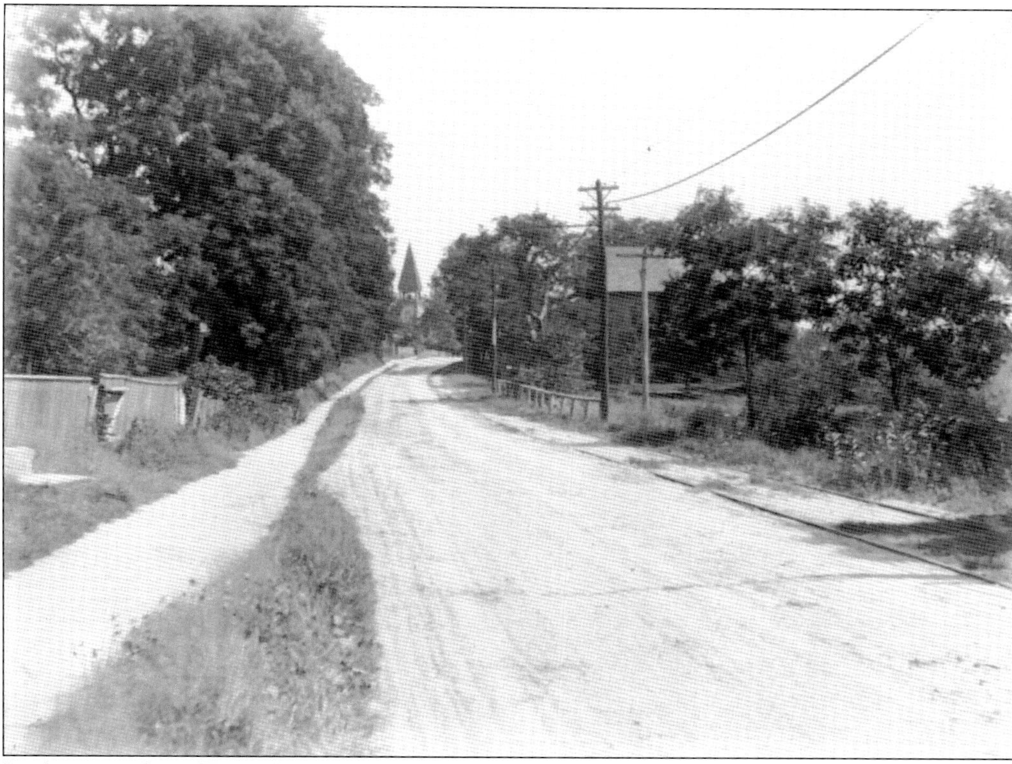

Looking north up Keene Street in 1906, one can see the spire for the Bourne United Methodist Church (left) and, at right, the Briggs-McDermott house. The tracks going up the right of the dirt road are for the trolley, or electric car, that came over the bridge from Buzzards Bay.

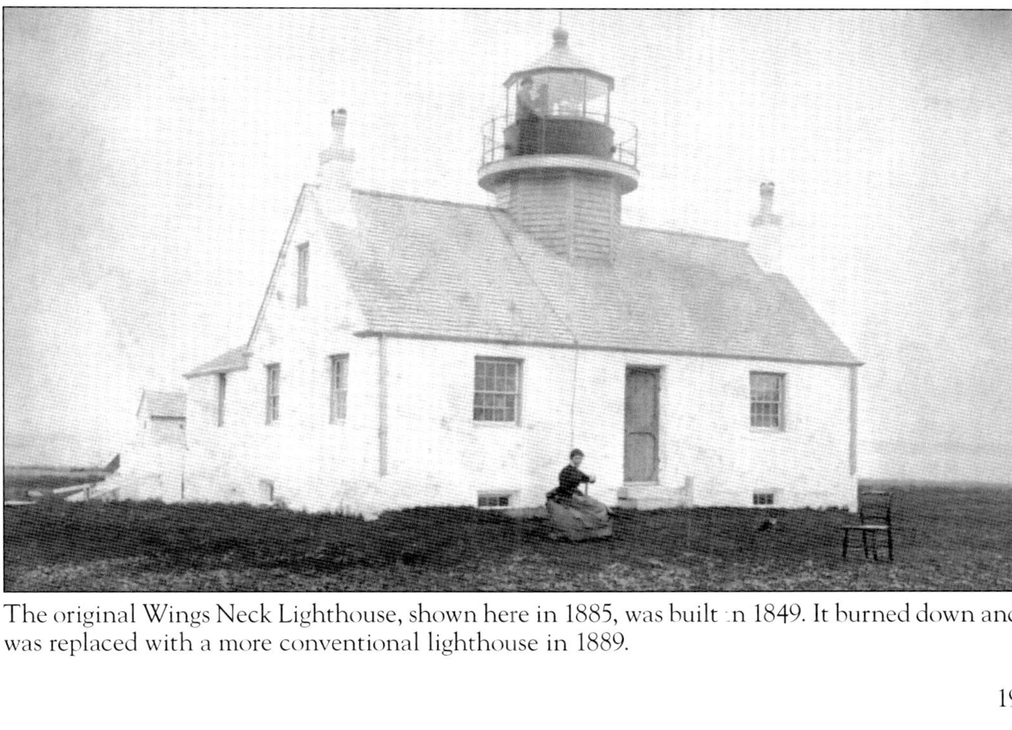

The original Wings Neck Lighthouse, shown here in 1885, was built in 1849. It burned down and was replaced with a more conventional lighthouse in 1889.

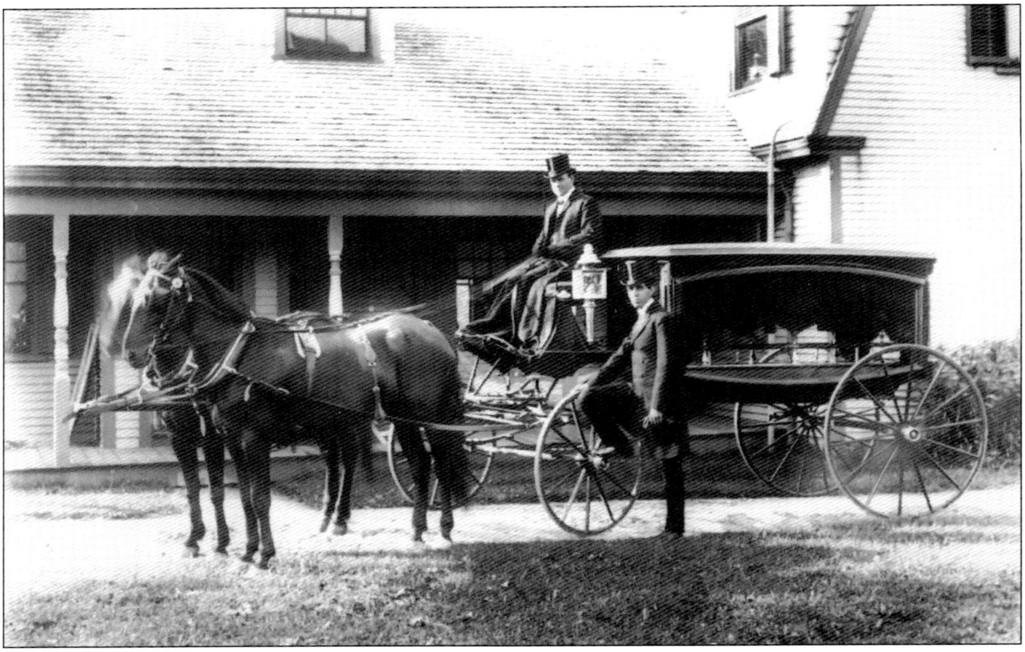

Bourne undertaker Edward "Ned" Nickerson poses in front of his horse-drawn hearse in 1910 in front of the home of Annie Philips on Old Bridge Road. Nickerson was the first undertaker in Bourne and much in demand in those early days. The hearse driver is Bill Sheperdson. The hearse and pair of black horses were hired from the stable of Sanford Irving Morse of Sandwich in 1895.

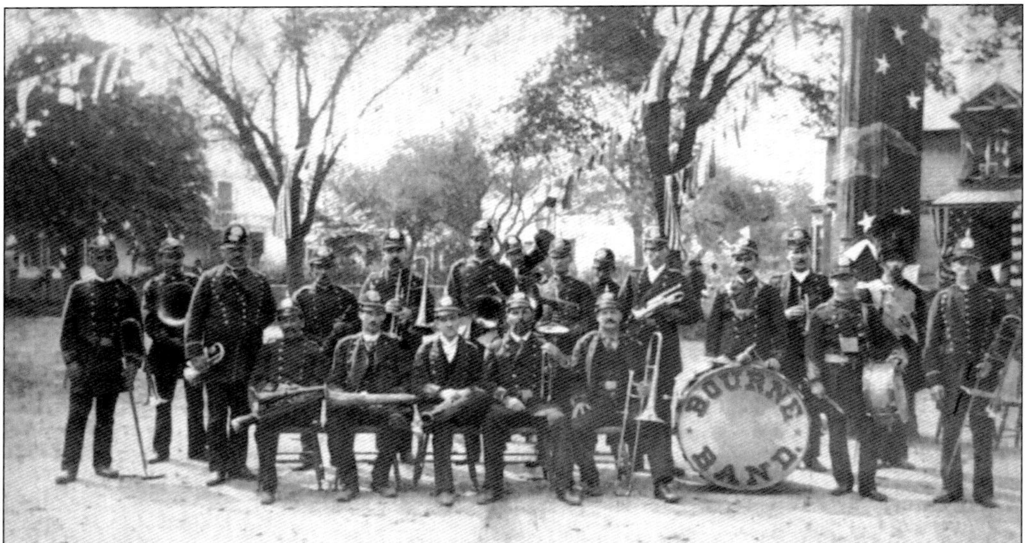

Musicians in the Bourne National Band pose for a photograph after playing in a parade in Sandwich in the late 19th or early 20th century. In 2013, the Bourne Historical Society acquired one of the original hats seen in this photograph. Musicians who are identified include Ordello Swift (far left, with trombone), William Gidley (third from right, with bass drum), F. Eldridge (second from right, with snare drum), and William C. Weeks (far right, with trombone).

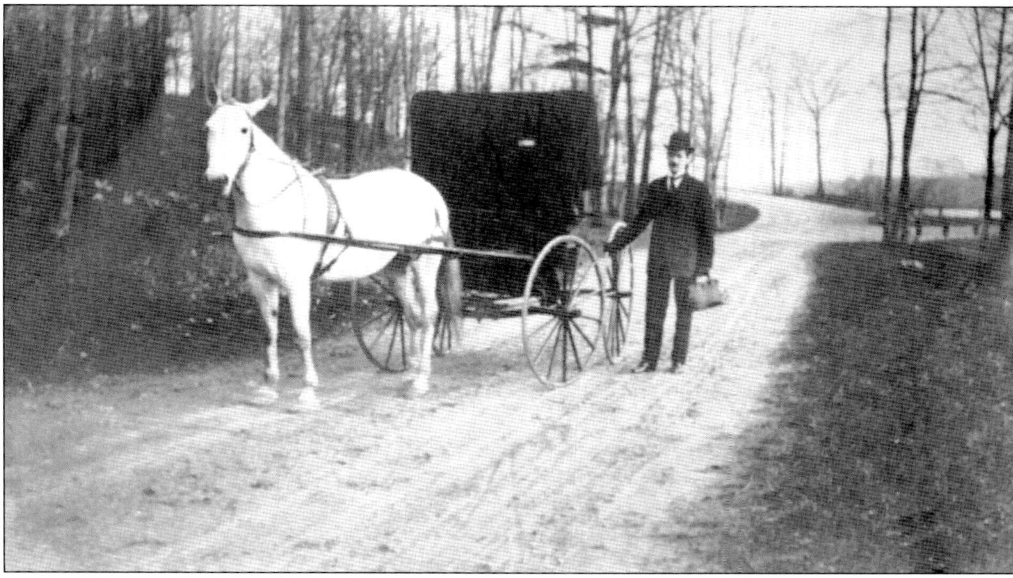

Dr. Ernest Francis Curry, the company doctor for Keith Car and Manufacturing Company, holds his medical bag while standing with his horse and buggy, which took him on his house calls in Sagamore and Sandwich. Curry was a well-known figure in the early 20th century.

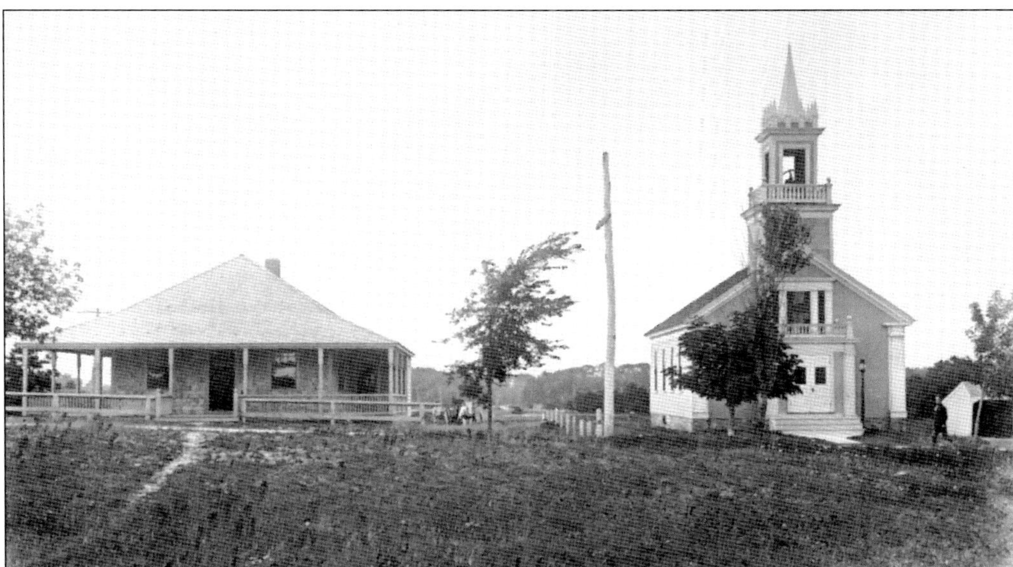

The Travelers Club (left) and the Pocasset Baptist Church stand side by side in this c. 1900 photograph. The Travelers Club building is now the Pocasset Community Club and remains in the same spot, but the church has been moved about 200 yards down the road to a new location.

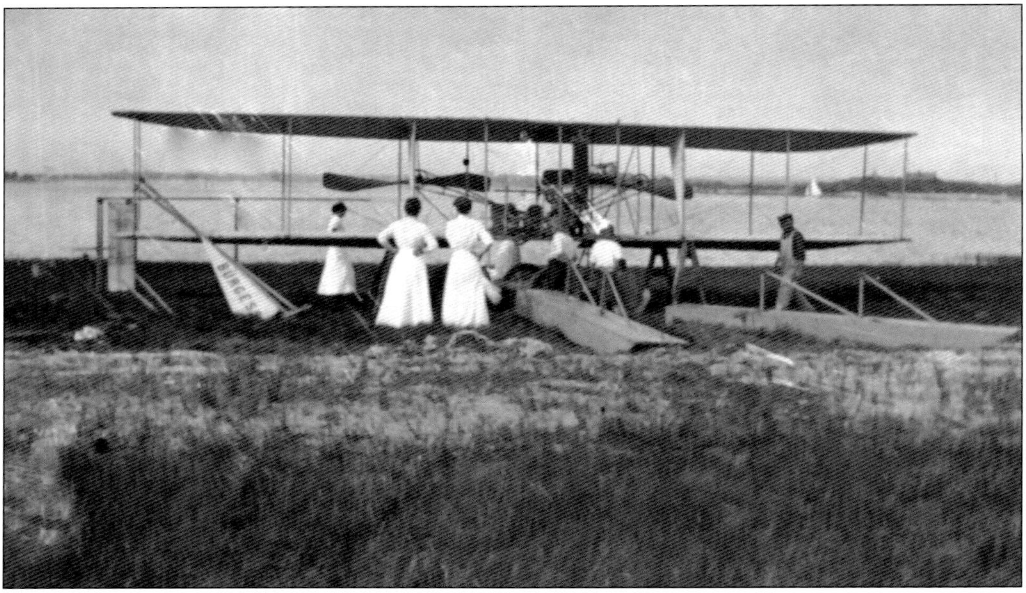

This c. 1910 photograph shows a group of people preparing a biplane for flight on Scraggy Neck in Cataumet. The plane was designed by William Starling Burgess and Augustus Moore Herring, who formed the Herring-Burgess Company and reportedly made the first flight on Cape Cod.

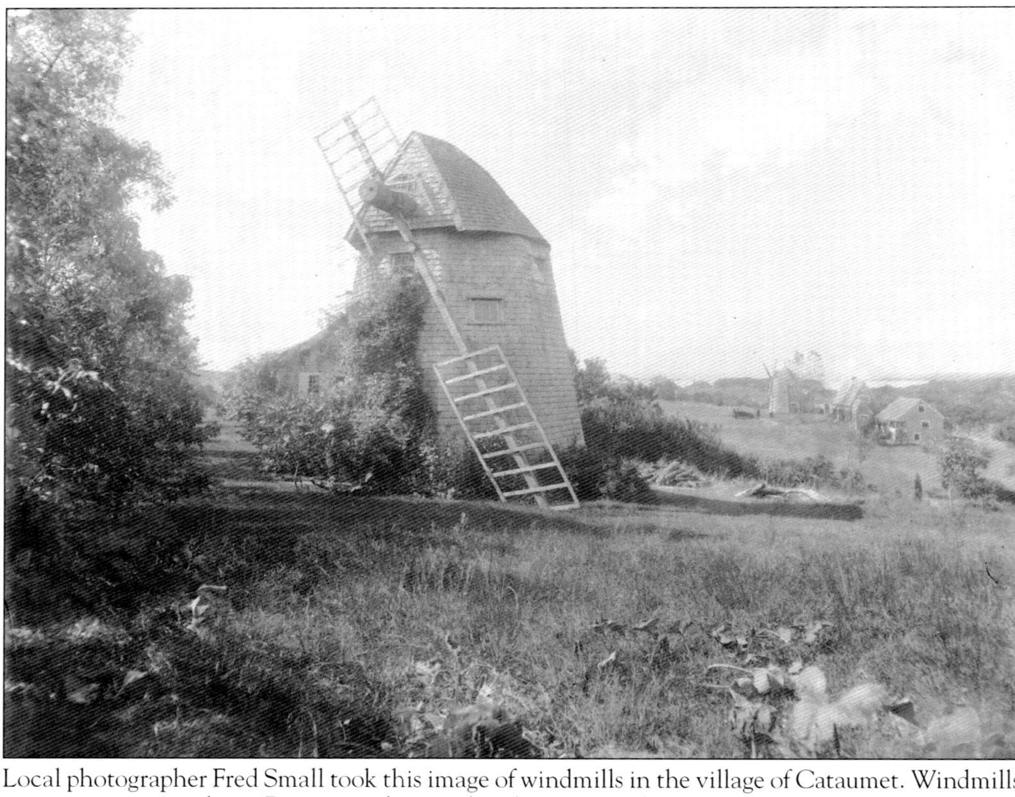

Local photographer Fred Small took this image of windmills in the village of Cataumet. Windmills were a common sight in Bourne and around early Cape Cod in general.

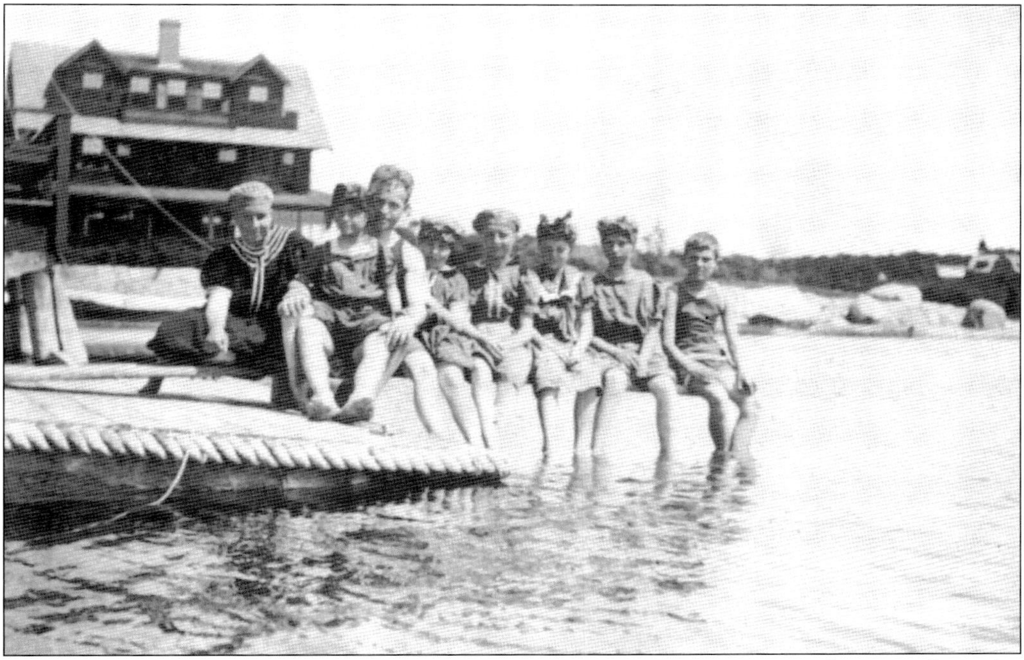

As evidenced by these swimmers all lined up on a dock and ready to get wet, there was fun to be had in the summer in Cataumet village. This photograph would have been taken around 1910 to 1920, as evidenced by the swimming costumes.

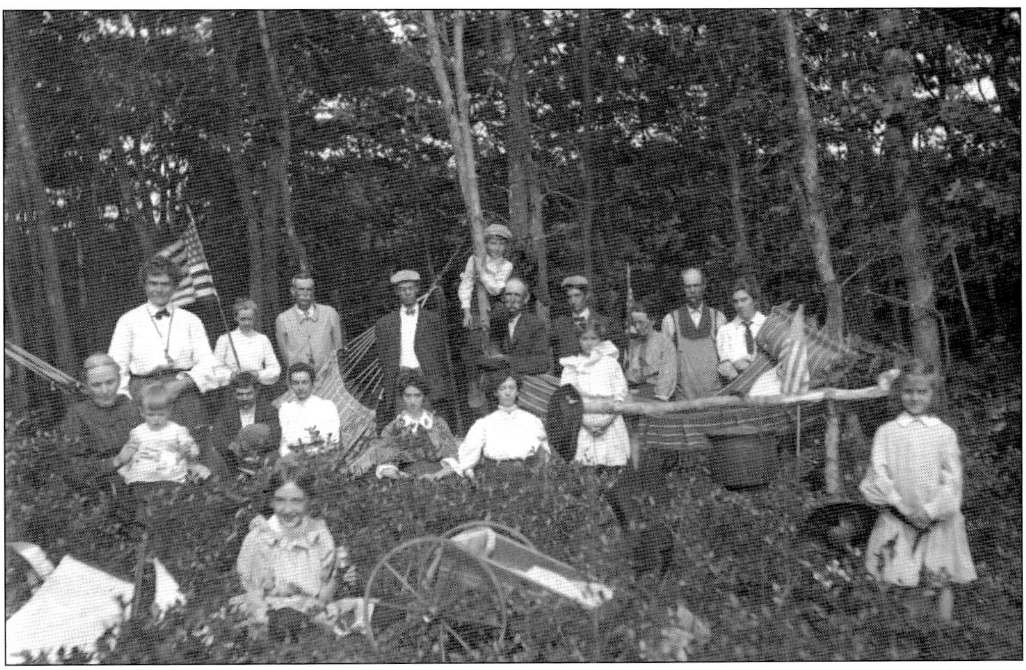

Picnickers pose for the camera during Fourth of July festivities in 1907. Picnics were a favorite summer pastime for visitors and locals alike. A group would hike to one of the scenic locations in and around Bourne, spend the day eating and socializing, and, if lucky, take photographs.

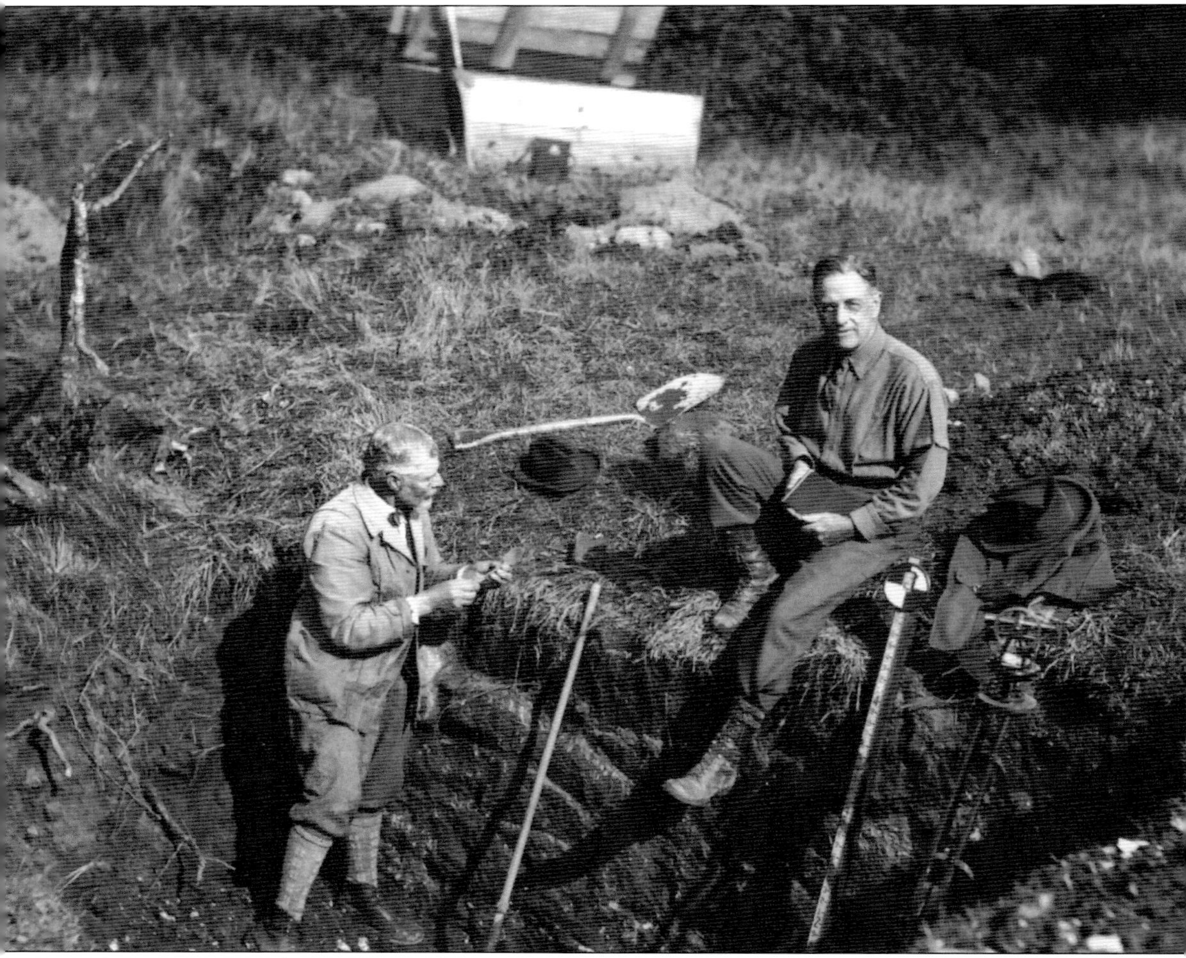

Bourne Historical Society founder Percival Hall Lombard (right) and Nathan Bourne Hartford excavate the cellar holes of the Aptucxet Trading Post in 1926. Hartford holds a colonial spoon found in the dig. The Aptucxet Trading Post, also called the old Dutch Trading Post, was the first trading post of the Pilgrims and was reconstructed by Lombard and Hartford on the old foundations. This is the site where the Pilgrims, including military leader Miles Standish, indentured servant John Howland, and second governor William Bradford, came to retrieve the corn they had garnered from a local tribe. When they saw the site, they knew it would be a great spot for trade with the Dutch New Amsterdam (later New York) colony.

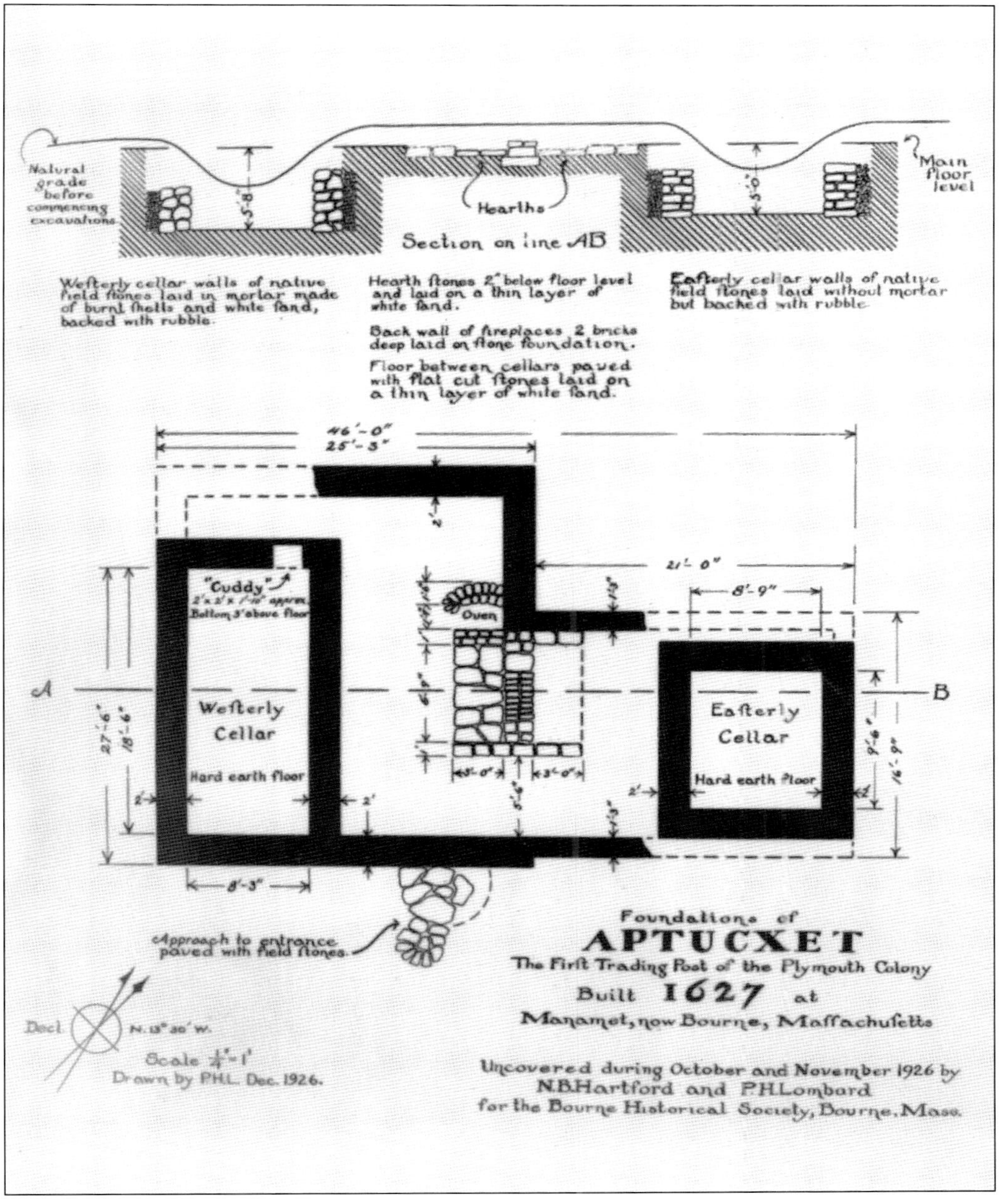

This diagram made by Lombard shows the foundations that were found along with the hearth and doorsteps.

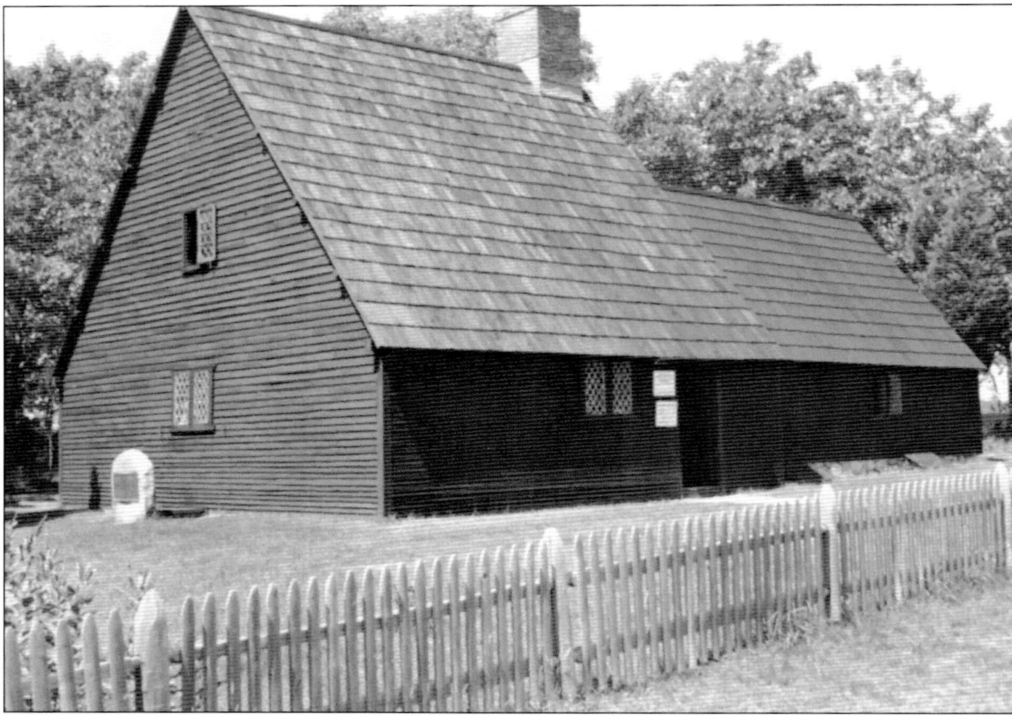

The restored trading post was built on the uncovered foundation stones and followed the same footprint as the original. The inside of the main room features a large hearth and area for heating a large pot, possibly for making beer.

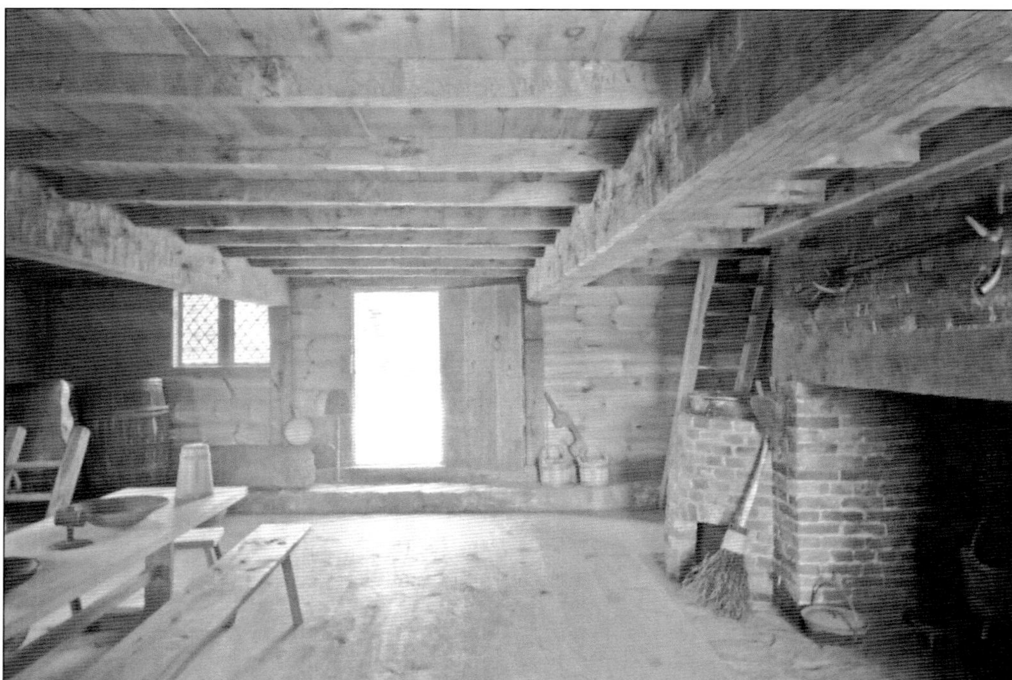

Two

All Around the Town

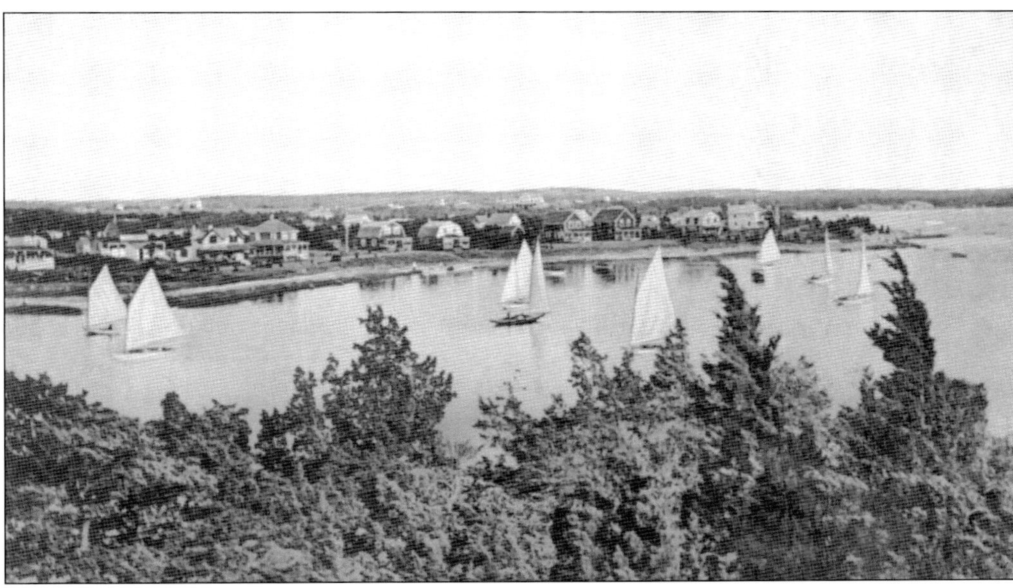

The view in this 1930s photograph of Circuit Avenue on Patuisset Island, taken from across the water at Bassetts Island, evokes summertime on Cape Cod. Local sailboat races were held on a weekly basis.

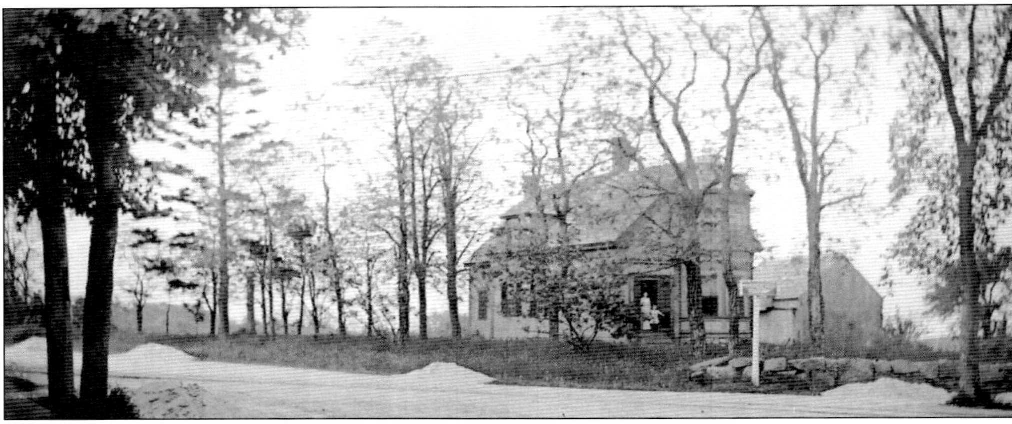

The area in Bourne village called Trading Post Corner seems incomplete in this c. 1900 photograph. Pictured is one of two Captain Blackwell houses, located on the corner of County Road and Shore Road, which were built by Deacon Gershom Ellis for his daughters, who both married Blackwell men. The house and the barn behind it still stand and are lived in and maintained by descendants of the original Blackwell family. In the doorway are Abby Walker Blackwell and her daughter Agnes Pearl Blackwell.

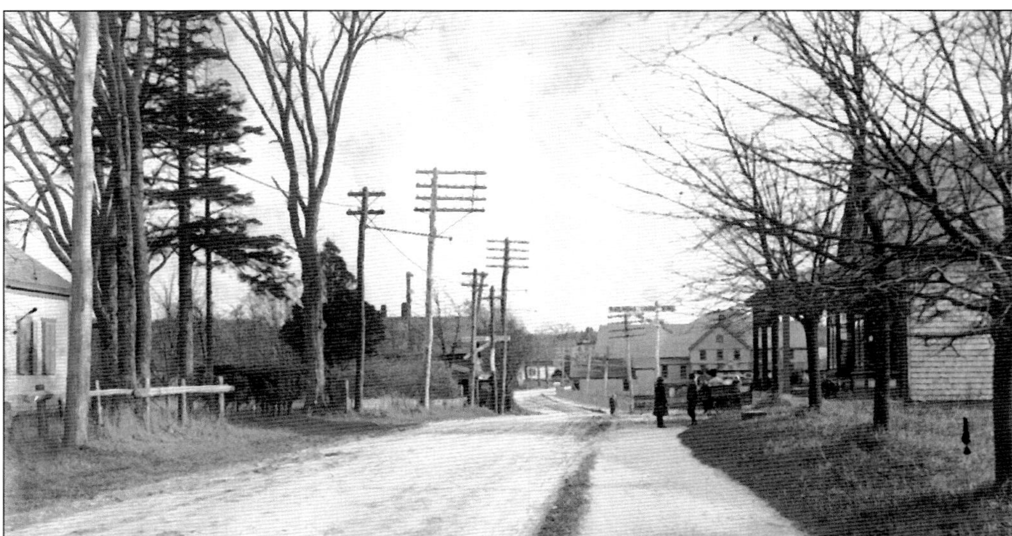

This 1909 view looking south across the Monument River Bridge shows the railroad tracks on the left side of the road with the old stone bridge and Welcome Hall in the center of the photograph. Welcome Hall burned down in 1912.

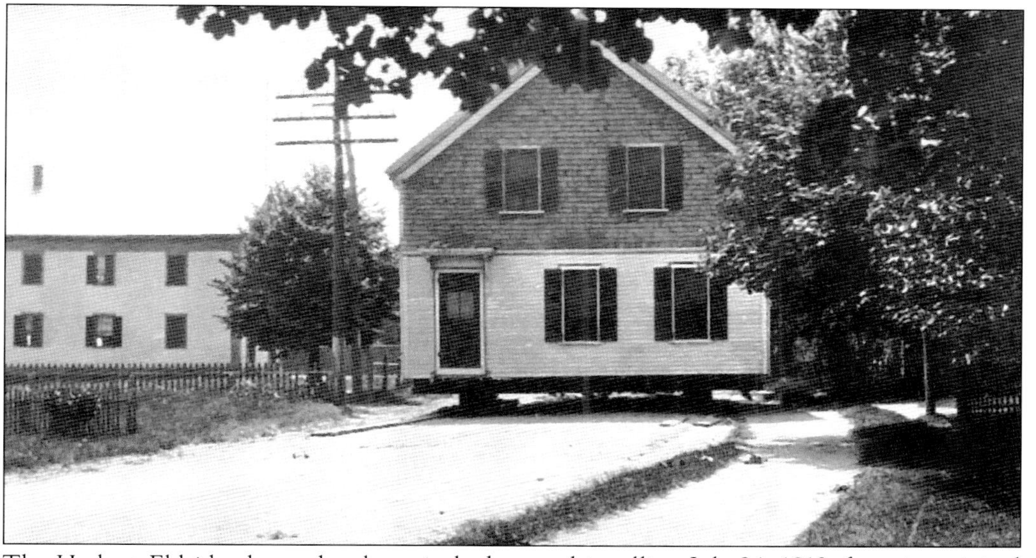

The Herbert Eldridge house has been jacked up and is rolling July 24, 1912, from its original location in the middle of the area designated for the Cape Cod Canal. It was moved to the current location on Shore Road in Bourne Village and can still be seen today.

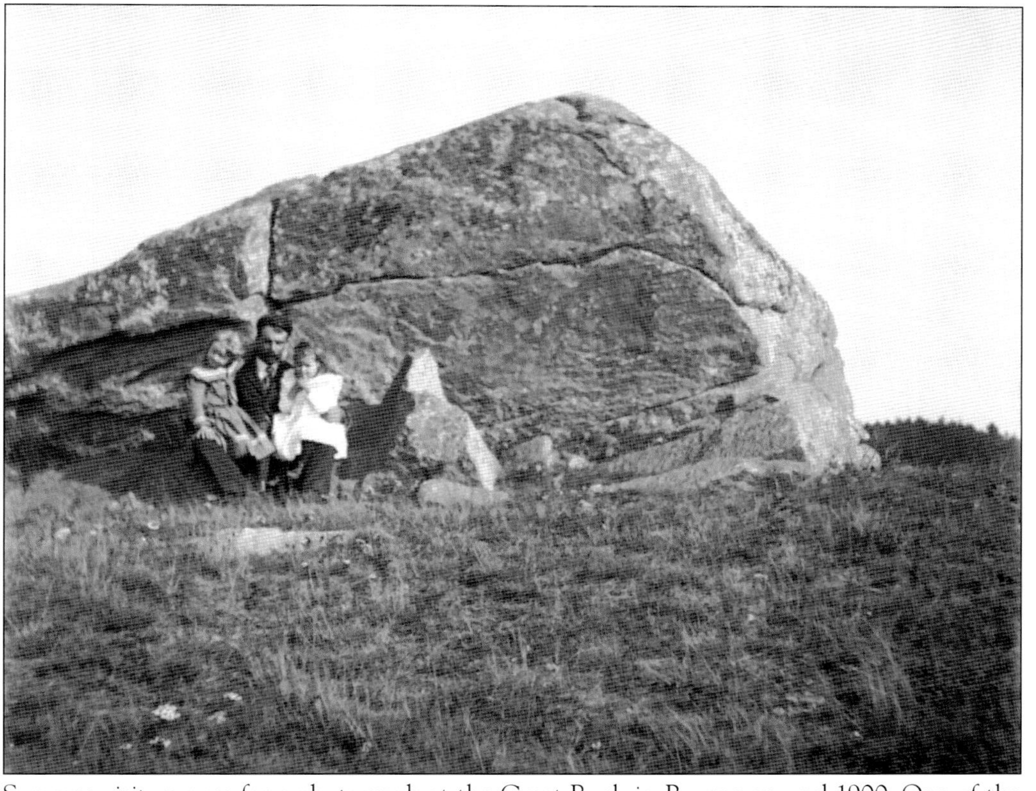

Summer visitors pose for a photograph at the Great Rock in Bourne around 1900. One of the favorite pastimes for visitors and locals alike was to hike to scenic rock outcroppings for picnics and photographs.

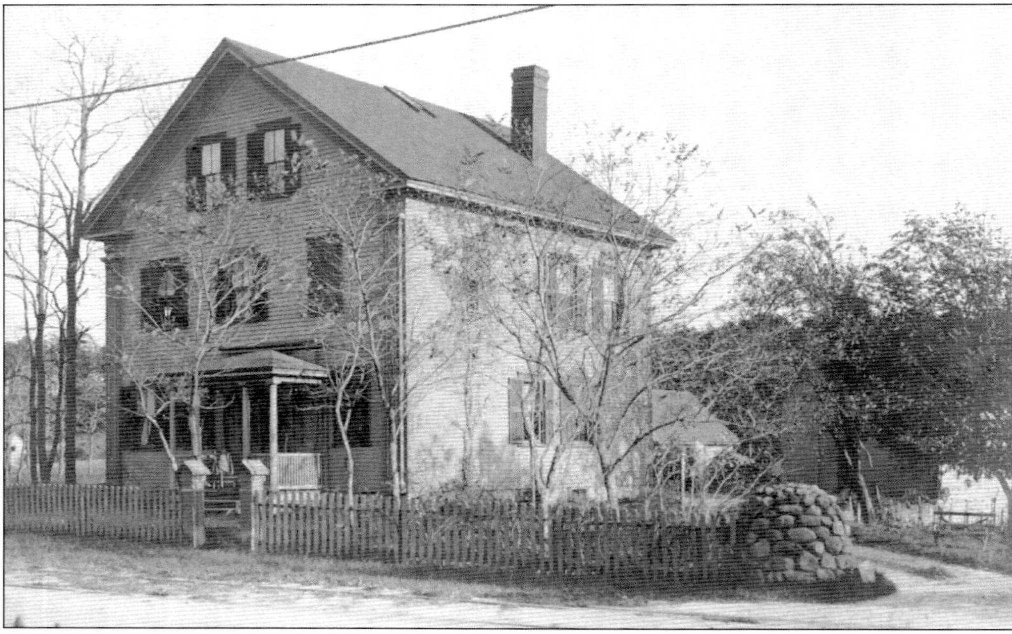

Seen here in the early 20th century, the Briggs-McDermott House, located on Sandwich Road in Bourne Village, was slated for demolition in the 1970s but was saved by the Bourne Society for Historic Preservation, who maintain it in Victorian style. Originally built in 1802, it was placed in the National Register of Historic Places in 1981.

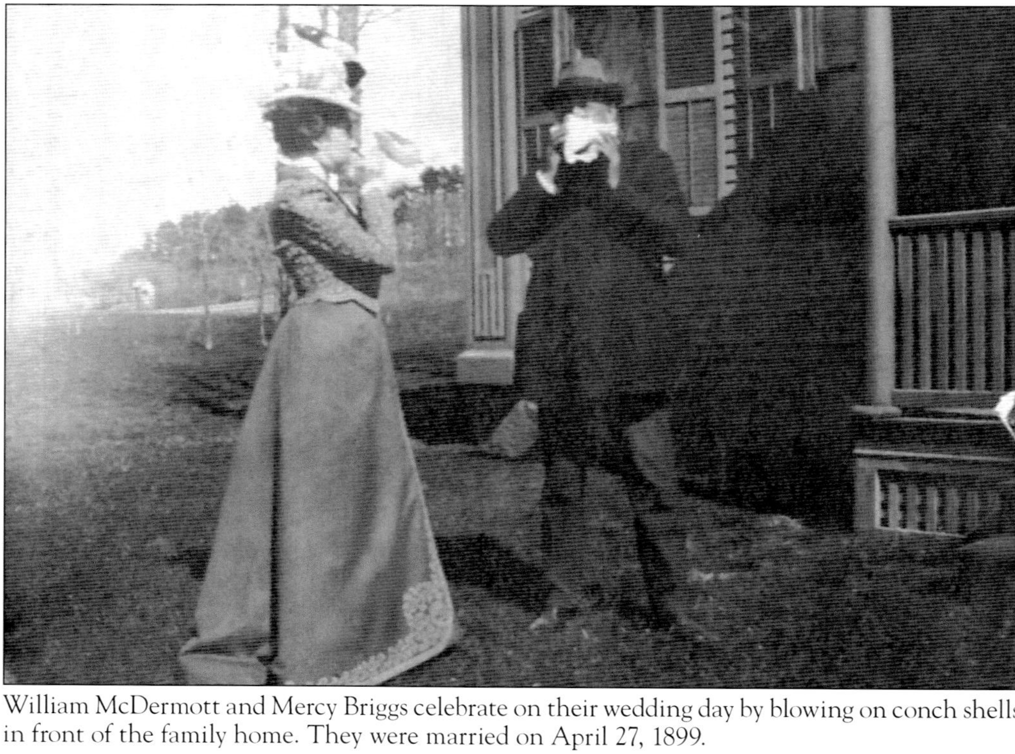

William McDermott and Mercy Briggs celebrate on their wedding day by blowing on conch shells in front of the family home. They were married on April 27, 1899.

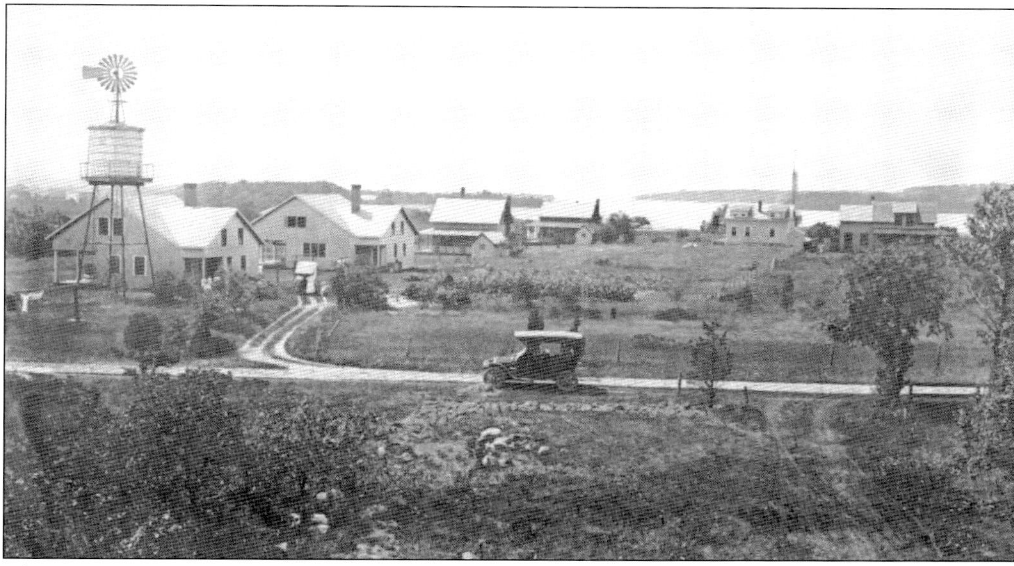

This c. 1915 view of Pocasset village looks out over Buzzards Bay. The village of Pocasset got its name from the Native American tribe that lived in the area.

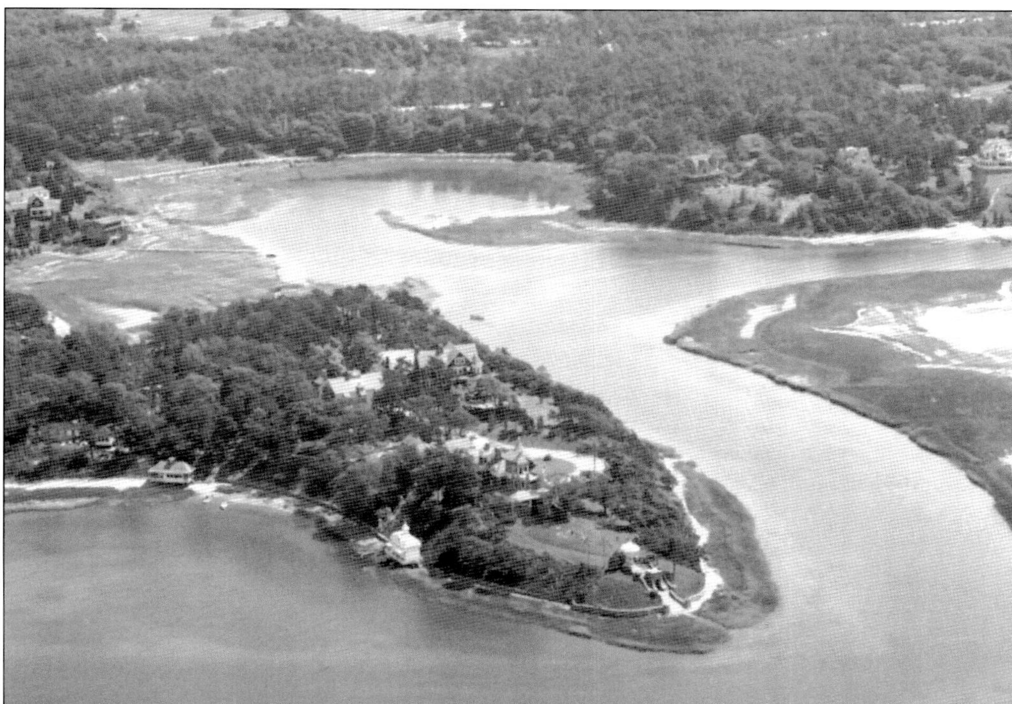

An aerial view of Amrita Island taken after the 1944 hurricane shows the Baxendale residence, the bathing pavilion (left), and the tomb where the Baxendales, their adopted son, and their dog Rex are buried. The bathing pavilion came down in the storm and was not rebuilt. The tomb bears the legend "Love is Eternal" and can only be seen properly from across the water. (Photograph by Ben Harrison.)

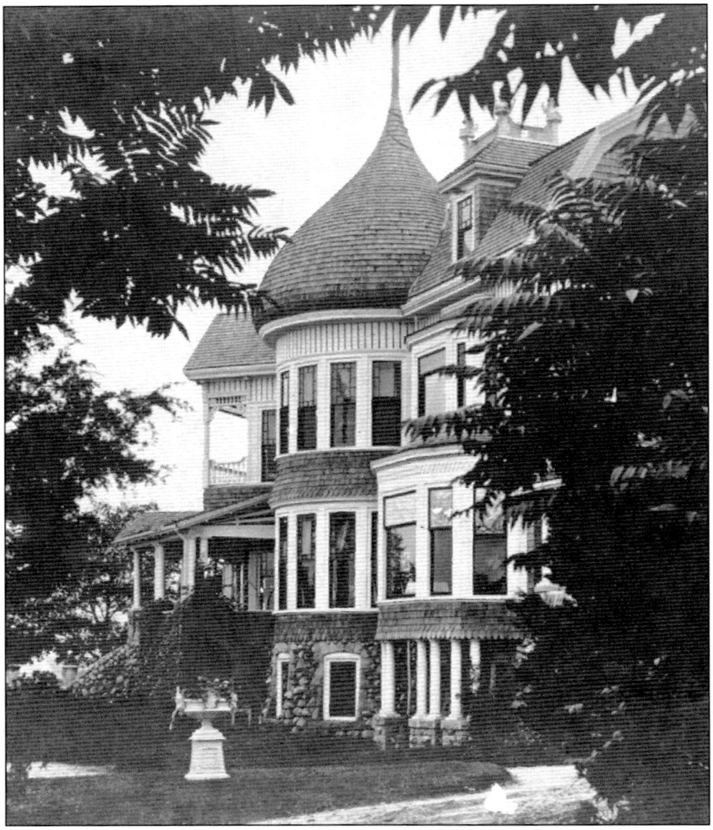

This 1906 photograph shows the Baxendale residence on Amrita Island. Though the house was enlarged in the 1980s, it retains its old-world charm to this day. Thomas and Esther Baxendale bought the six-acre island in Cataumet in 1893 and built the house in the summer of that year. They named it Amrita, which means "youth-renewing water" in Sanskrit.

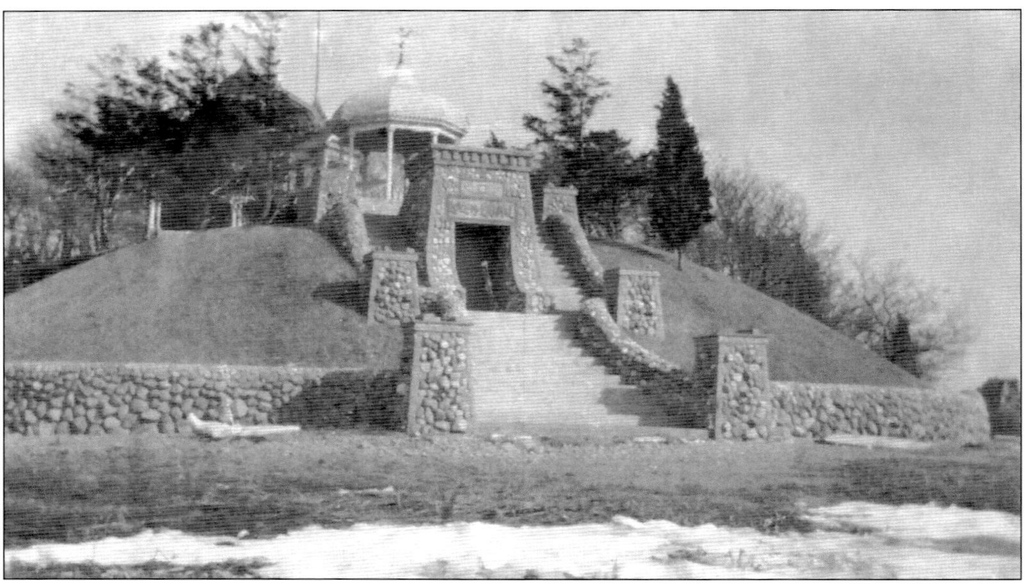

This c. 1910 winter photograph from the waters of Squeateague Harbor shows the tomb and the gazebo that once graced the top of it. The gazebo area was called Sunset Terrace by the Baxendales and was one of their favorite places to sit.

This undated photograph shows US president Grover Cleveland, who held the office of president twice. He was the only president to leave the White House and return four years later for a second term. Cleveland spent his summers in the Gray Gables neighborhood, and a special train station was constructed for him in that area.

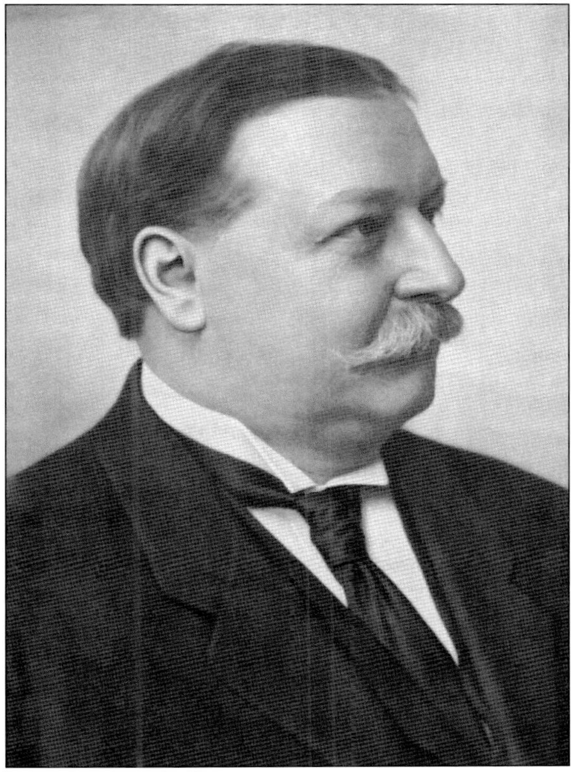

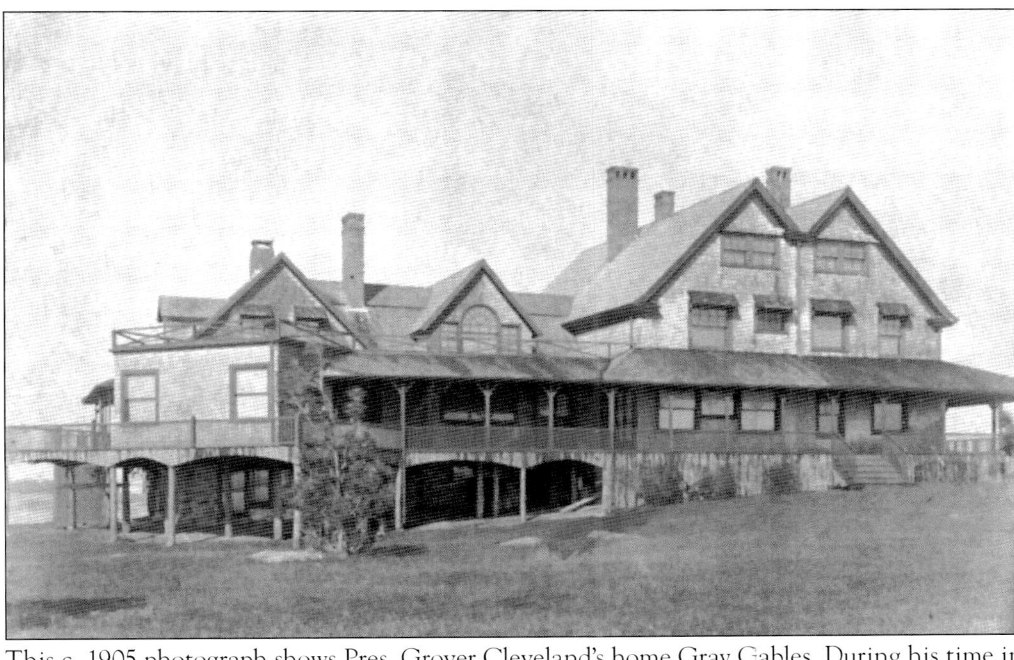

This c. 1905 photograph shows Pres. Grover Cleveland's home Gray Gables. During his time in the town of Bourne, one of his favorite activities was fishing in the waters of Buzzards Bay with his friend and neighbor, the actor Joseph Jefferson.

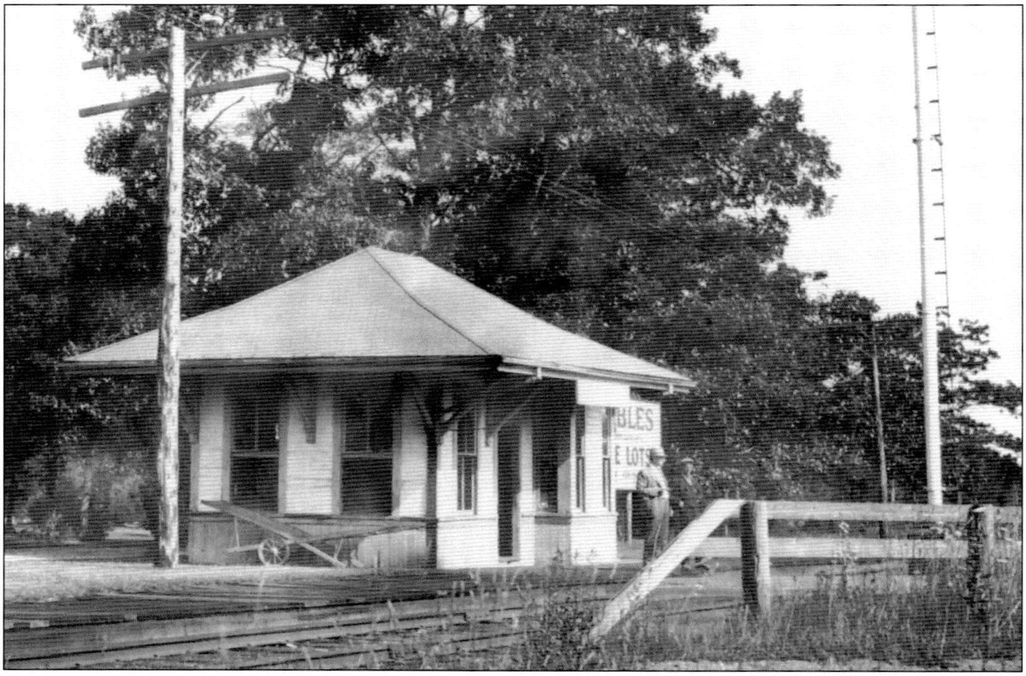

Passengers wait at the Gray Gables Railroad Station in this c. 1905 photograph. Local lore says that the train station was built for Cleveland because when he and the White House entourage came for the summer, their group interrupted the river traffic for too long while coming over the river. The problem was solved with the Gray Gables train station, at which Cleveland could hop off and walk to his house.

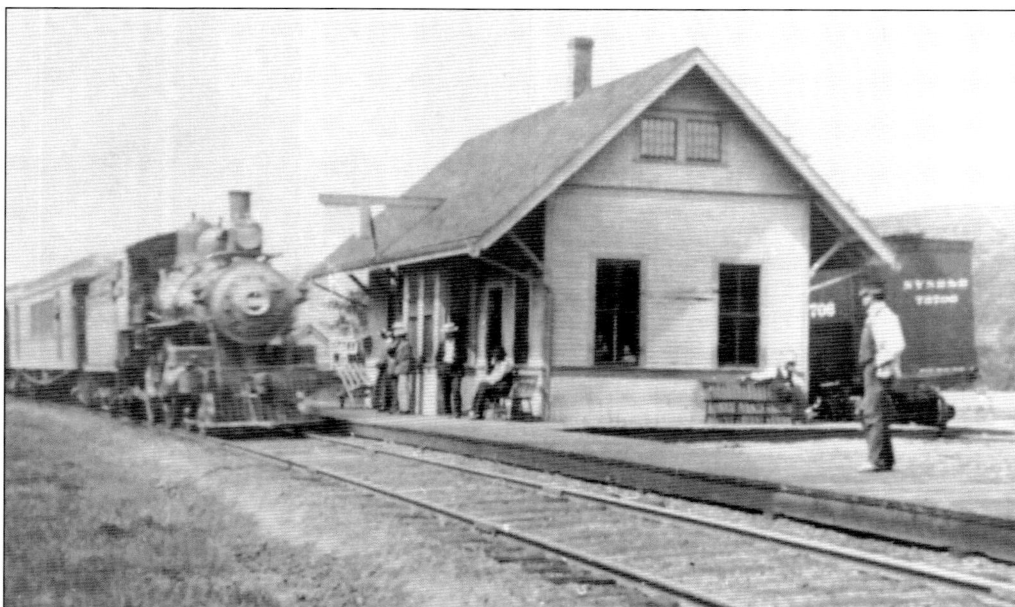

In this c. 1900 photograph, passengers sit outside the Bournedale train station as the train pulls in. Railroad travel was a favorite way to come to the Cape in the early 20th century.

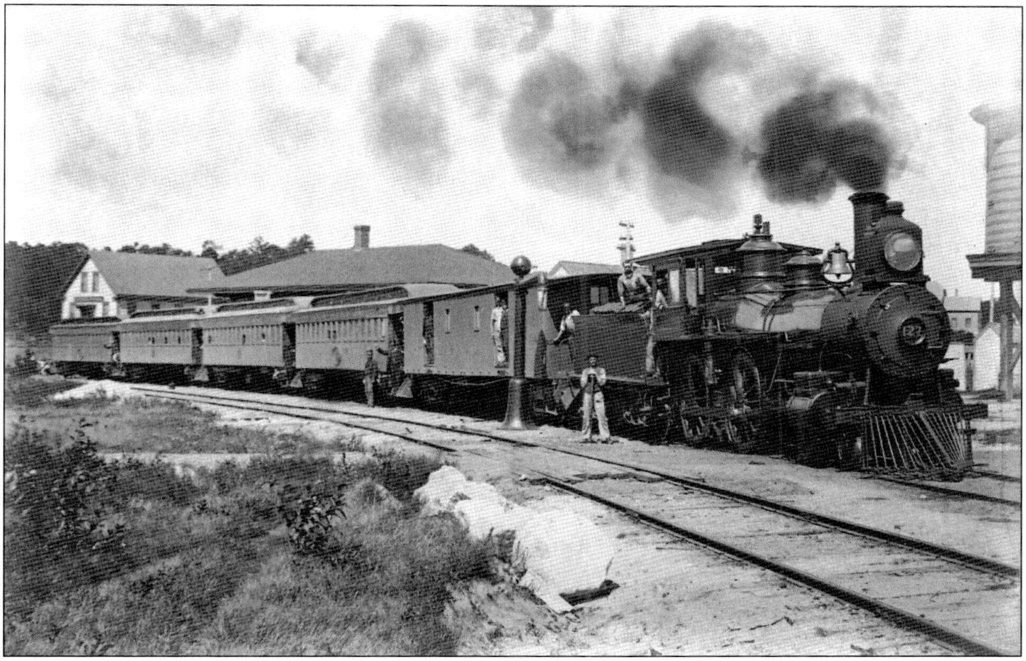

Smoke pours from the coal-fired engine of the Old Colony Railroad as it pulls into the train station at Buzzards Bay Village in the early 1900s. The conductor and the yard crew show their faces for the photograph.

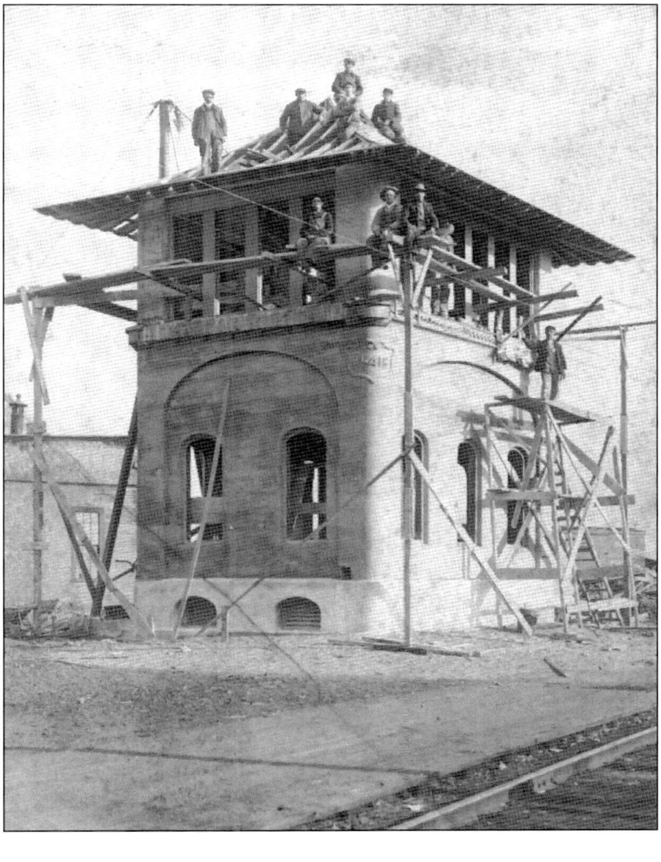

Construction workers sit on the tower during the building of the Buzzards Bay train station for the New York, New Haven & Hartford Railroad in 1912.

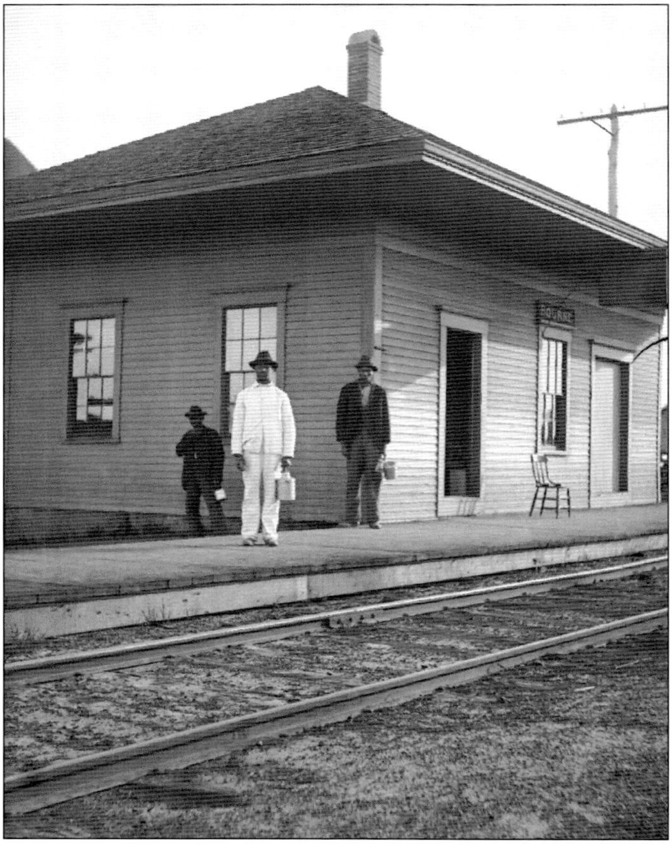

Laborers wait to catch a train at the Bourne Railroad Station. The trains that ran through this station followed the rails down to the beach and the summer cottages.

A train pulls into the Monument Beach Station in this c. 1910 photograph. The tracks and station are still in existence today, and a new railroad company is trying to start the service up again, at least from Boston to Buzzards Bay.

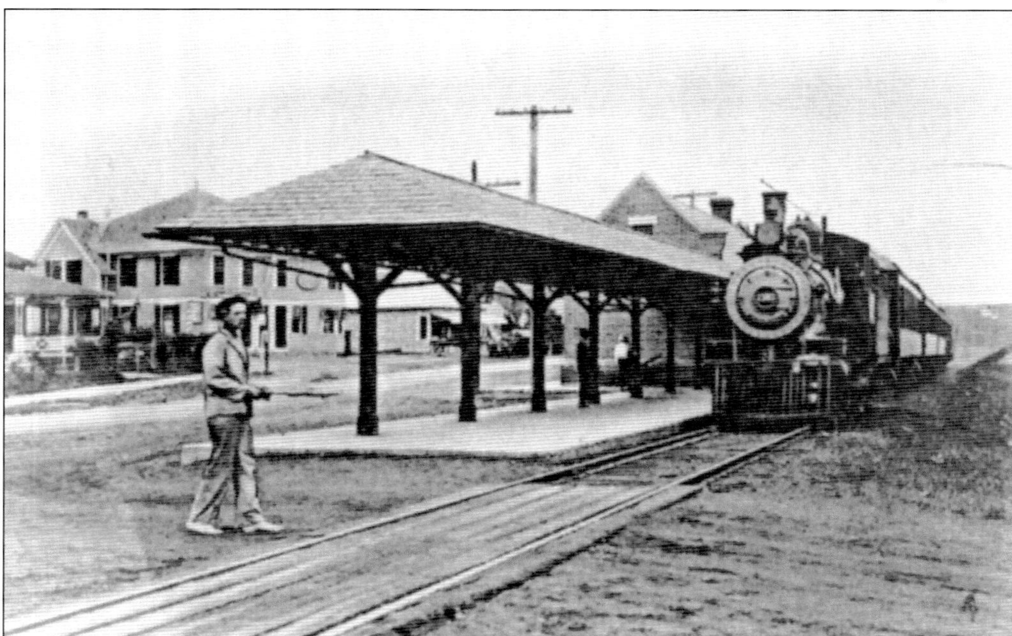

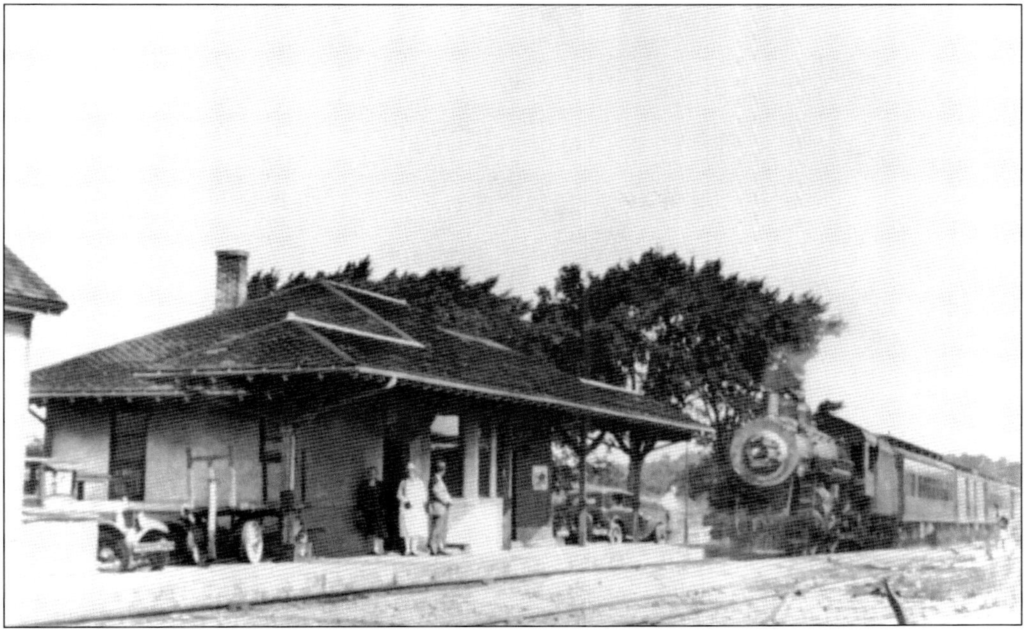

Passengers wait for the train to pull in at the Pocasset Train Station in this c. 1920 photograph. There were originally two stations in this popular little village, but one was eventually moved away and became a home. Although the station was eventually taken down, the lampposts have been saved and preserved at the Aptucxet Trading Post Museum.

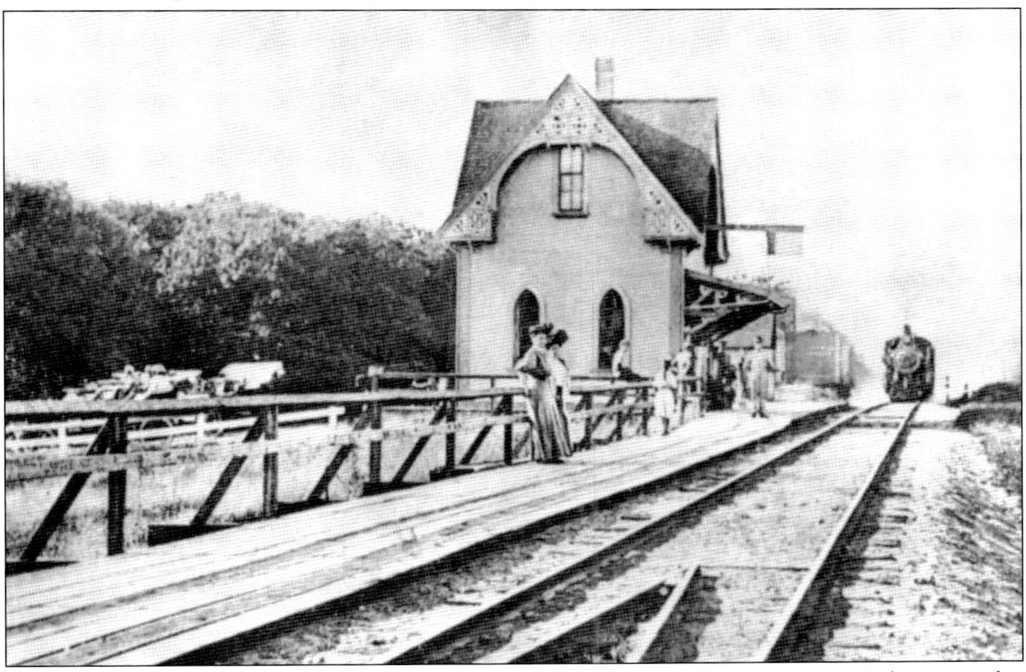

Women wait on the platform as the "Dude Train" pulls into Cataumet Station. The men who came from Boston and points north on the weekends were the "dudes." They came for short stays while their wives and children enjoyed the Cape Cod summers for longer periods of time.

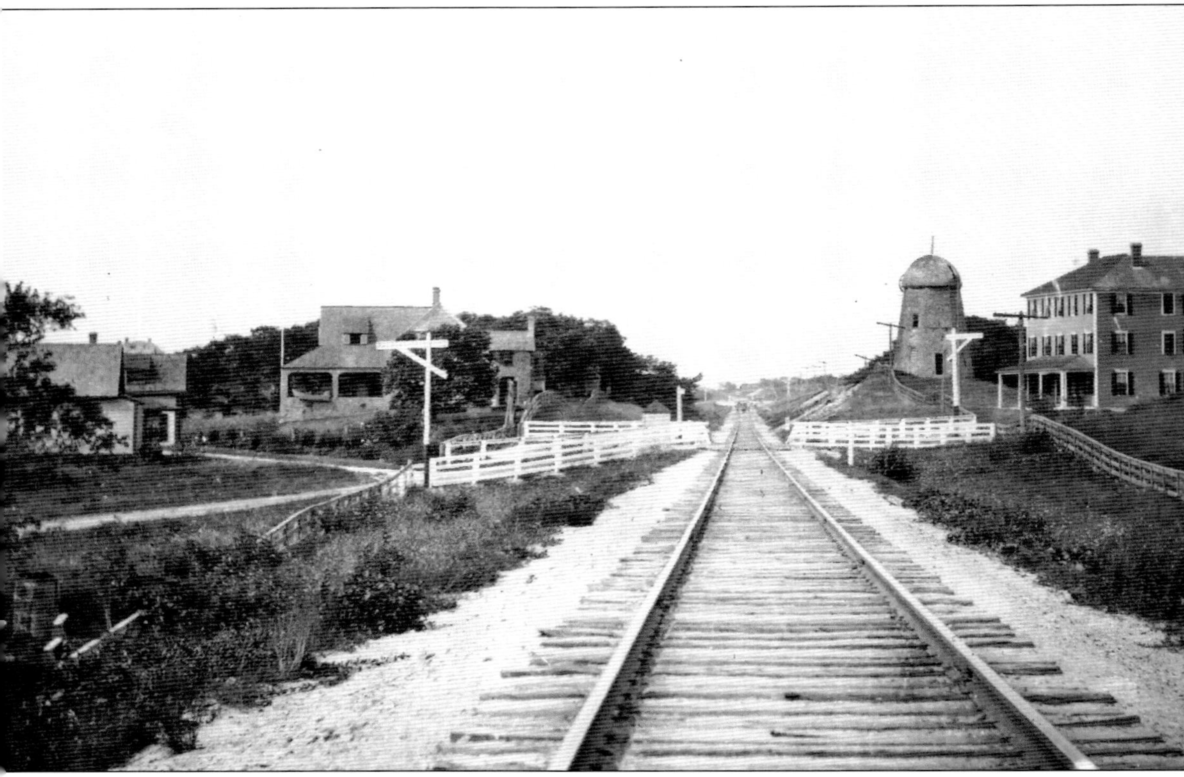

The Aldrich house (right) and windmill can be seen at the railroad crossing at Red Brook Harbor in the village of Cataumet in this c. 1910 photograph.

Three

Bridges and Connections

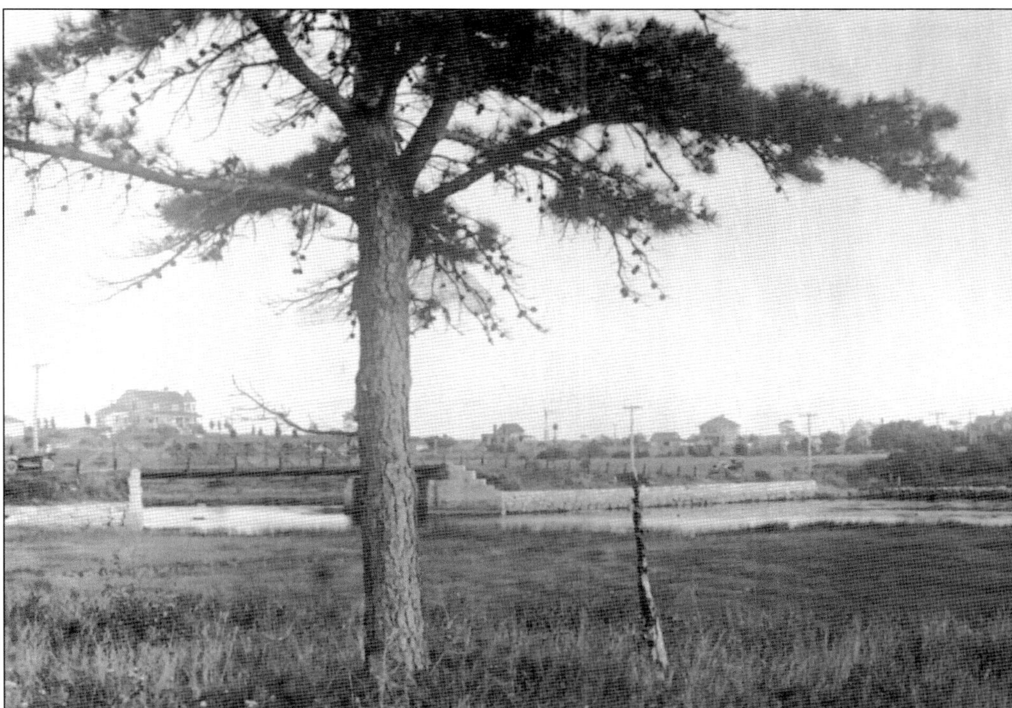

This pre-1915 photograph shows the bridge crossing the Barlow River, now called the Pocasset River, with the village of Pocasset in the background. The bridge, which is completely different now, is locally called the "Singing Bridge" for the noise it makes when a car goes over it.

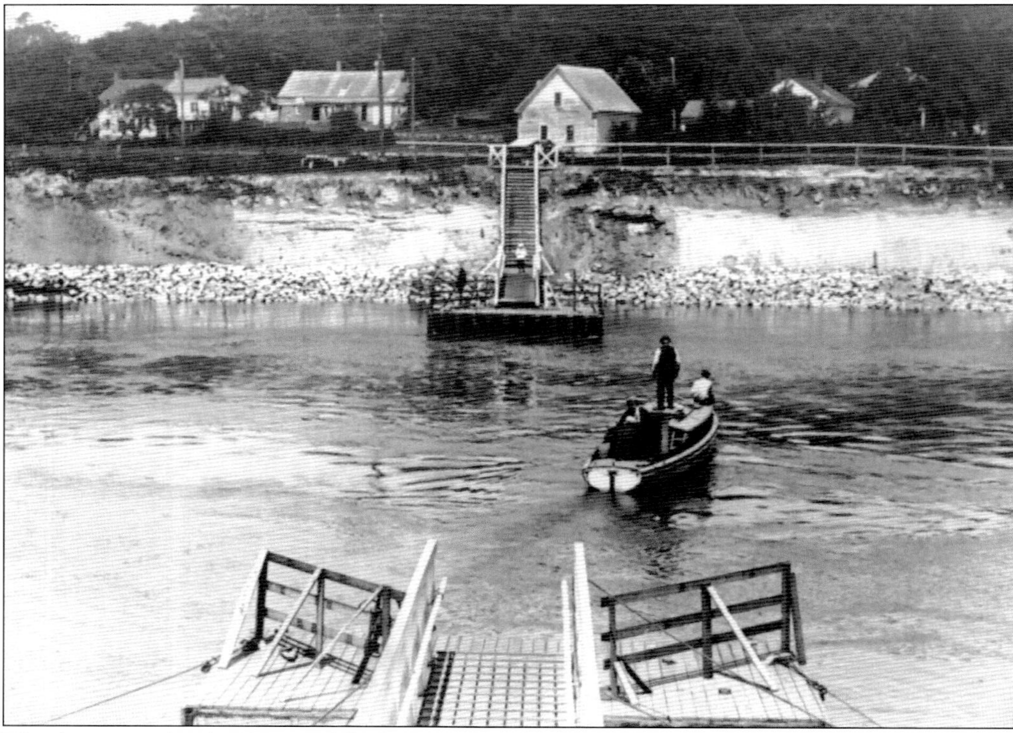

The ferryman for the Bournedale ferry takes a group across the Cape Cod Canal in this 1913 photograph. With the digging of the canal, the Bournedale railroad station wound up on the south side of the canal, thereby making it difficult for locals to catch the train to Boston. The little ferry was much used in those days.

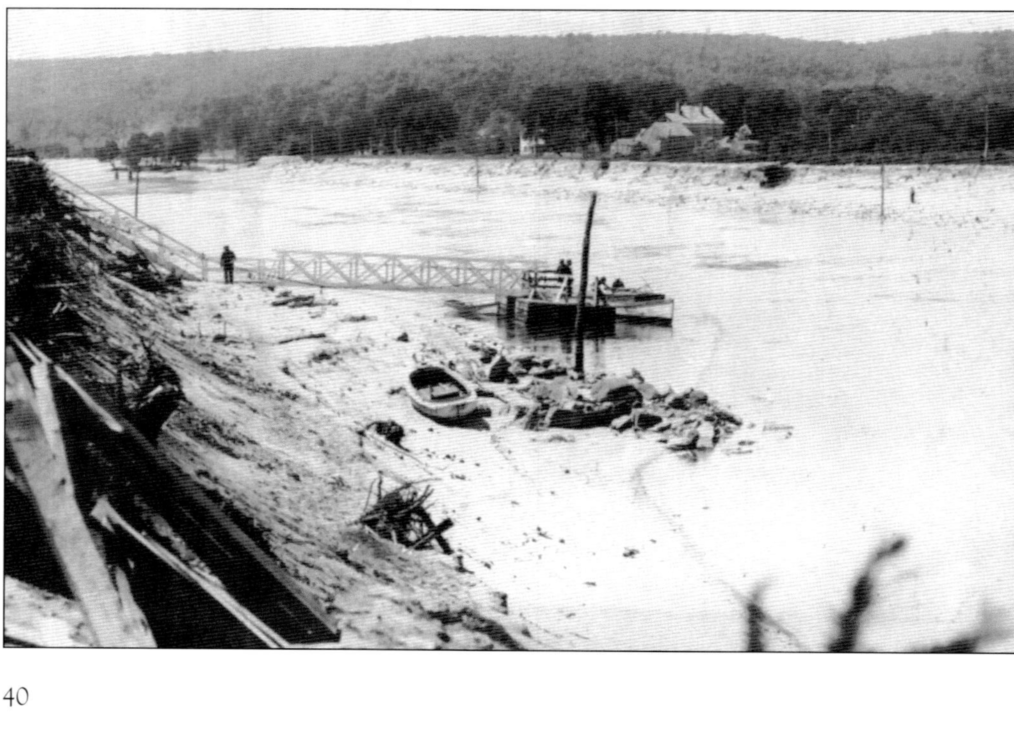

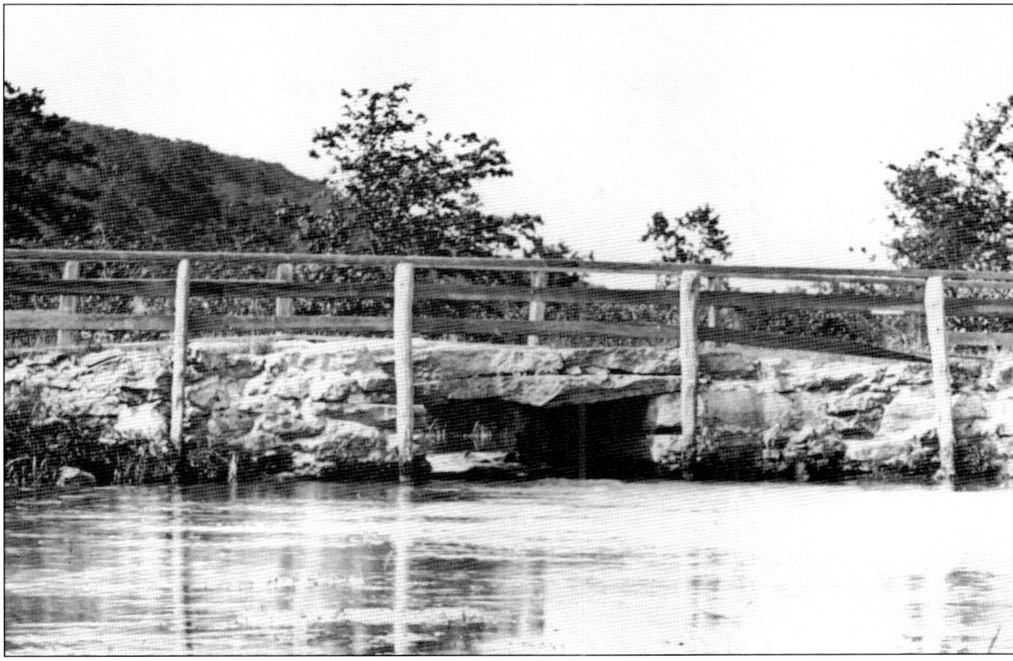

The Collins Farm Bridge is seen from the waters of the Monument River. This was the first bridge over the river.

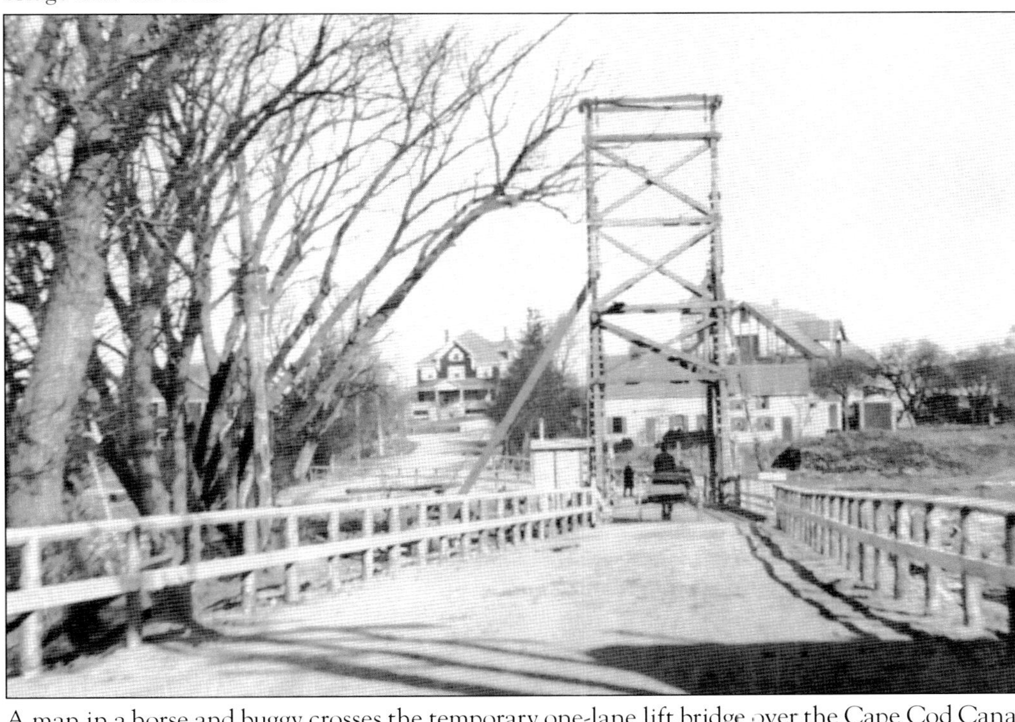

A man in a horse and buggy crosses the temporary one-lane lift bridge over the Cape Cod Canal at Sagamore in 1912. The bridge was built mostly for workers getting to and from the Keith Car and Manufacturing Company.

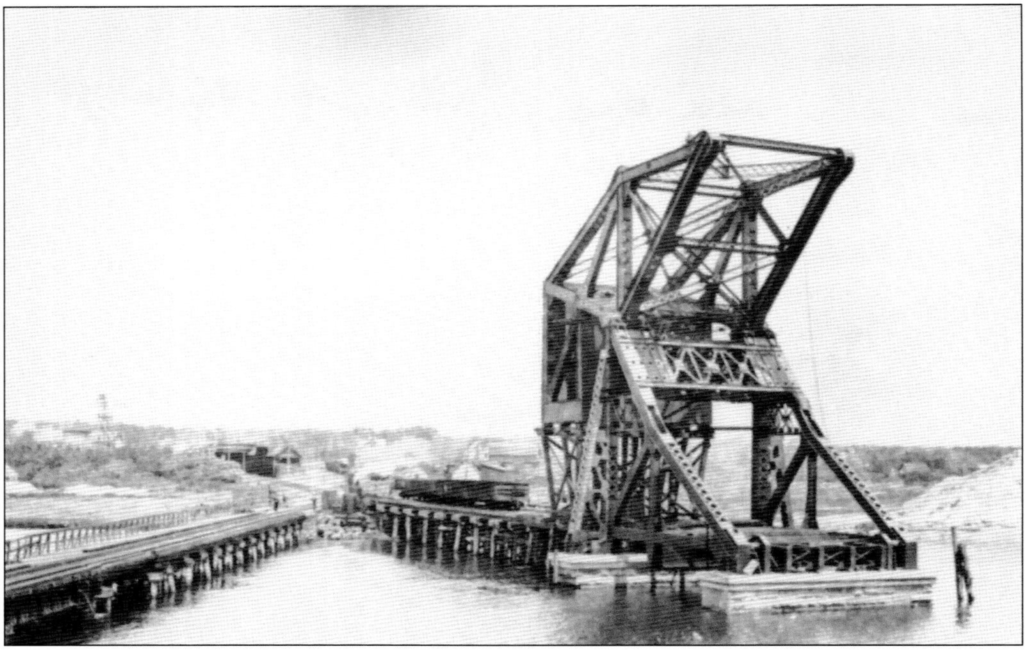

With the original train bridge on the left, the bascule railroad bridge over the Monument River is only partially built in this c. 1909 photograph. The bridge had a span of 160 feet and a 140-foot opening for vessels to pass through when raised.

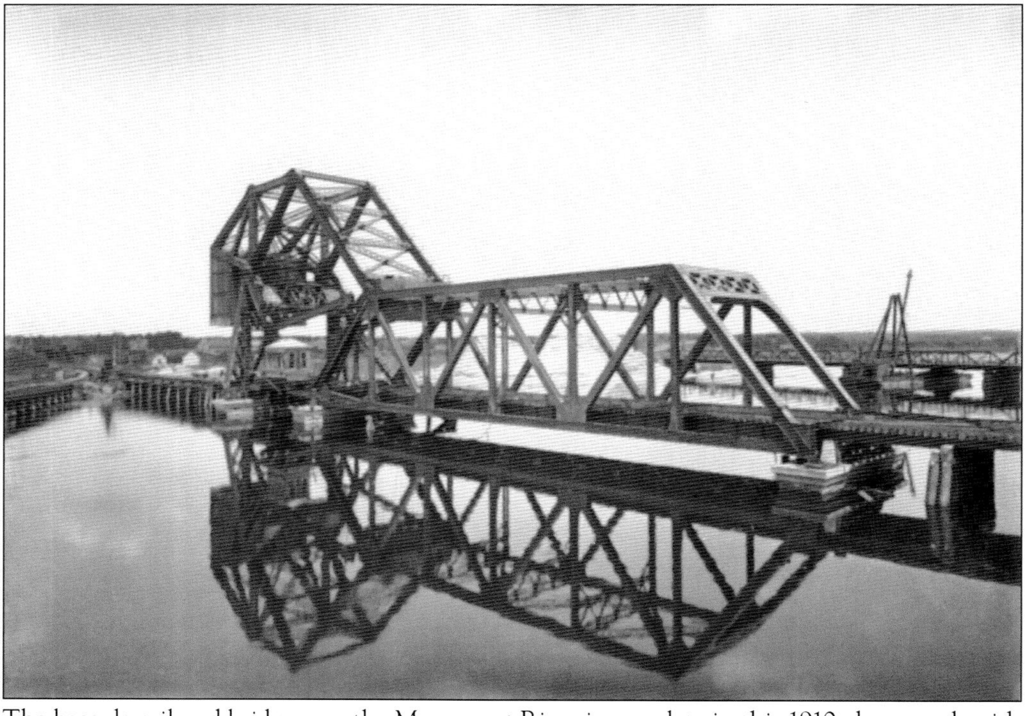

The bascule railroad bridge over the Monument River is complete in this 1910 photograph with the original train bridge on the left.

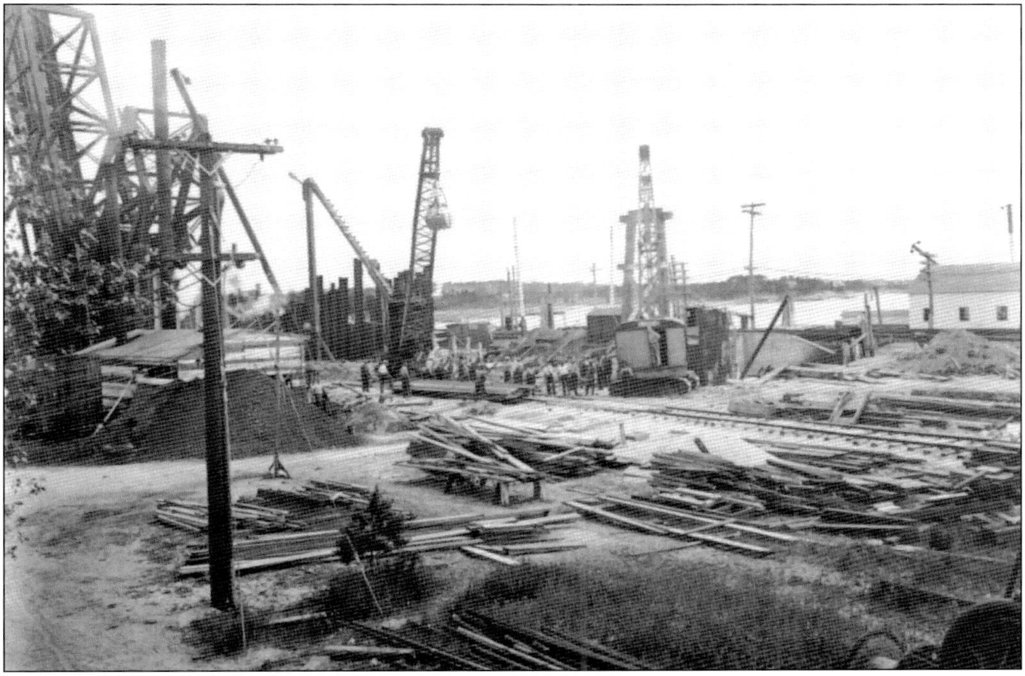

Construction of the new railroad vertical-lift bridge is in process, with the sheet piling of the north main pier partially driven in on June 26, 1934. The old bascule bridge can be seen at left.

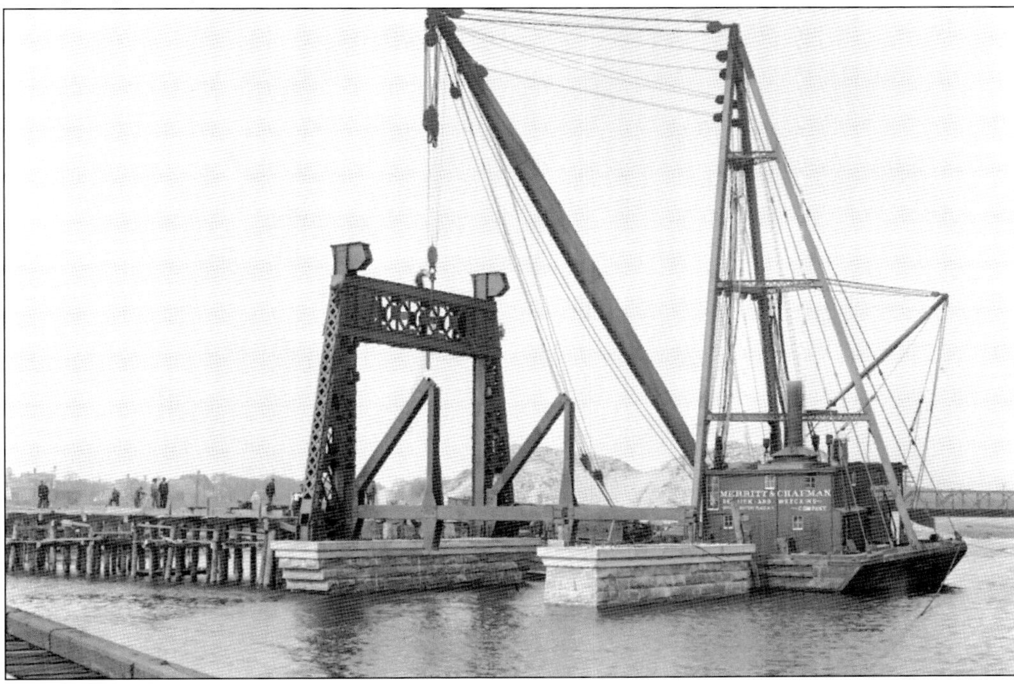

A crane on a dredge guides a piece of the bascule railroad bridge into place as men watch on the dock in this 1909 photograph. Construction of the bridge began in 1909, and it opened for trains two years later.

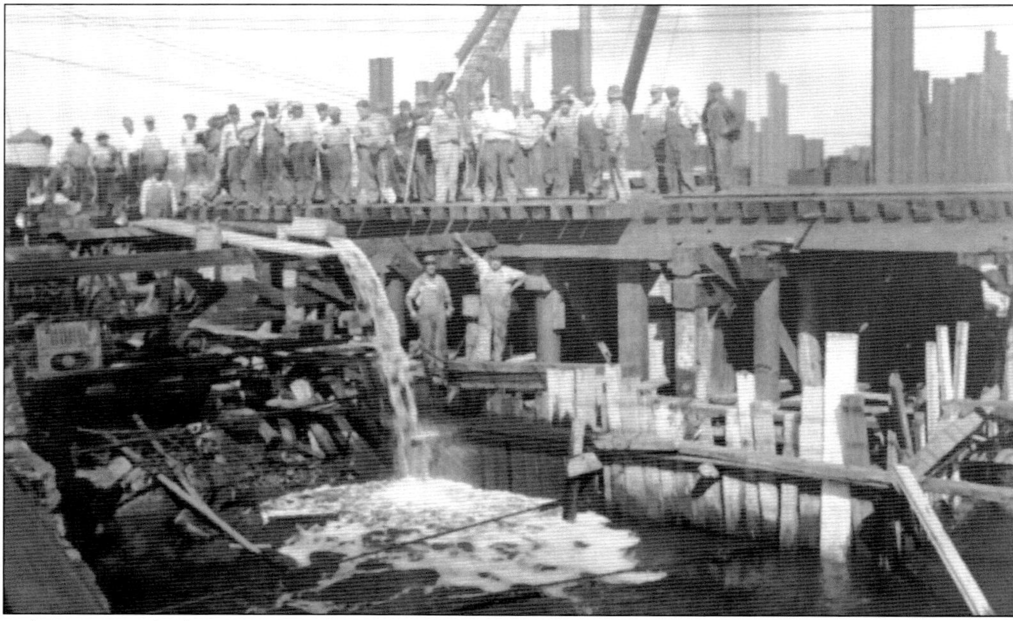

Laborers watch during construction of the auxiliary cofferdam around the main cofferdam of the north main channel pier on September 26, 1934. Also shown are the pieces shoring up the existing trestle so trains could continue to go over the river.

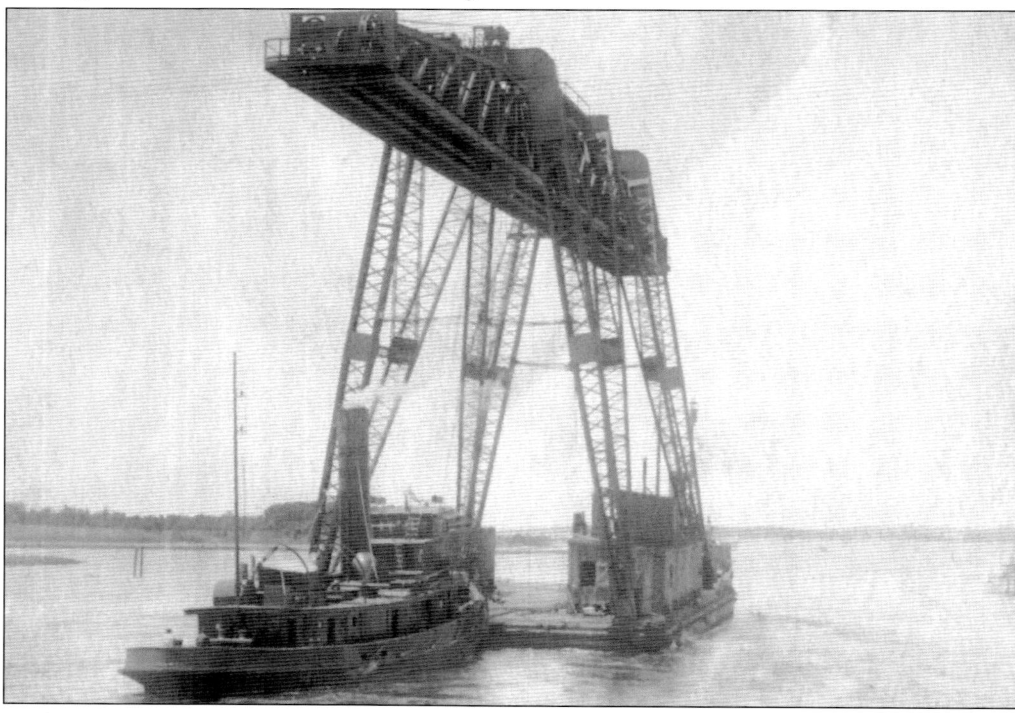

Looking like a space alien, a piece of the railroad bridge is moved by tugboat across the waters in this undated photograph. When completed, the one-track bridge had clearance above mean high tide of 135 feet.

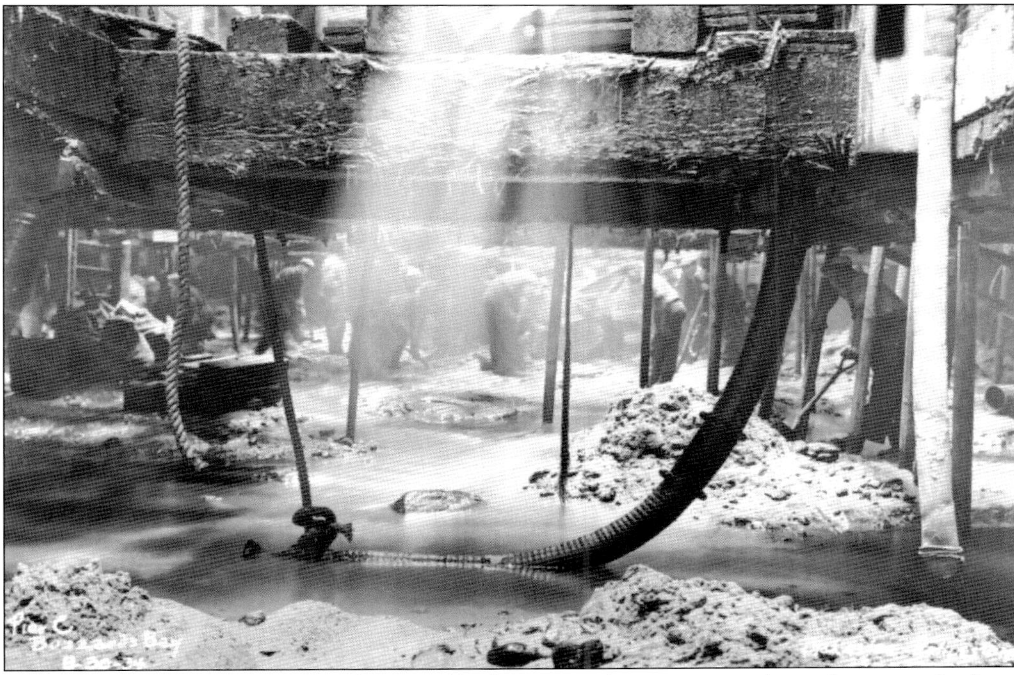

The bottom of the sheet-piling cofferdam can be seen in this photograph from August 30, 1934.

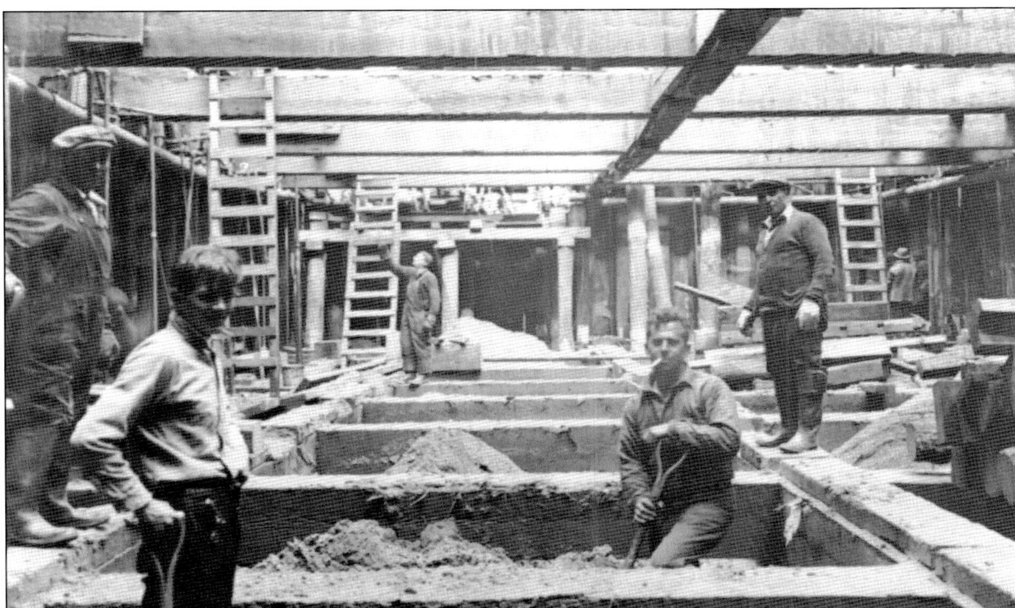

During construction of the railroad bridge, workmen pose for a photograph from the interior of the cofferdam of south pier on April 2, 1934.

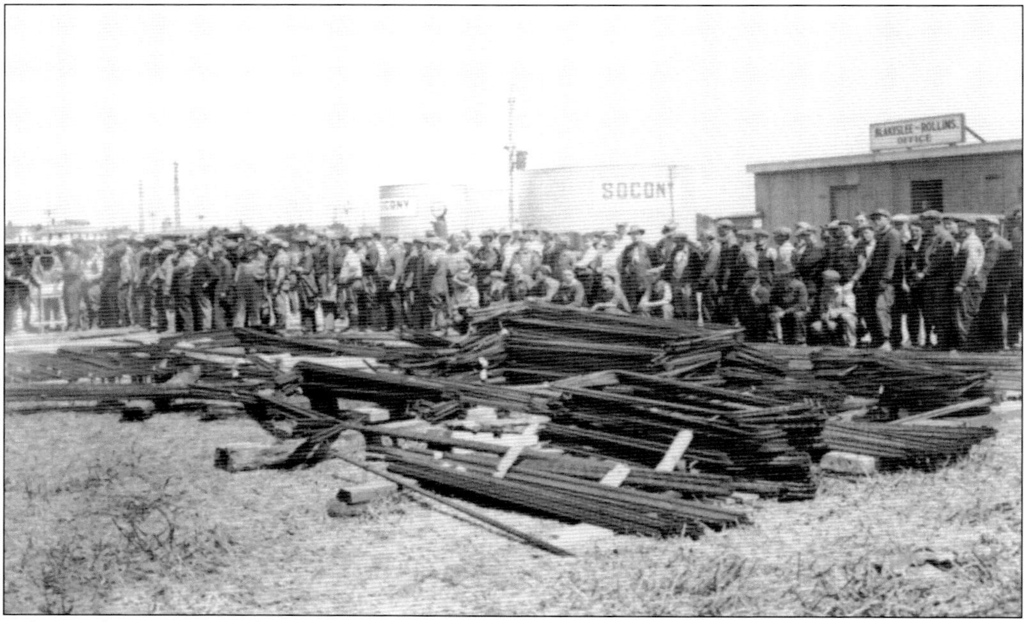

Laborers line up on payday, April 18, 1934. The modern lift bridge was built within 60 feet of the original bascule bridge to minimize track realignment.

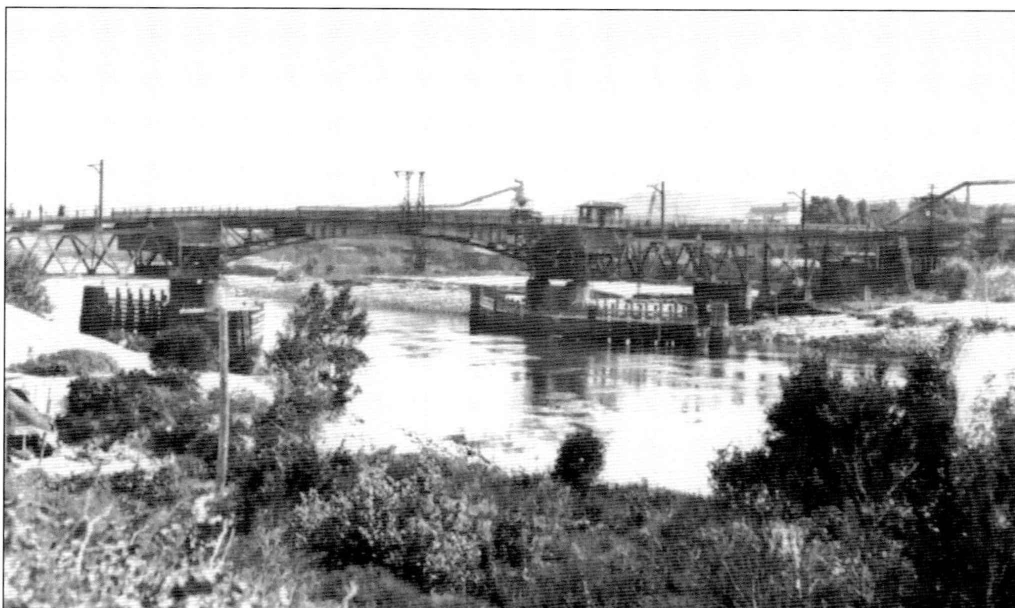

A ship passes under the old Sagamore drawbridge in this photograph. The bridge was completed in 1912.

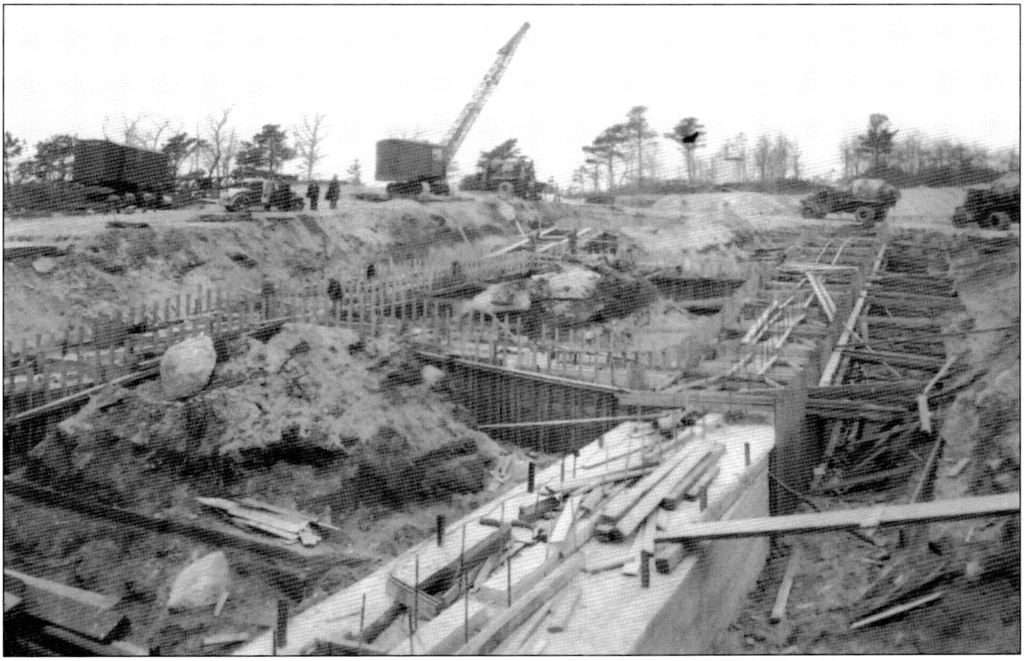

Pieces are laid in place for the abutment of one of the highway bridges being built over the Cape Cod Canal around 1933. Both highway bridges were constructed between 1933 and 1935 and have a clearance of 135 feet above mean high tide.

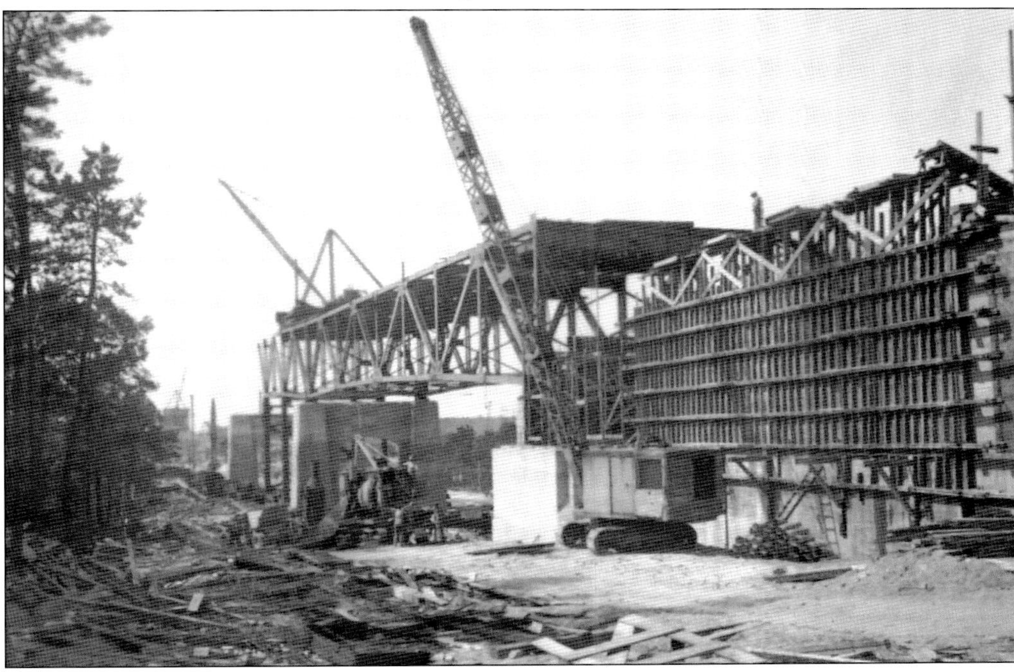

Construction of the Sagamore Highway Bridge crawls toward the north side of the Cape Cod Canal in this 1934 photograph. Both highway bridges and the vertical lift railroad bridge are owned and maintained by the US Army Corps of Engineers.

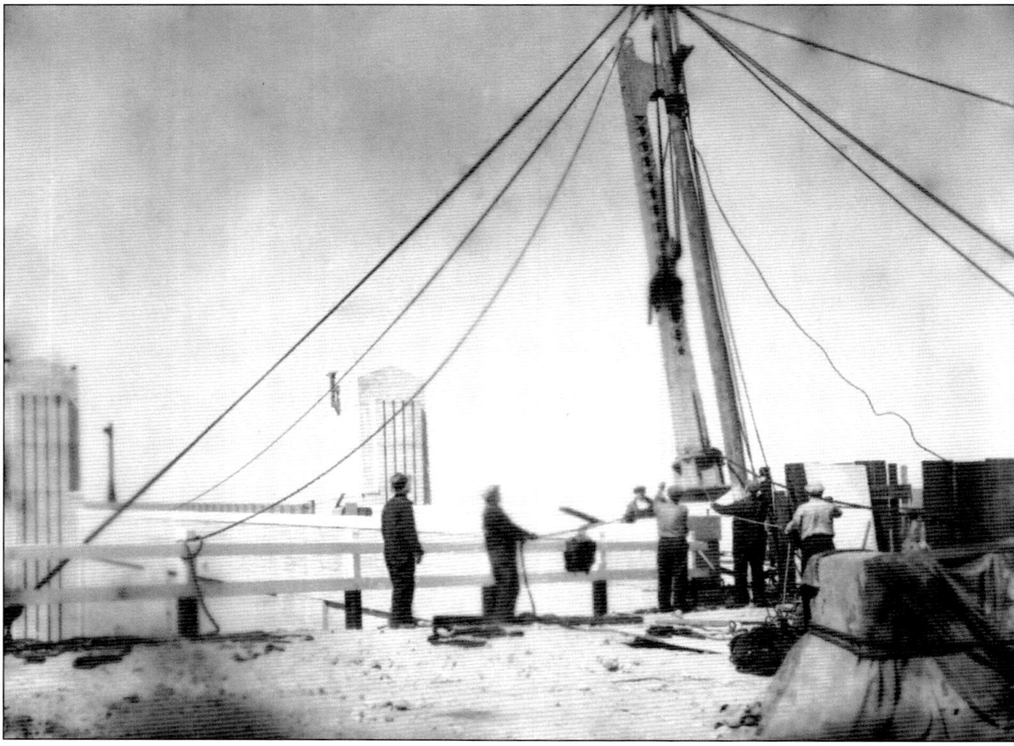

Laborers raise the posts for the bridge suspension during construction of the Sagamore Highway Bridge around 1934. Both highway bridges have horizontal clearance of 480 feet.

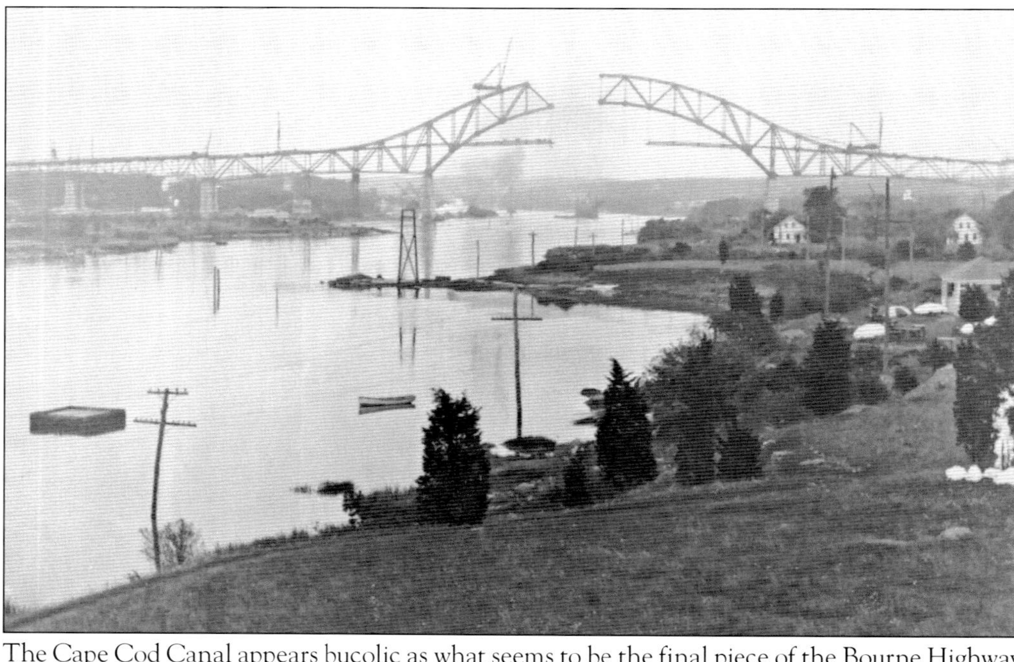

The Cape Cod Canal appears bucolic as what seems to be the final piece of the Bourne Highway Bridge hangs suspended in 1934.

Four

The Cape Cod Canal

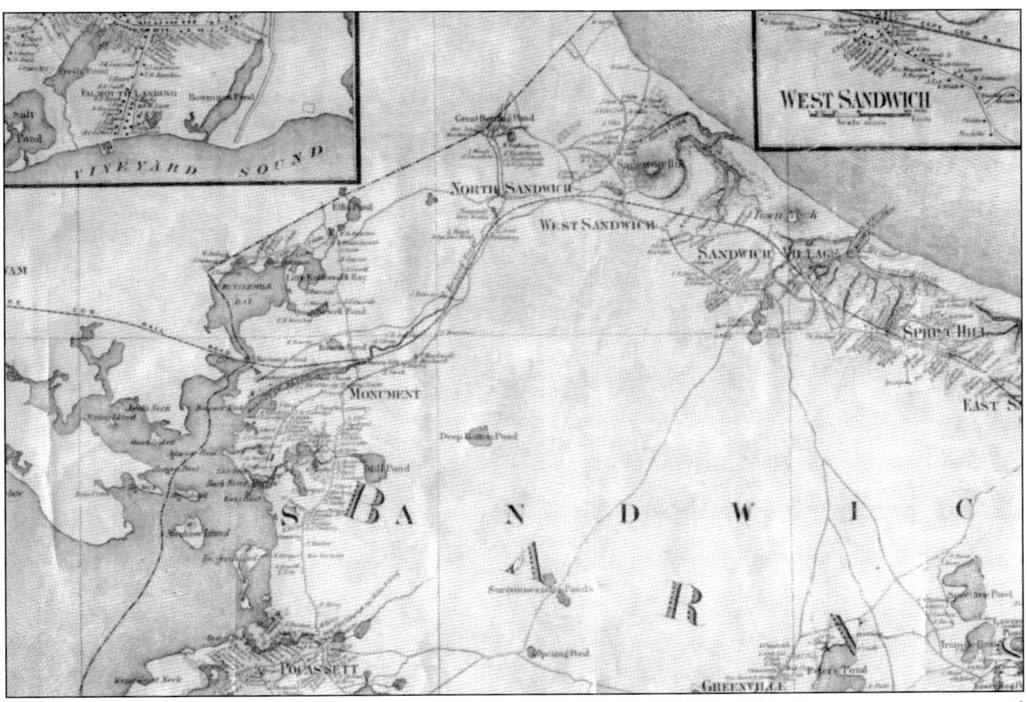

This 1858 map shows the area that would become the Cape Cod Canal before construction and also before Bourne was incorporated. With the vision of easier trading with the Dutch, the idea of a canal began with Pilgrim military leader Miles Standish in 1623.

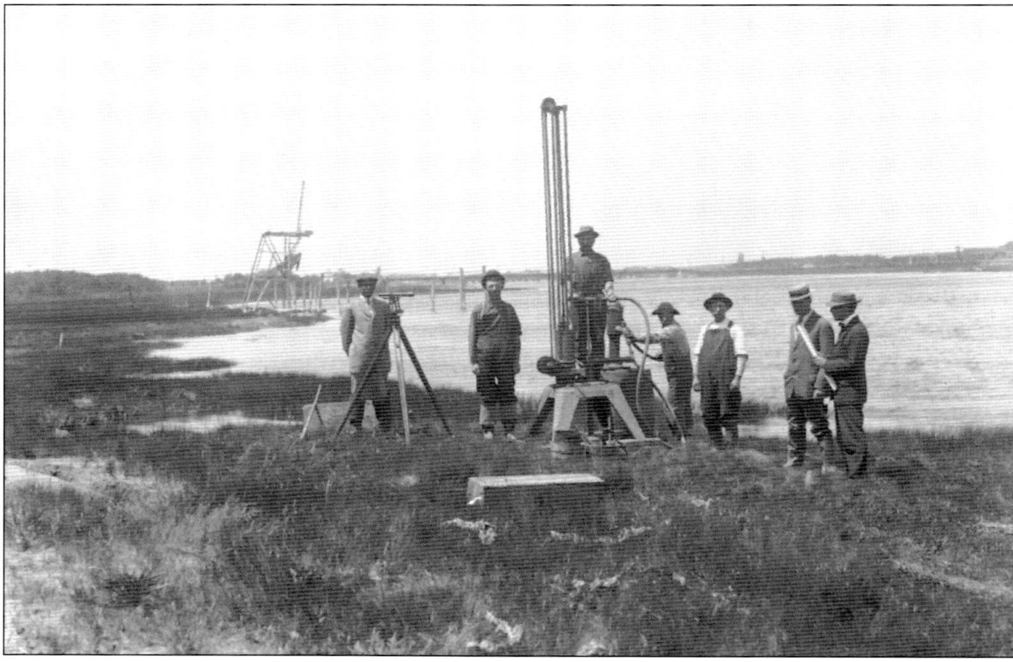

In this pre-1914 photograph, surveyors for the Cape Cod Construction Company take borings in preparation for the digging of the Cape Cod Canal. The Cohasset Narrows Bridge can be seen in the background.

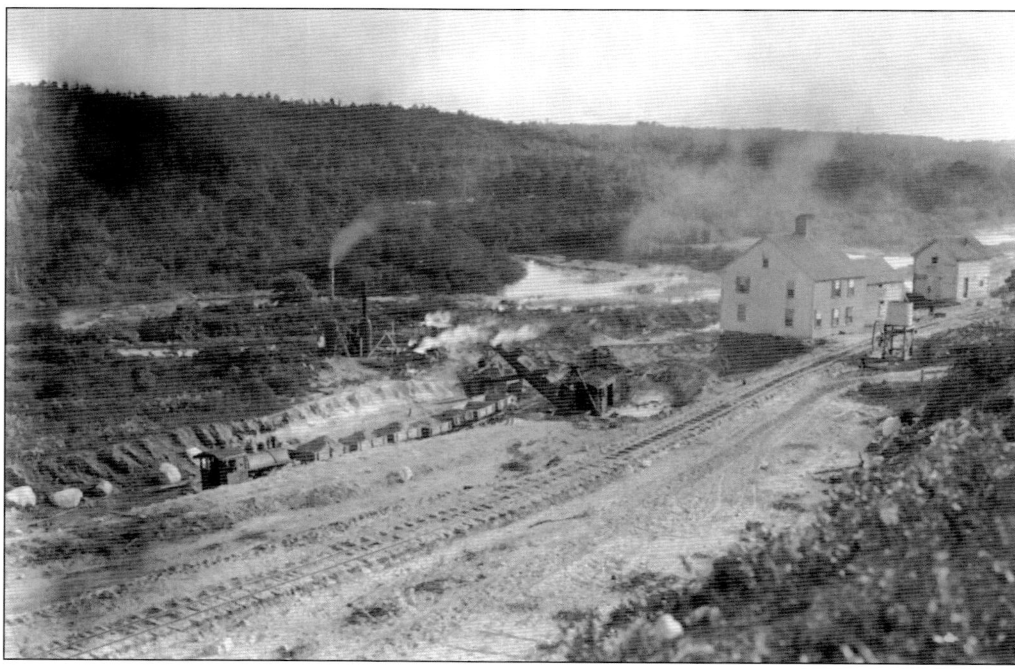

A steam shovel removes dirt from the Collins Farm area of what will become the Cape Cod Canal. Dry digging was one of the main ways dirt was removed from the canal area. Steam shovels built into boxcars were utilized to carry the debris out of the area on makeshift rails.

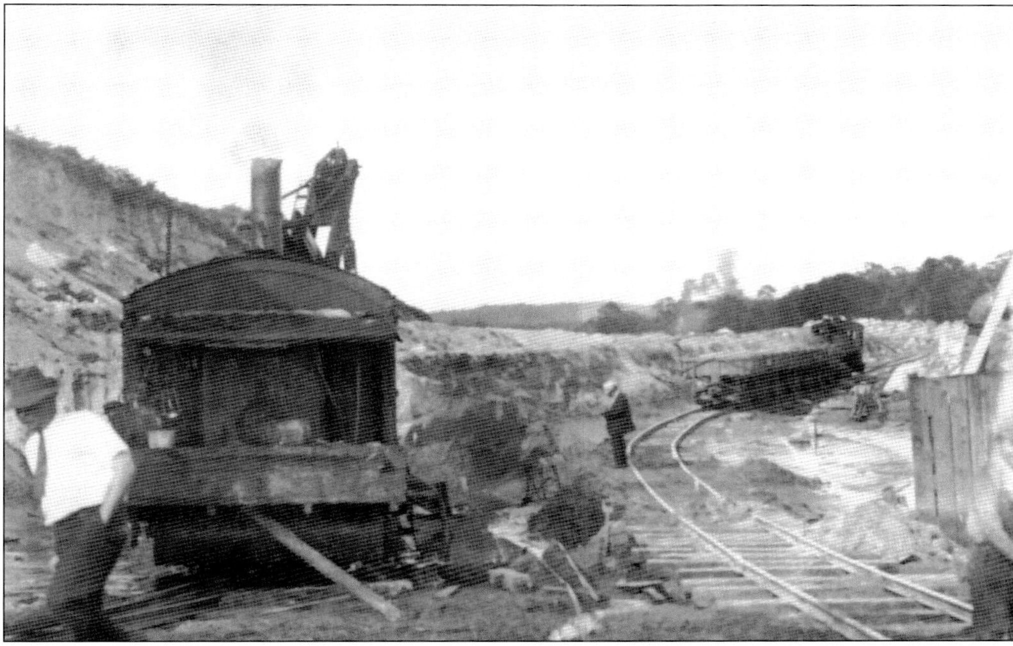

Laborers and others can be seen in the area where dry digging is going on in the Cape Cod Canal. The train cars at left are used to carry the dirt out of the canal path.

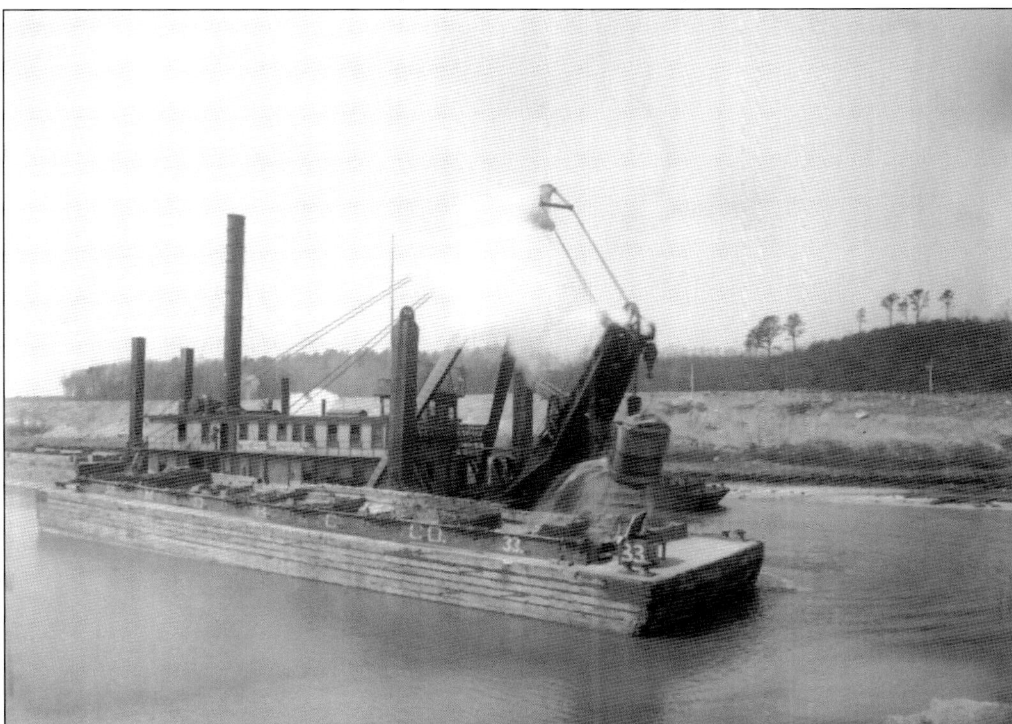

The dredge *Governor Herrick* hauls up dirt and debris from the bottom of the Cape Cod Canal during this phase of digging under the water. The canal officially opened in 1914.

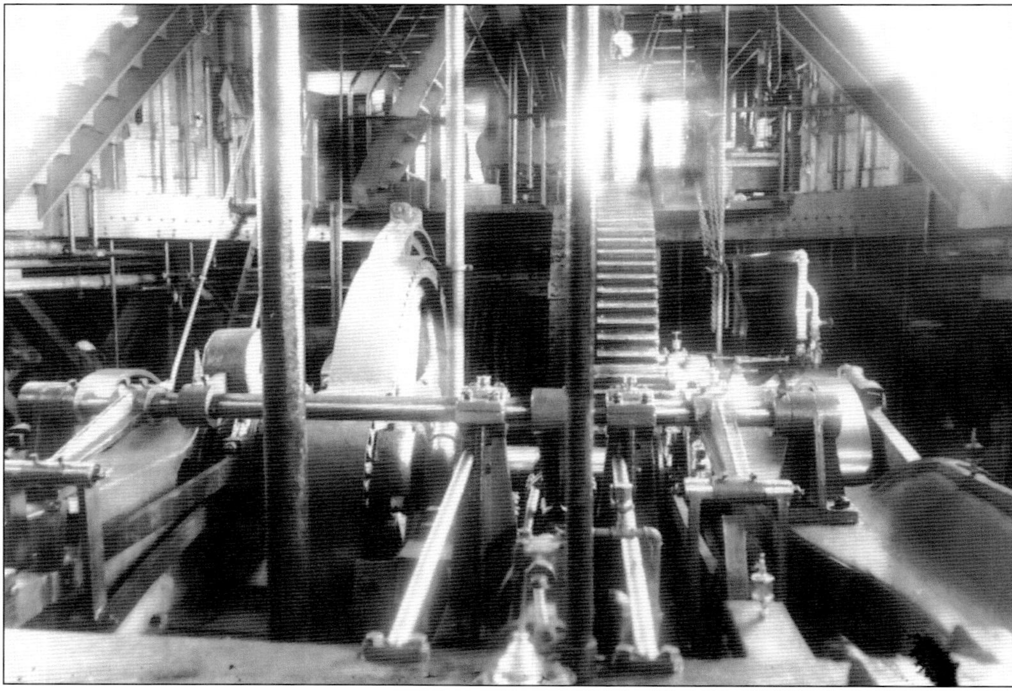

The engine room of the dredge *Governor Herrick* is full of wheels and cogs. The *Governor Herrick* was assembled in Sagamore near the Keith Car Works, and it began work in 1912.

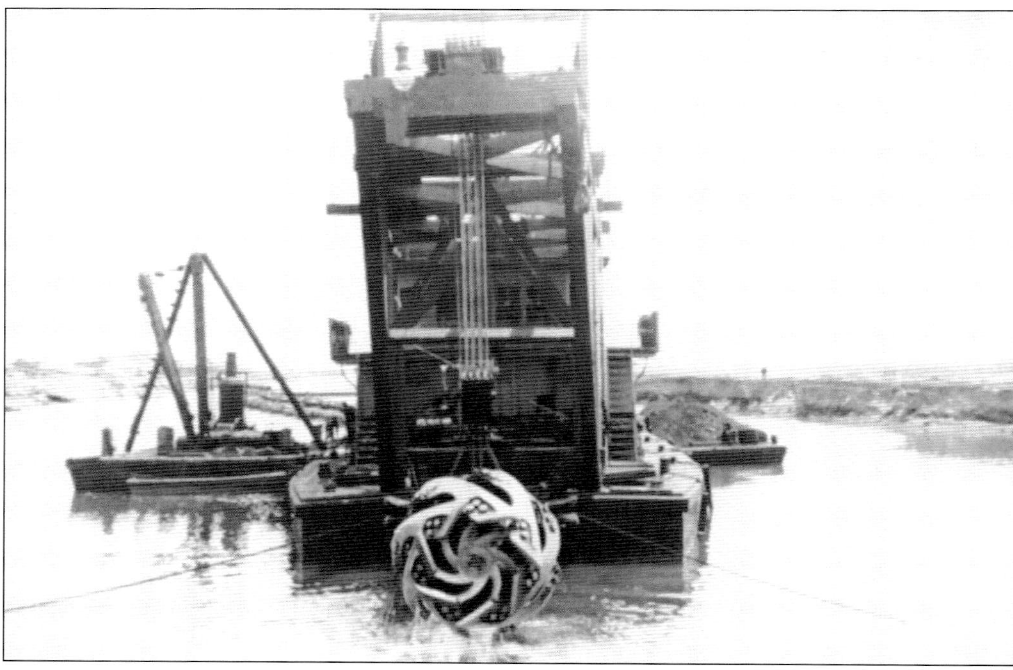

A hydraulic dredge head spins on the dredge General MacKenzie as it works in the Cape Cod Canal around 1910. The head loosened material that was drawn up by steam pumps and deposited along the banks of the canal.

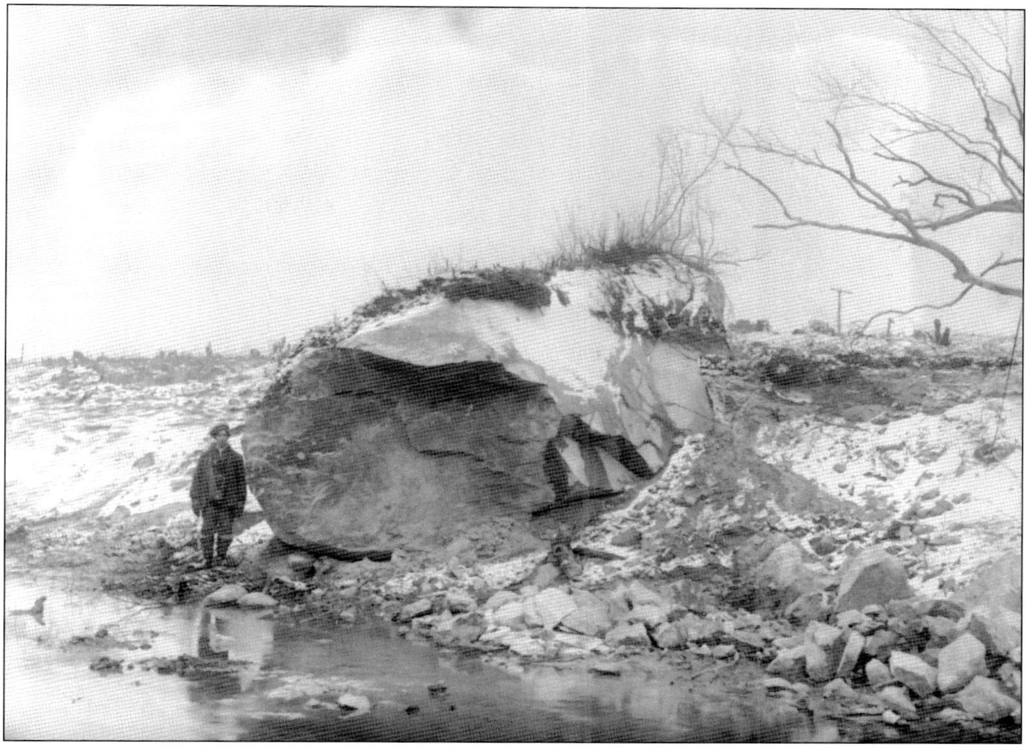

Called "Dynamite" by fellow workers, Charlie Venn gives perspective to the huge rocks found in the path of the canal in this c. 1912 photograph. Venn was the man responsible for setting the charges that blew up the boulders that had to be dealt with in the building of the canal.

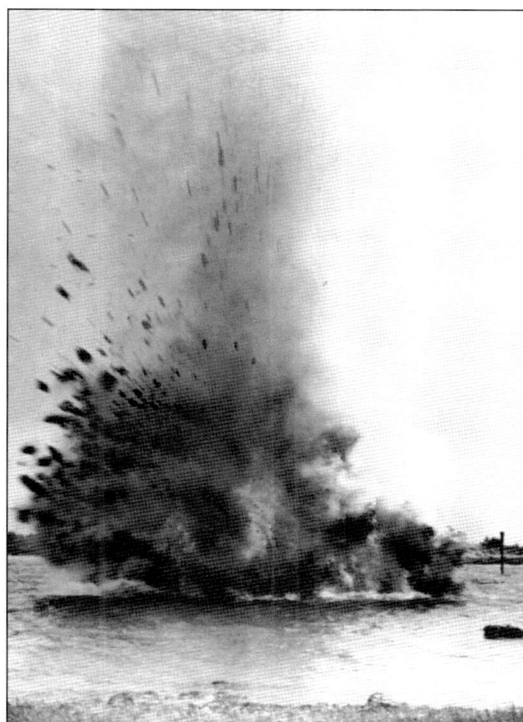

The giant rocks found in the path of construction were blown up on-site to make way for the dredging during the beginning phases of the building of the Cape Cod Canal around 1912.

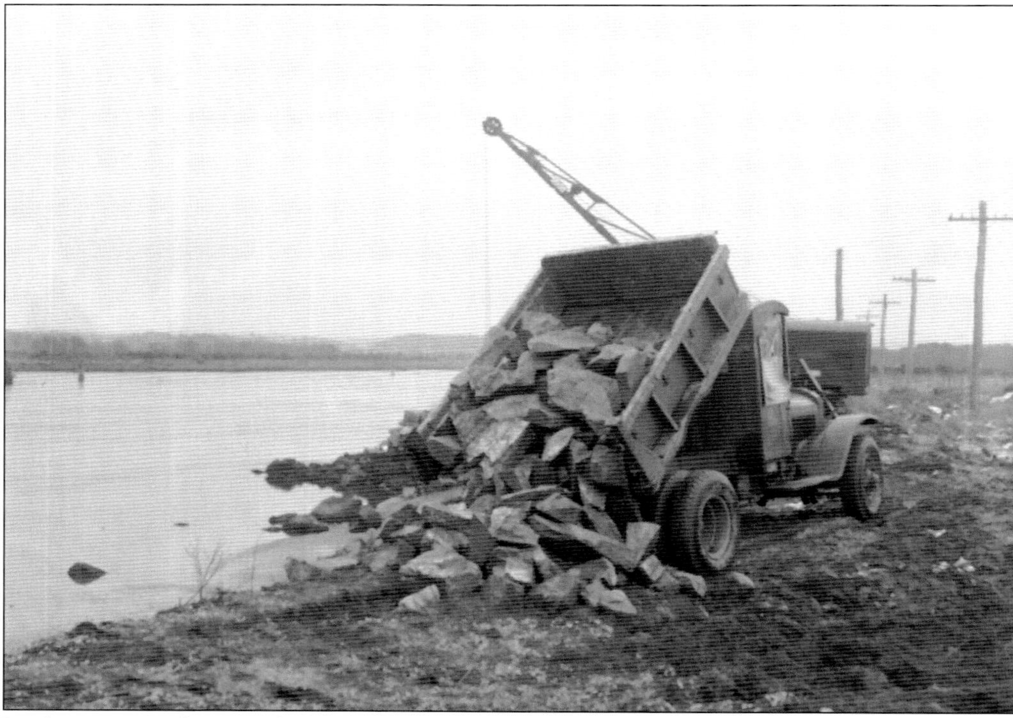

In this c. 1912 photograph, a truck delivers stones for creating the riprap that lined the Cape Cod Canal.

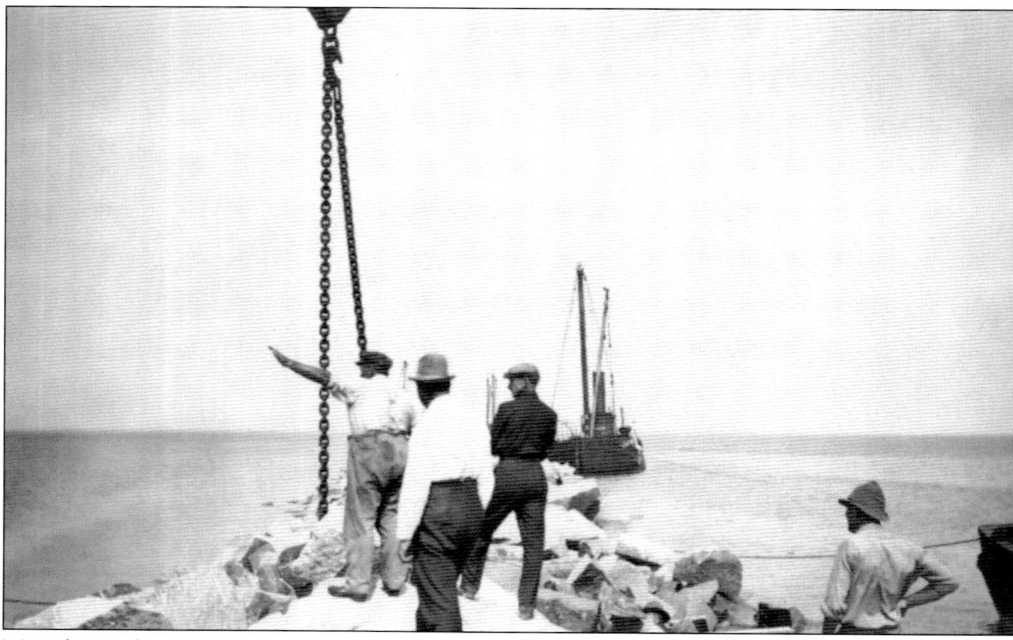

Men direct the placing of stones for the breakwater at the Sandwich end of the Cape Cod Canal. Some of the granite for the breakwater came from a quarry located in Blue Hill, Maine. The breakwater was completed in 1913.

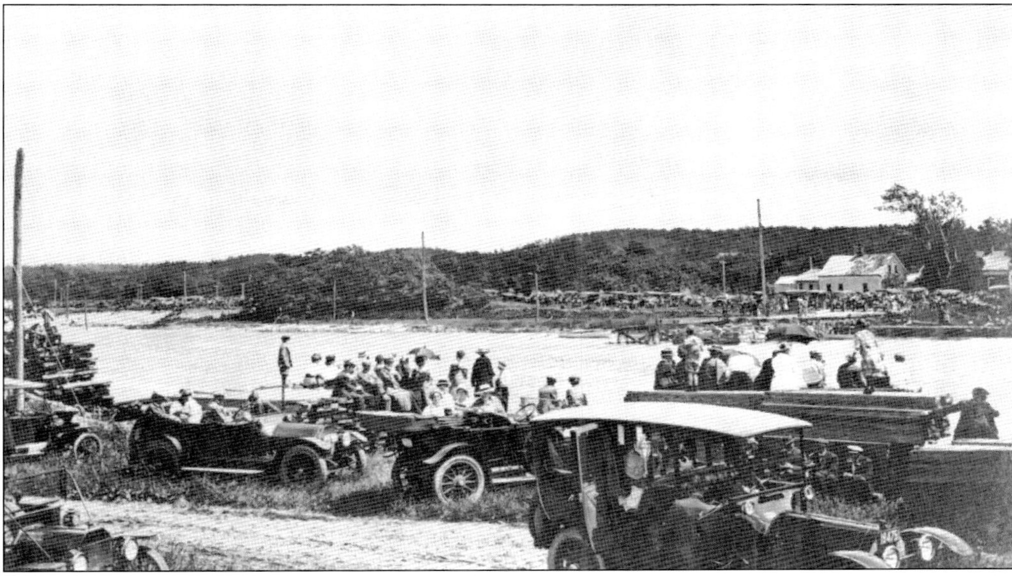

People came from far and wide and lined up along the water to watch the ship parade and other festivities that marked the official opening of the Cape Cod Canal on July 29, 1914.

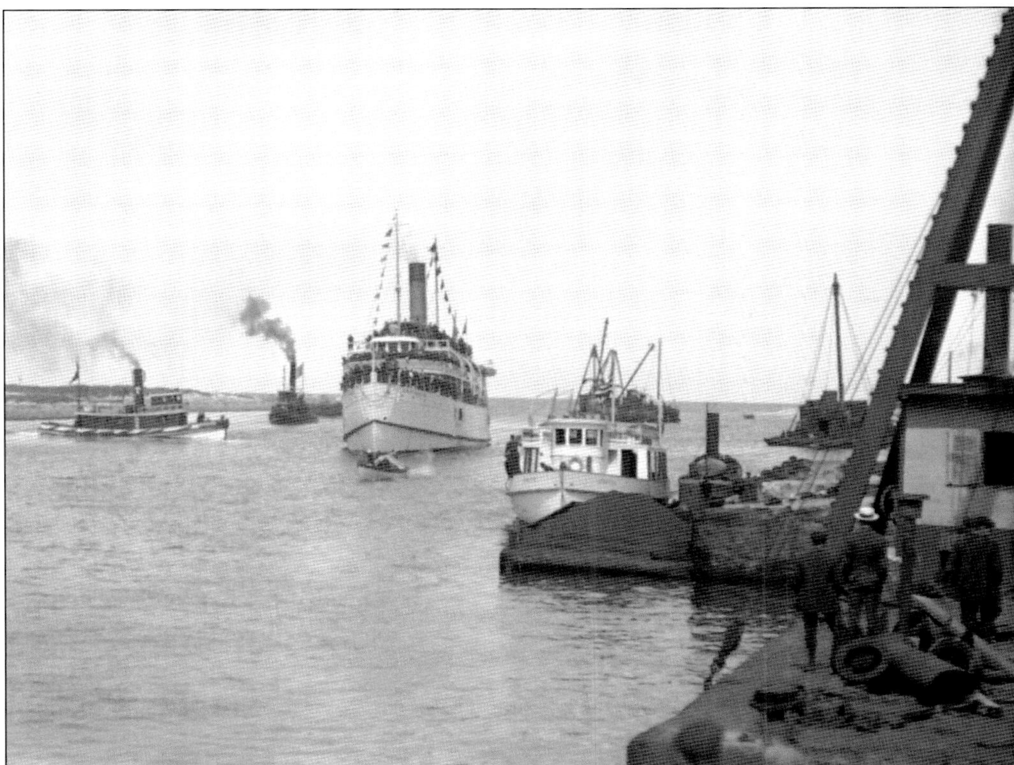

Filled with passengers, the commercial steamer *Dorothy Bradford* from the Provincetown Line enters the Sagamore end of the Cape Cod Canal in this c. 1915 photograph.

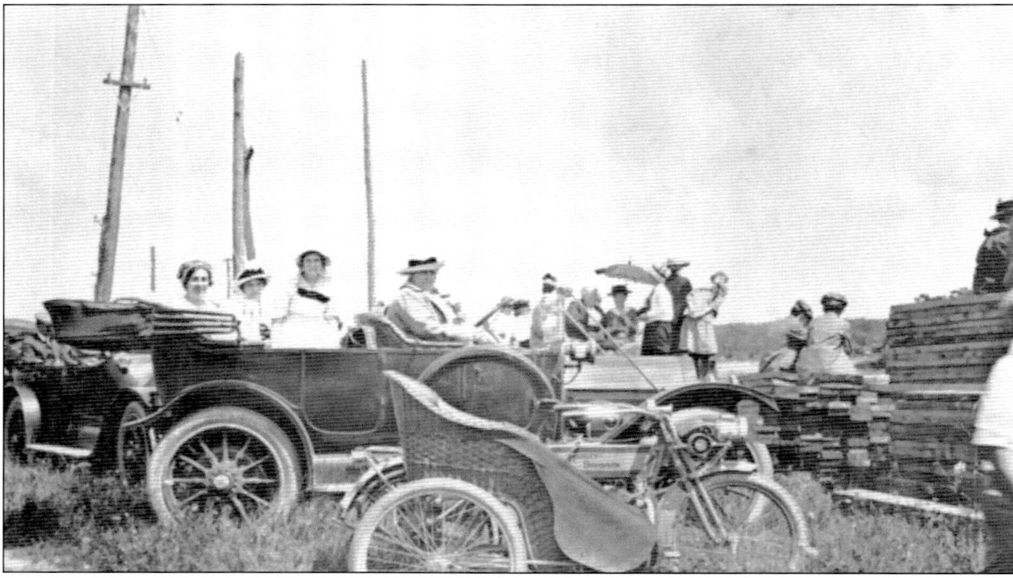

Alongside a Harley-Davidson motorcycle with a wicker sidecar, women in their finery line the banks of the Cape Cod Canal on opening day, July 29, 1914.

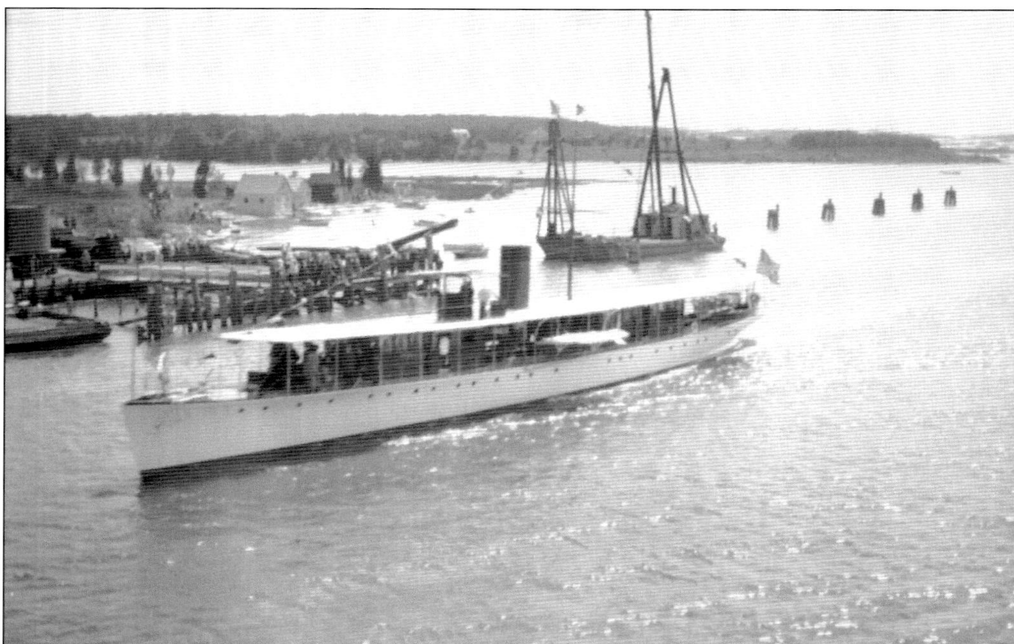

One of the many boats rigged out in finery enters the Cape Cod Canal to participate in the ship parade on opening day, July 29, 1914.

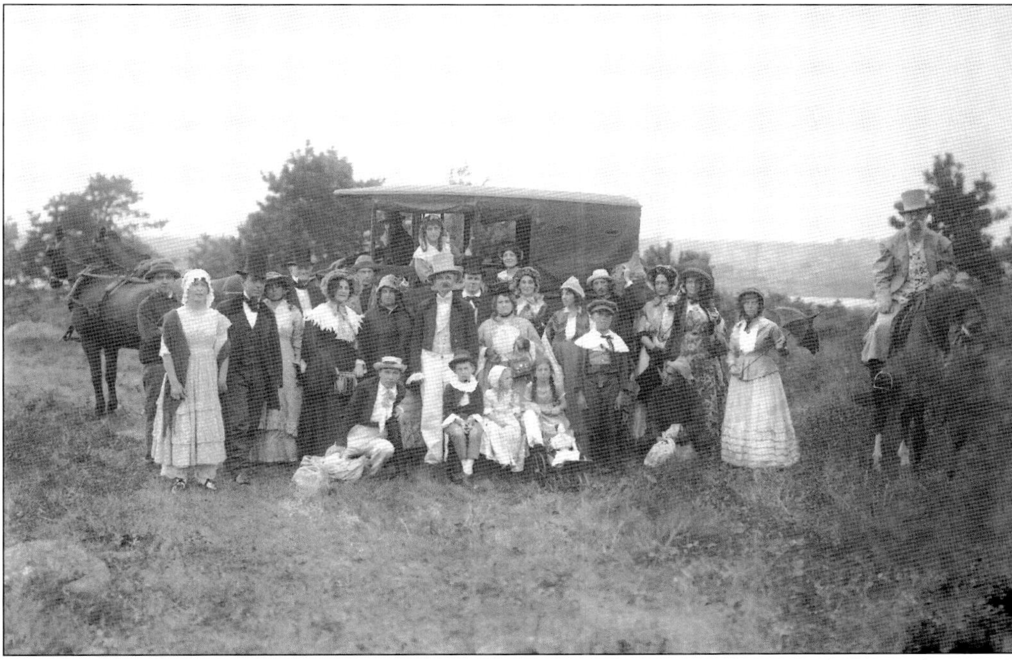

Local people dressed as many different characters pose for a commemorative photograph in early August 1914 during the Pageant of Cape Cod, part of the festivities for the opening of the Cape Cod Canal.

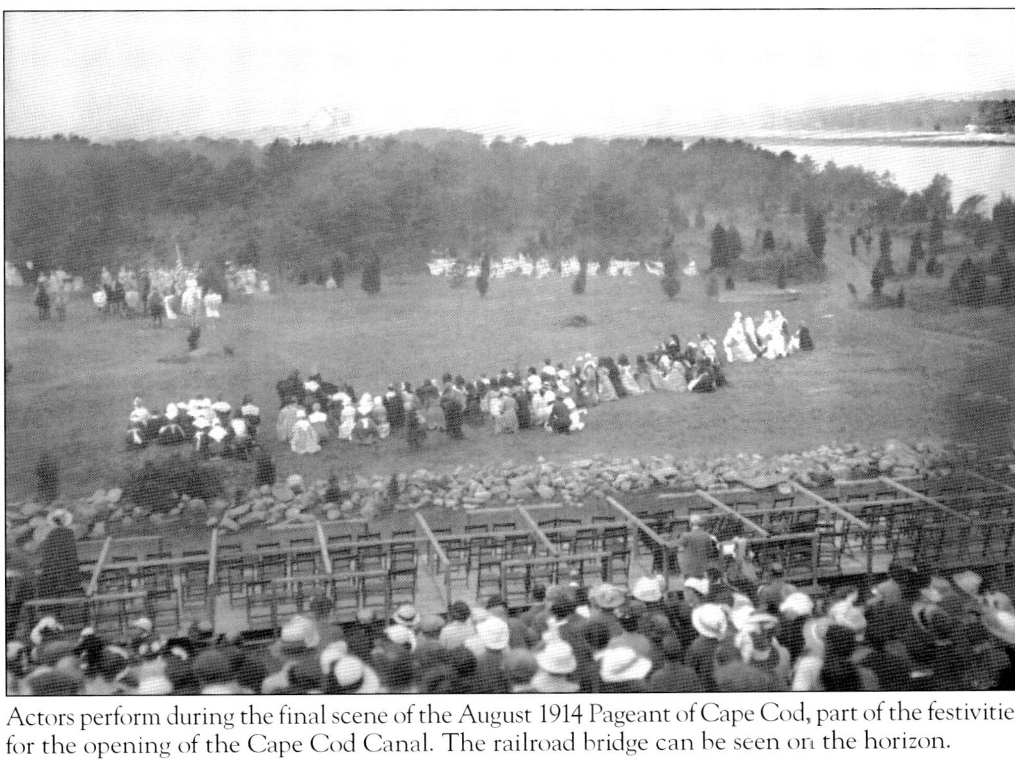

Actors perform during the final scene of the August 1914 Pageant of Cape Cod, part of the festivities for the opening of the Cape Cod Canal. The railroad bridge can be seen on the horizon.

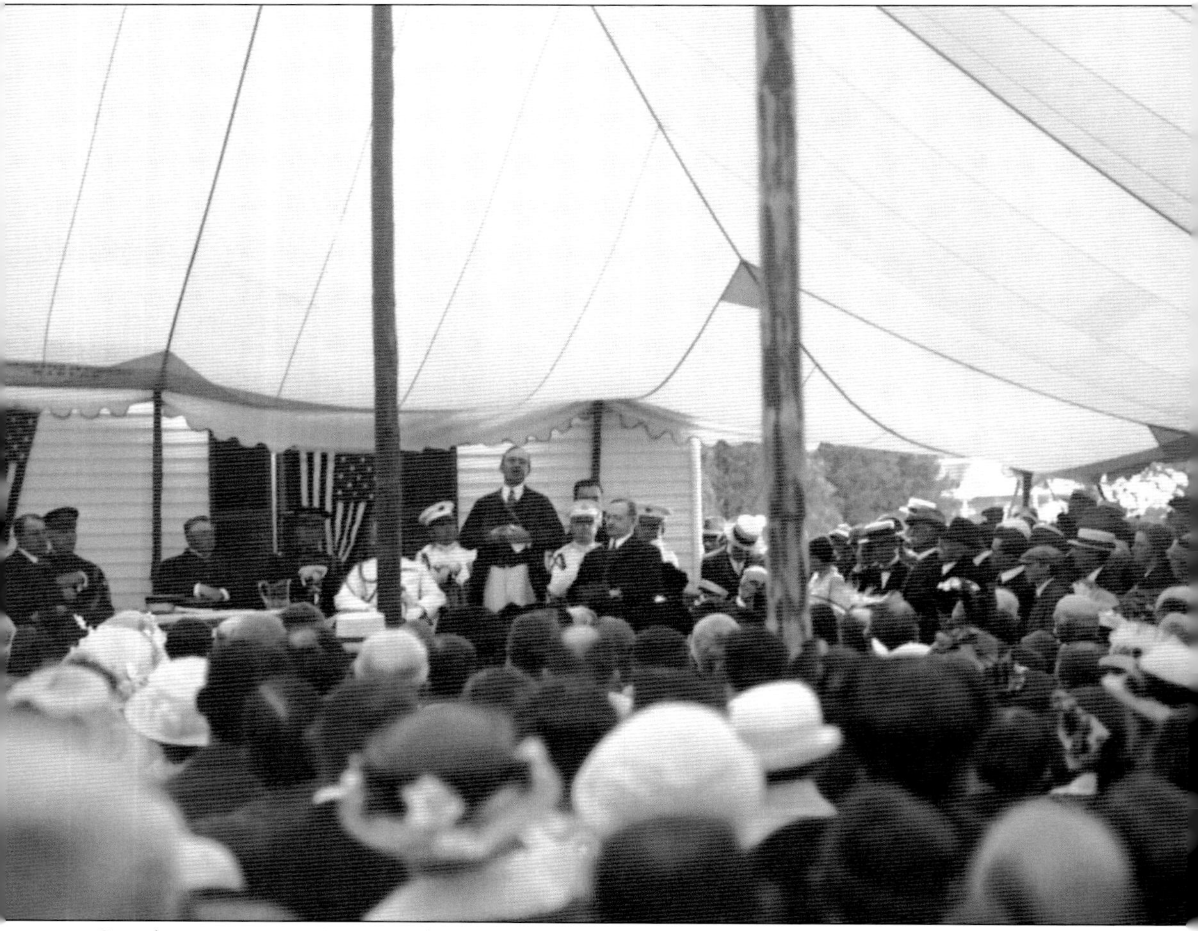

Canal entrepreneur August Belmont speaks during opening day ceremonies under the big tent on the banks of the Cape Cod Canal on July 29, 1914.

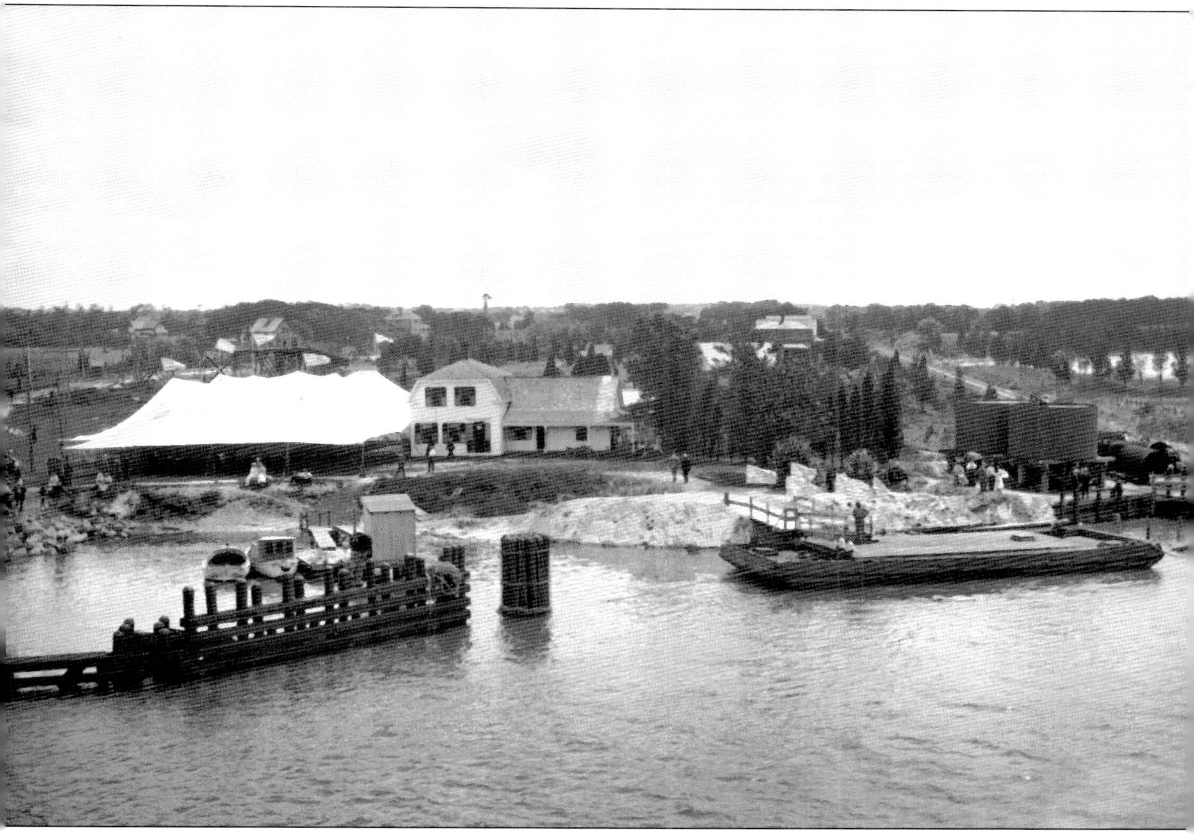

The pavilion is the setting for opening day speeches and festivities during the opening of the Cape Cod Canal on July 29, 1914. At right is the barge that took August Belmont and his group out to inspect the finished canal.

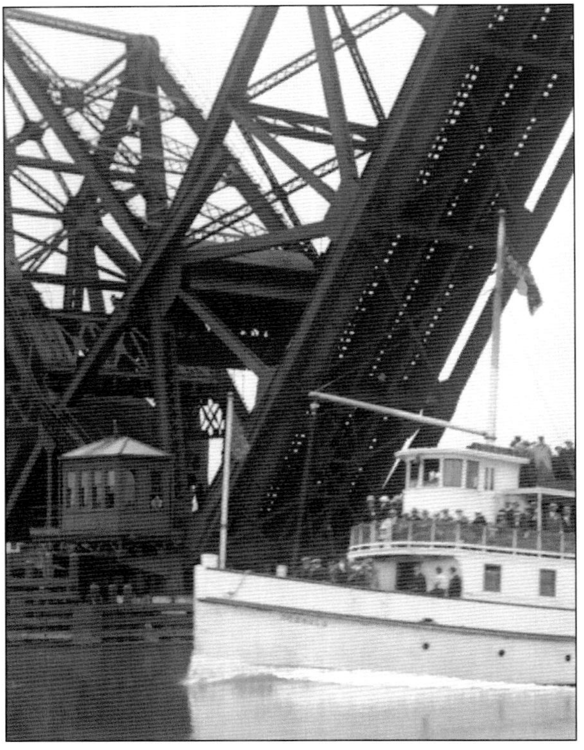

The bridge tender hangs out his window to watch as ships pass the railroad bridge and enter the Cape Cod Canal for the ship parade on opening day.

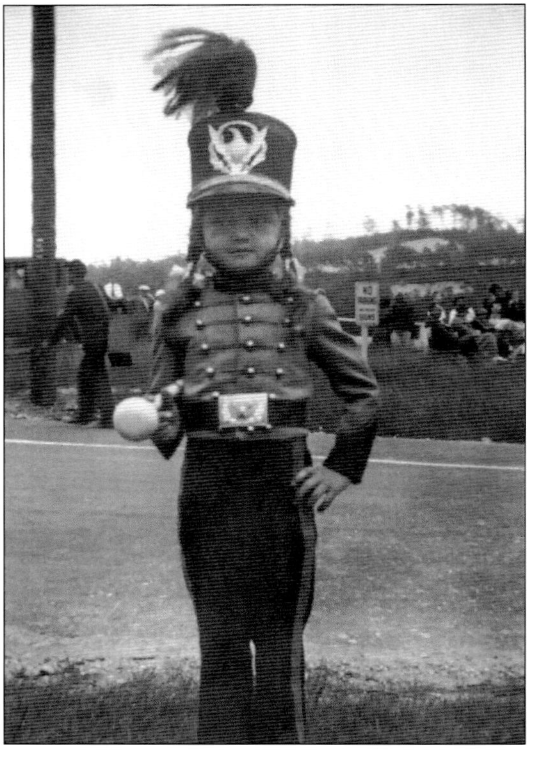

A little majorette poses for a photograph prior to the parade that was part of the festivities celebrating the opening of the Cape Cod Canal in July 1914.

Five

Business and Industry

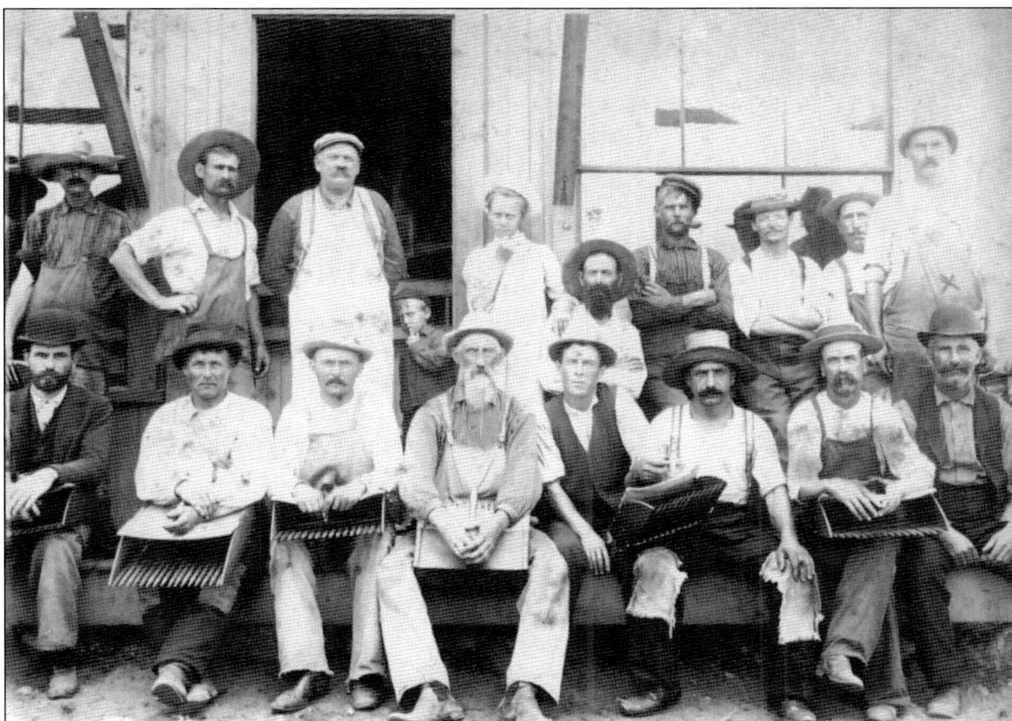

This c. 1900 photograph shows a group of cranberry-industry workers posing with their cranberry scoops. The wooden scoops were used for the dry harvesting of berries. The native peoples first used cranberries as part of the high-protein food called pemmican, a combination of berries, deer meat, and melted fat.

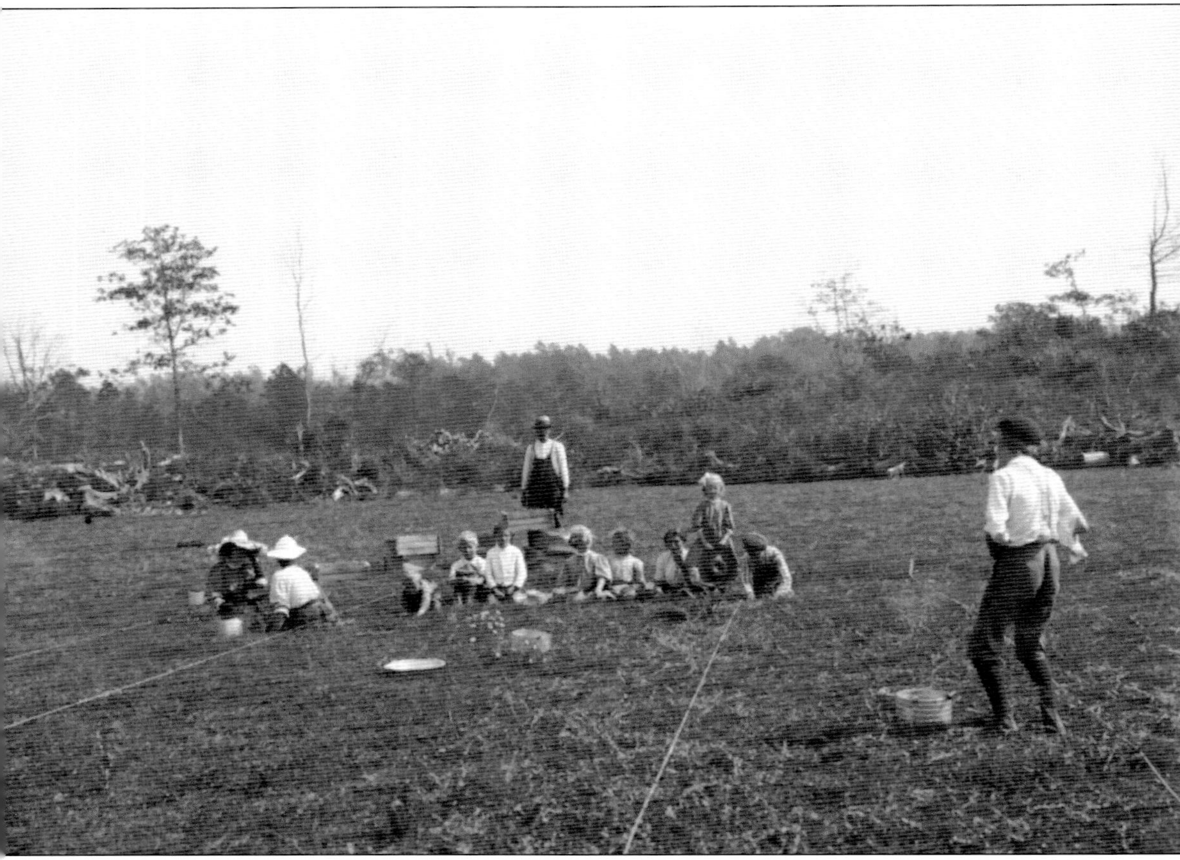

A group picks cranberries in this 1903 photograph. Whole families, including women and children, gathered in the bogs when the cranberries were ready for picking and helped get the crop in.

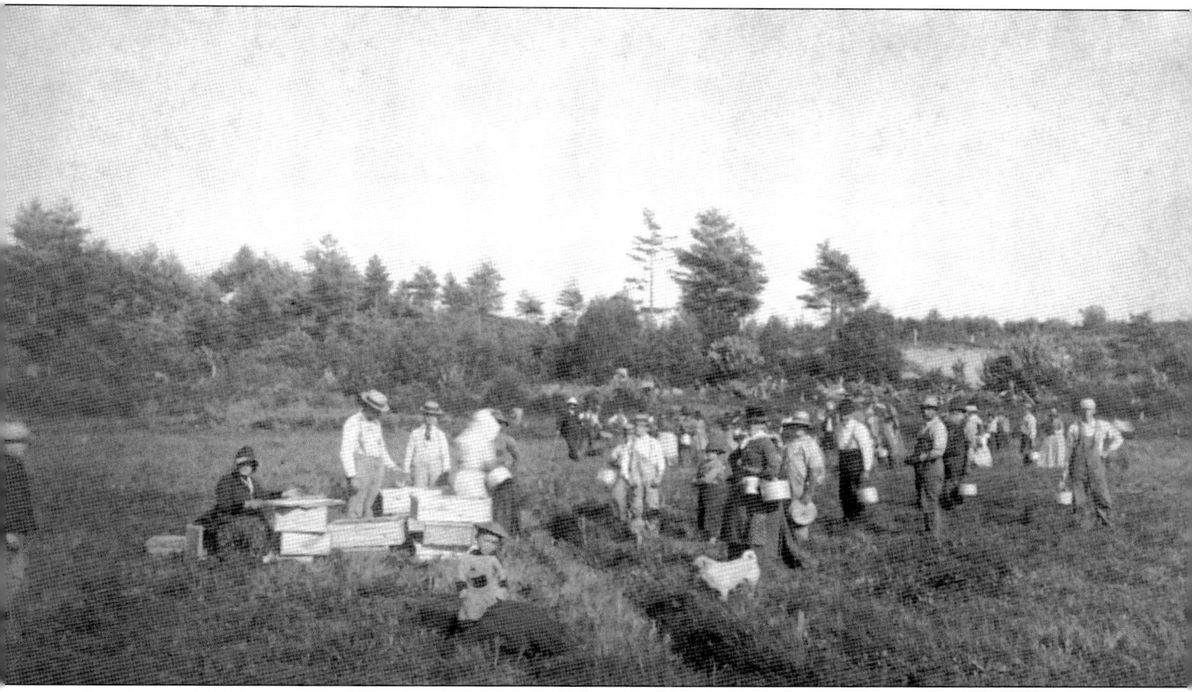

In this c. 1903 photograph, people line up with pails during the cranberry harvest to get their berries weighed and put into the wooden boxes that were used to send the cranberries to the plant. Cranberries were first cultivated on Cape Cod in 1816, and the first association of growers was formed by the 1870s.

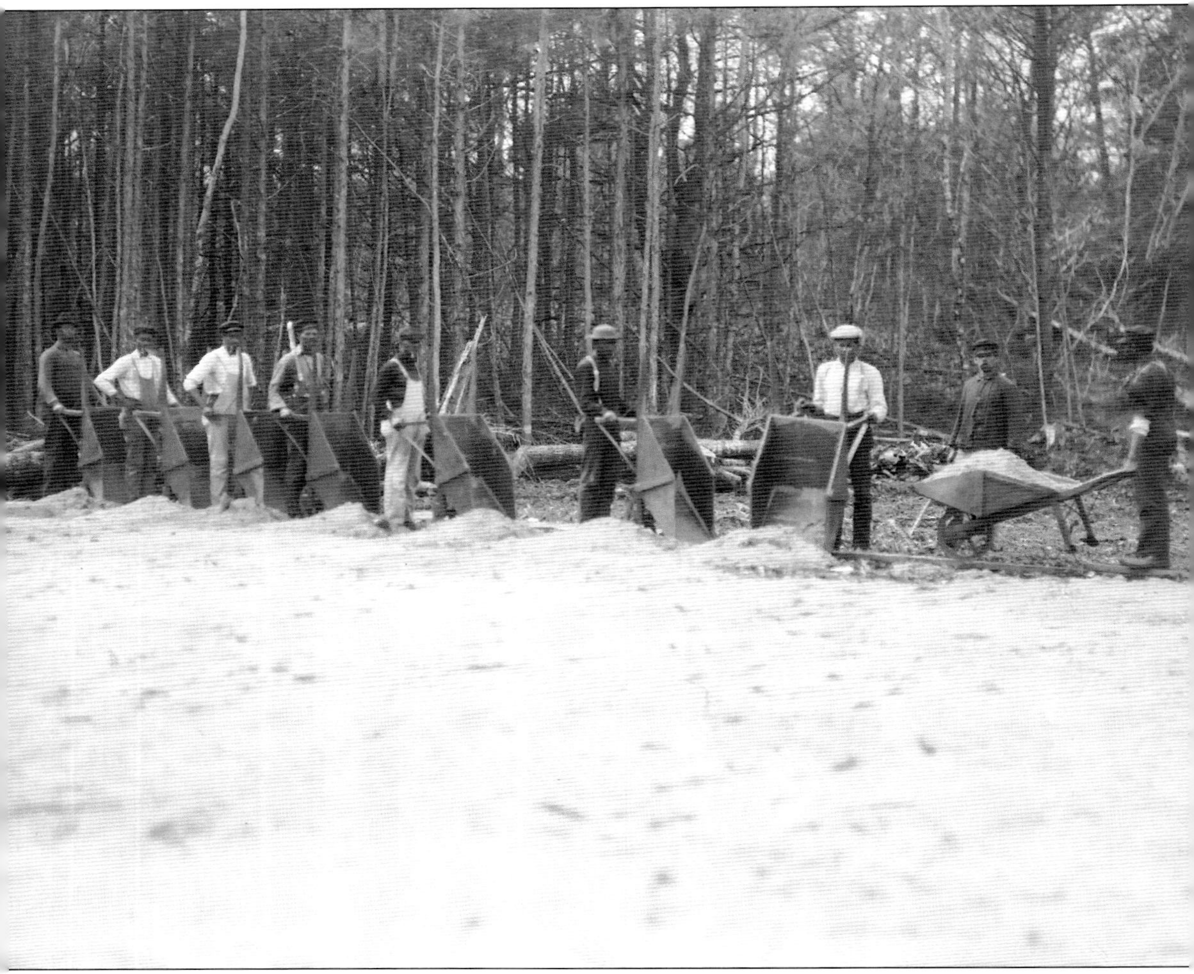

Laborers line up with wheelbarrows full of sand in preparation to sand the bogs for the next season of cranberry harvesting. Cranberries need sand, peat, gravel, and clay layered in beds, commonly known as bogs, to be successfully grown.

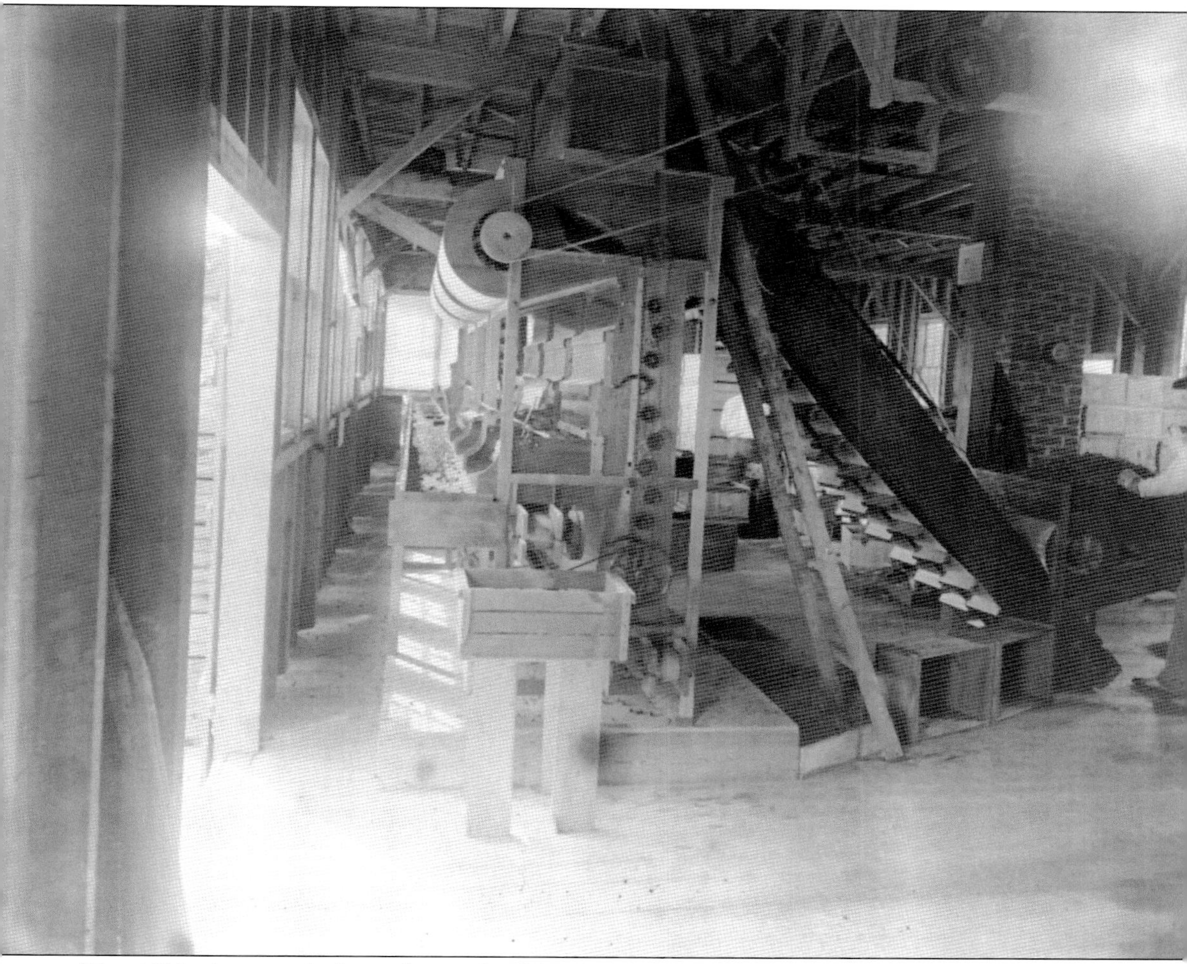

This 1930s photograph shows the inside of the Ocean Spray cranberry packing plant. Cranberries are one of three native North American fruits that are grown commercially; the other two are blueberries and Concord grapes.

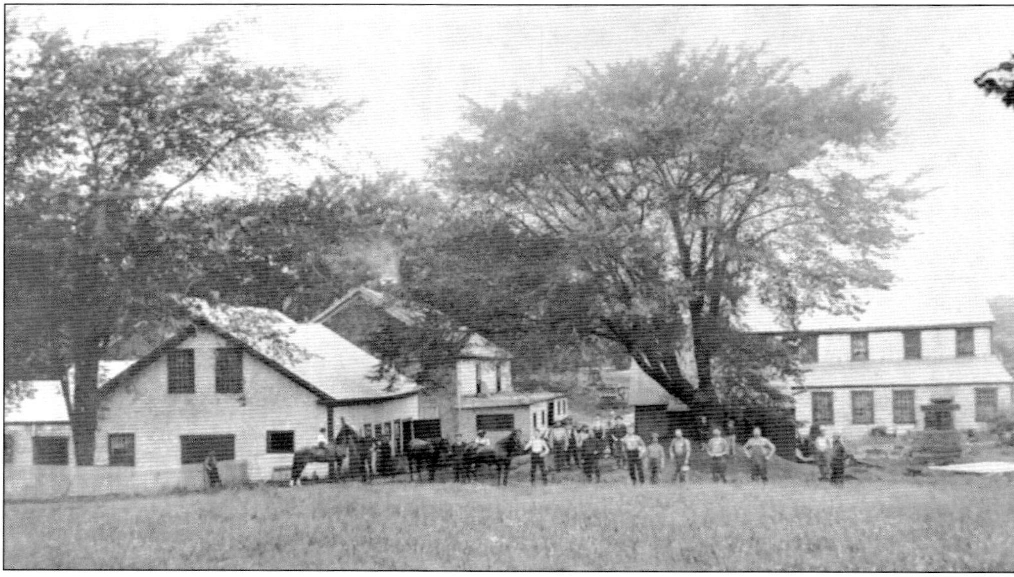

In this 1880s photograph, workers and horses pose in front of the Howard Foundry in Bournedale. The foundries in Bourne began with the discovery of bog iron in the local swamps and springs.

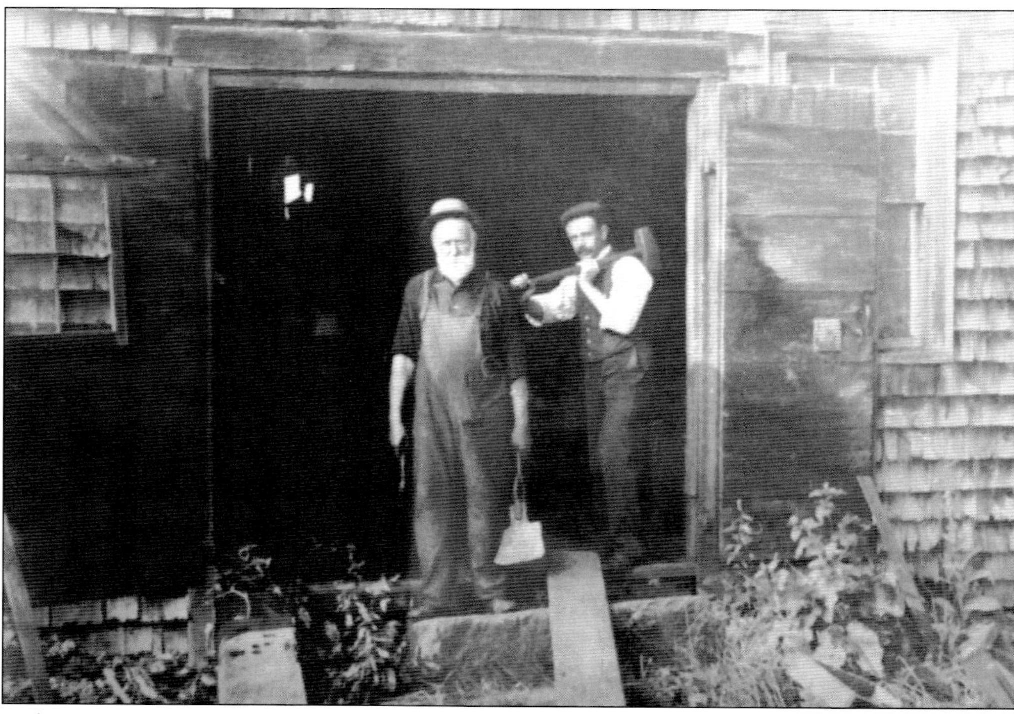

Holway Axe Factory owner Seth Holway (left) and his nephew Albert Holway hold their tools in the doorway of the axe factory in the village of Bournedale. The axes made in Holway's factory could be found all over the country and the world in those early days.

Foundry workers in Bournedale stand for a photograph around 1910. An iridescent, oily film on the surface of a body of water can be an indication of the presence of bog iron, one of the early industries in Bourne.

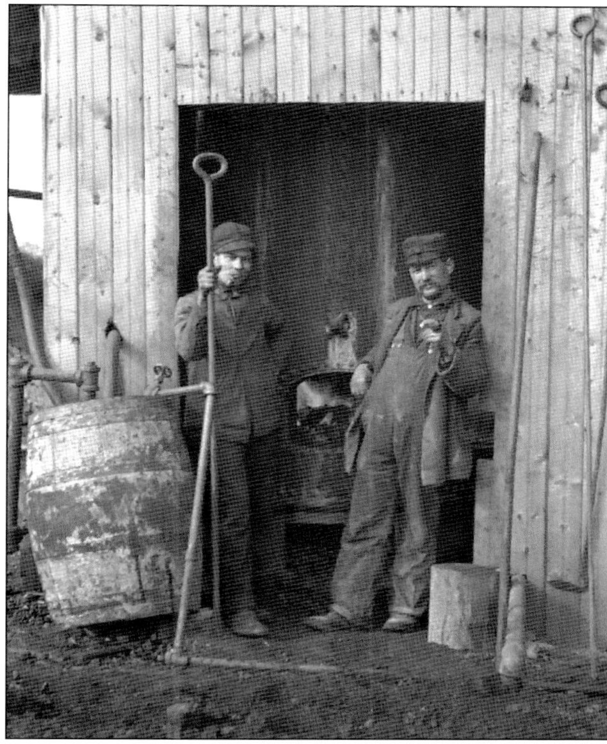

Workers pose around 1910 in front of the "fruit and confectionery" store, first operated by the Holt and Girard families, that still stands on Main Street in Buzzards Bay. Through the years, the building has housed many different commercial ventures.

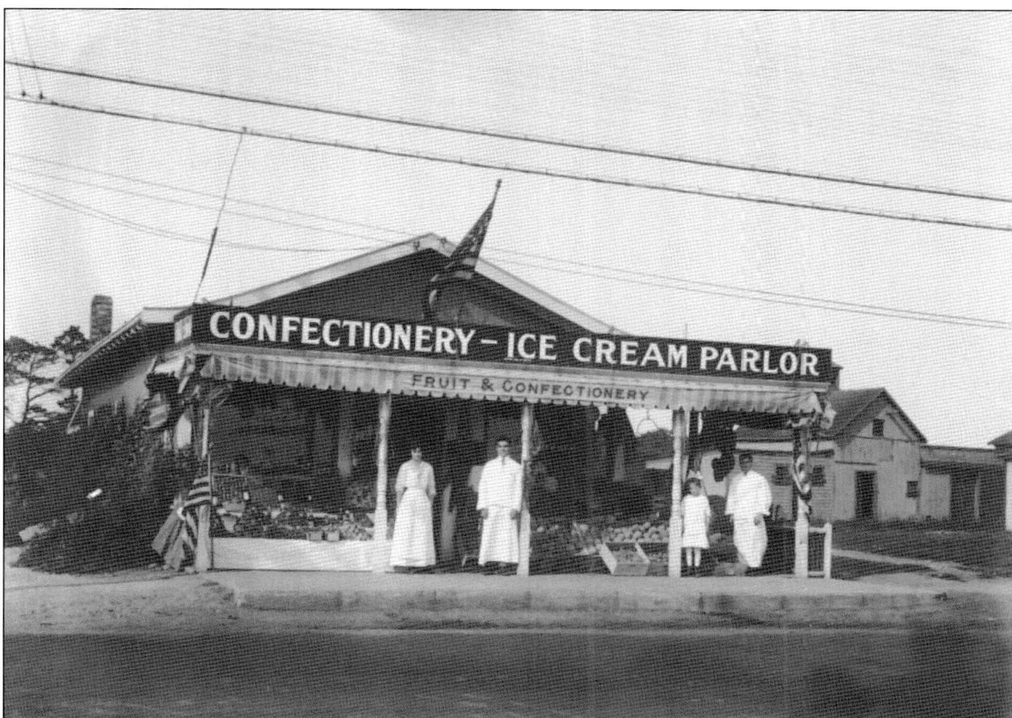

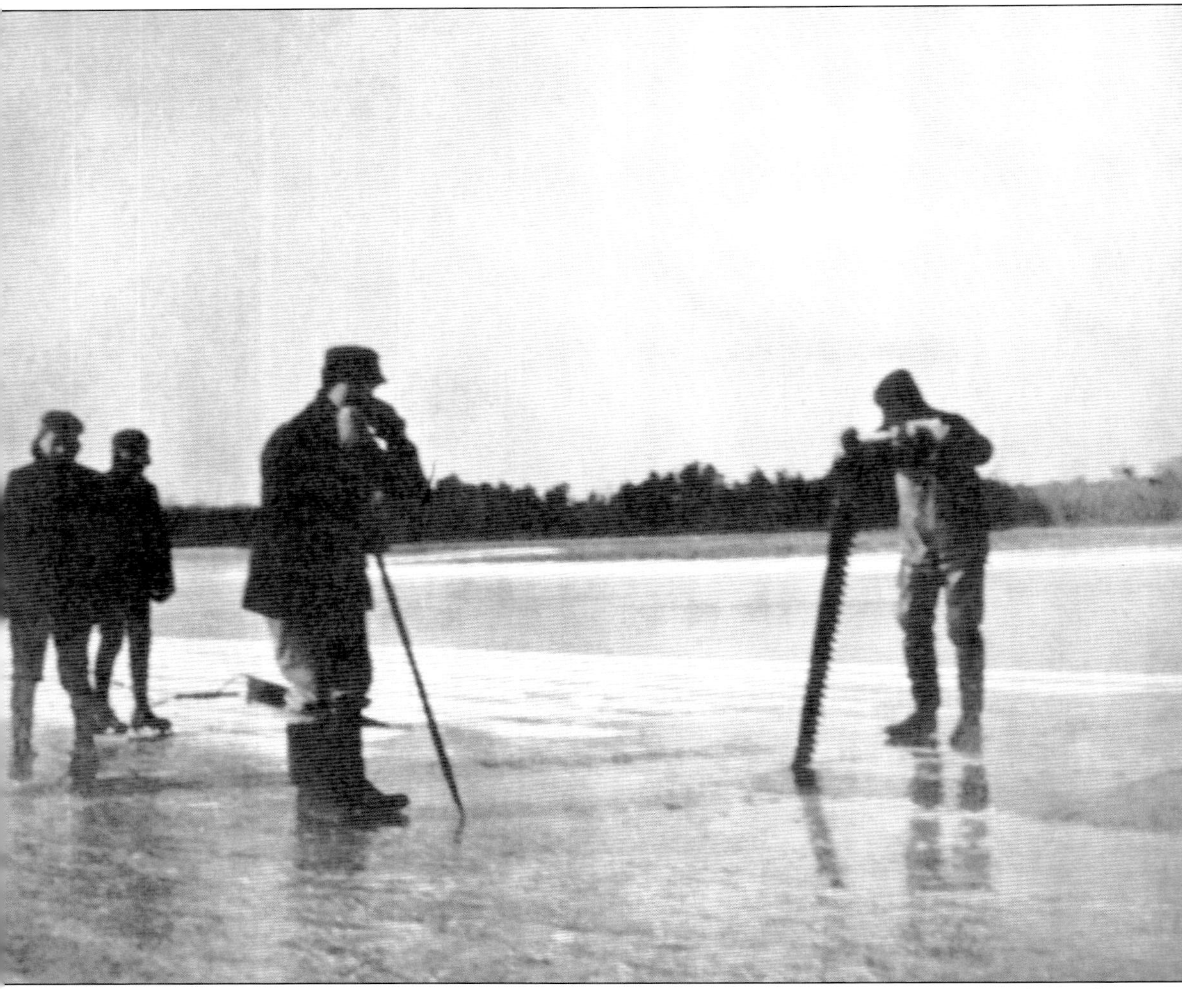

In this c. 1920s photograph, men sawing ice for winter storage cut through the frozen Nightingale Pond in Buzzards Bay with their long saws.

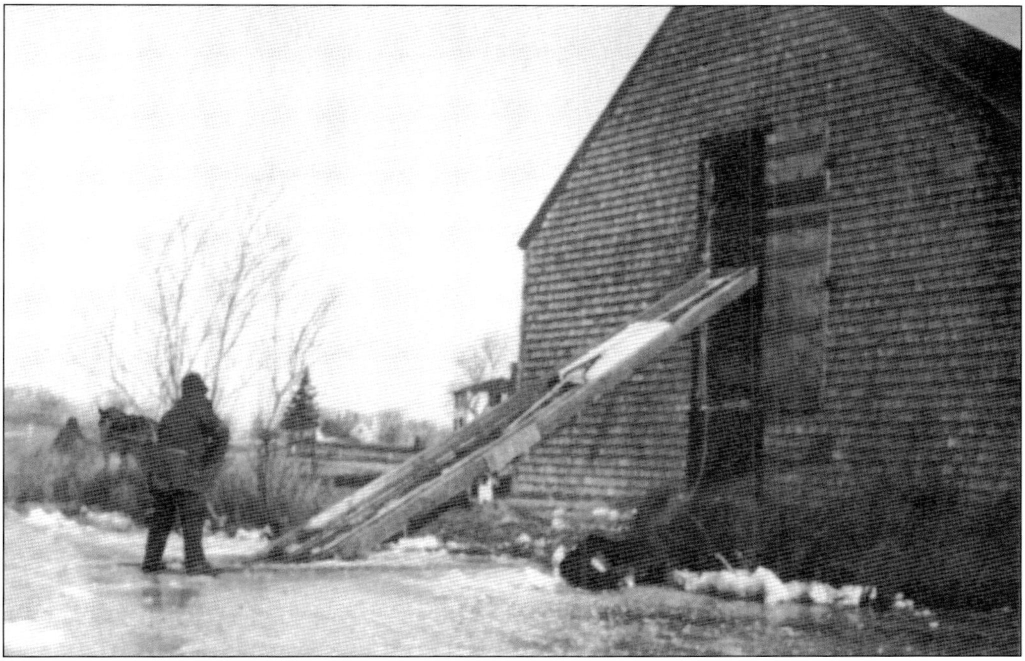

In this 1920s photograph, a block of ice is pulled up into one of the icehouses that belonged to Benjamin Bourne. Early in the 20th century, ice harvesting was gradually replaced by refrigeration and ice made in factories.

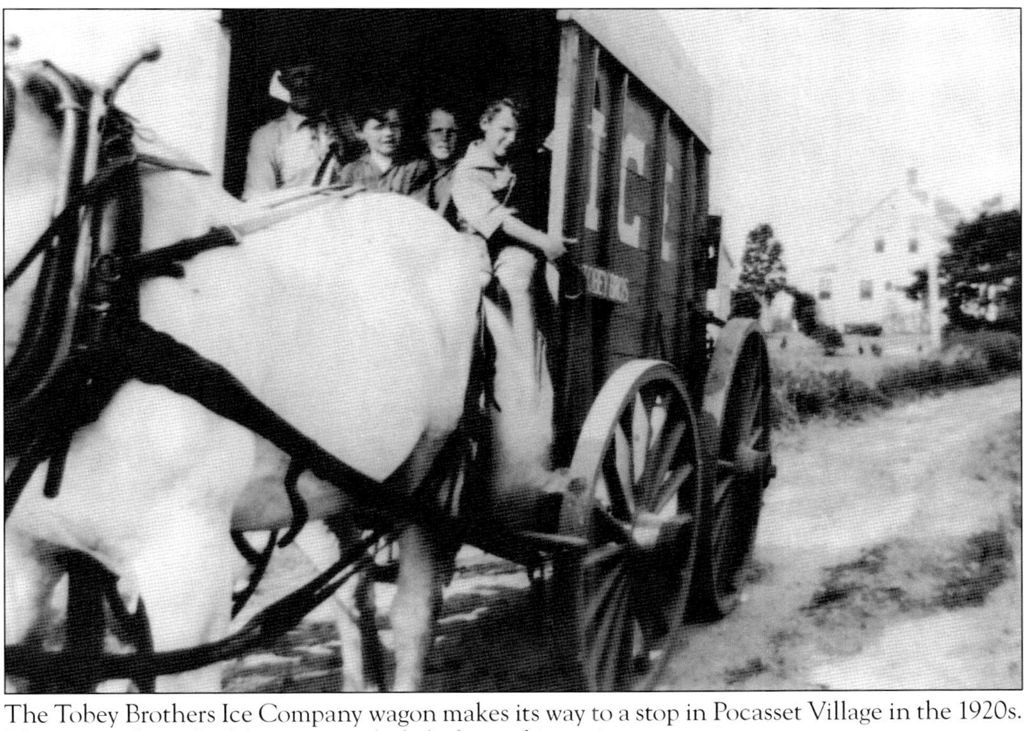

The Tobey Brothers Ice Company wagon makes its way to a stop in Pocasset Village in the 1920s. The ice truck made deliveries regularly before refrigeration was common.

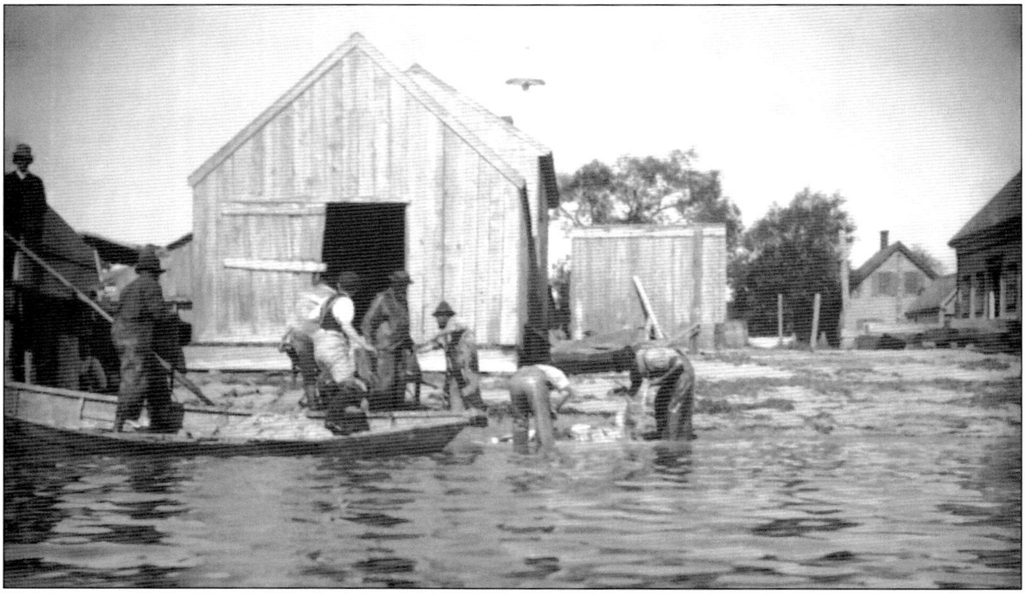

Fishermen clean their catch in front of one of the fish houses in Bourne around 1910.

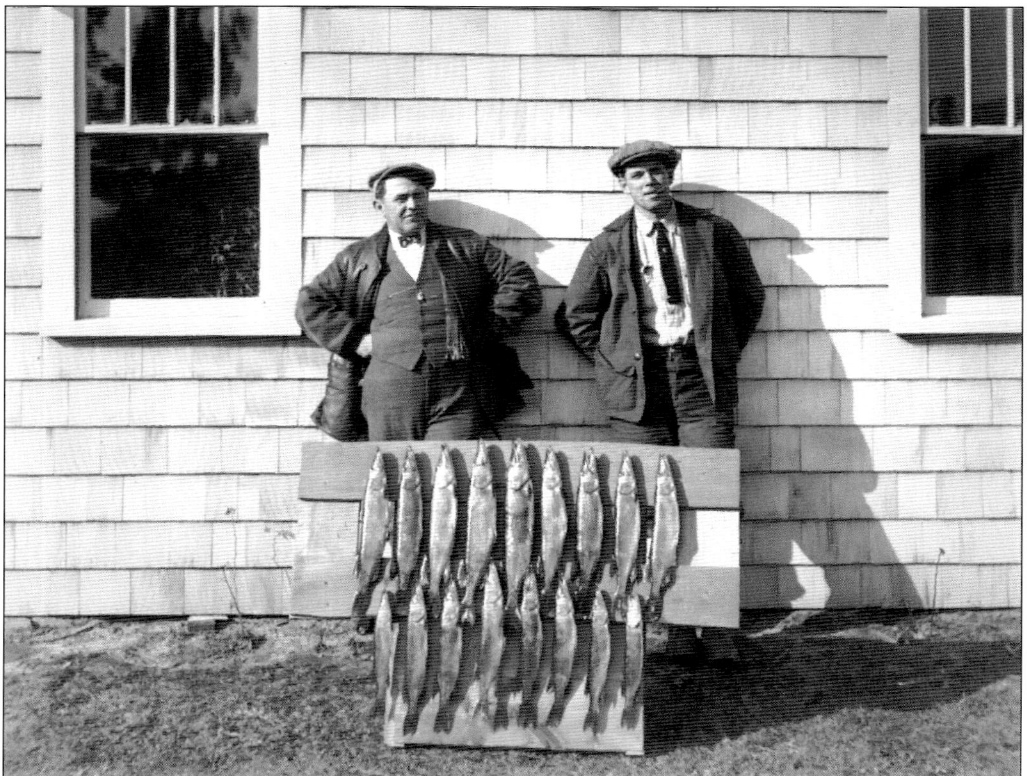

Two local men line up their fish and pose with their catch after a day of fishing in this photograph from the early 1900s. Fishing was a mainstay of the area commercially, locally for the table, and for sport.

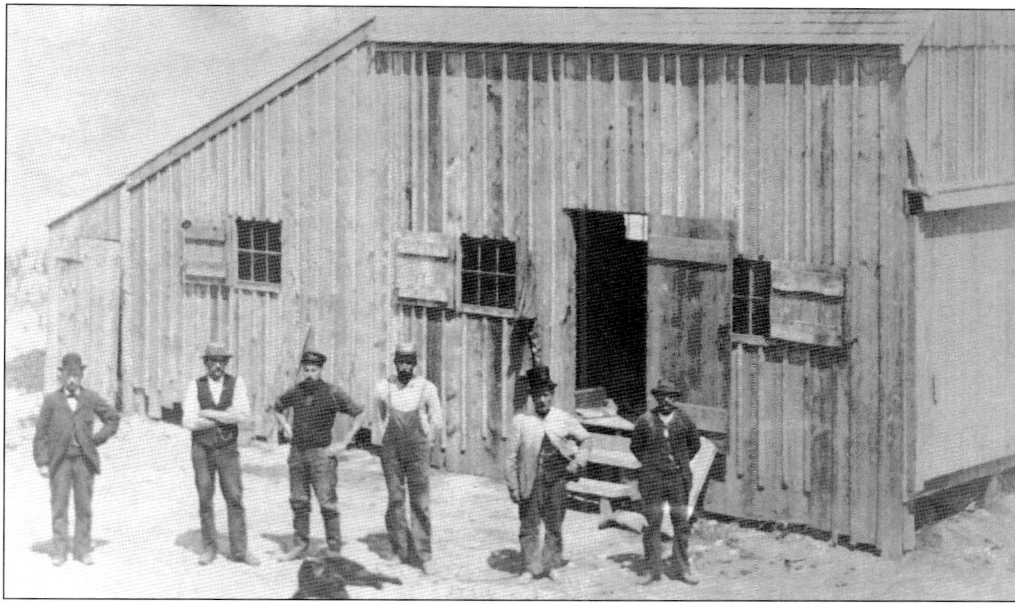

Workers stand in front of the Sagamore Fish Weir Company building around 1905. Sagamore Fish Weir stockholder Emory Gibbs, a local of the area, is at right; the others are unidentified.

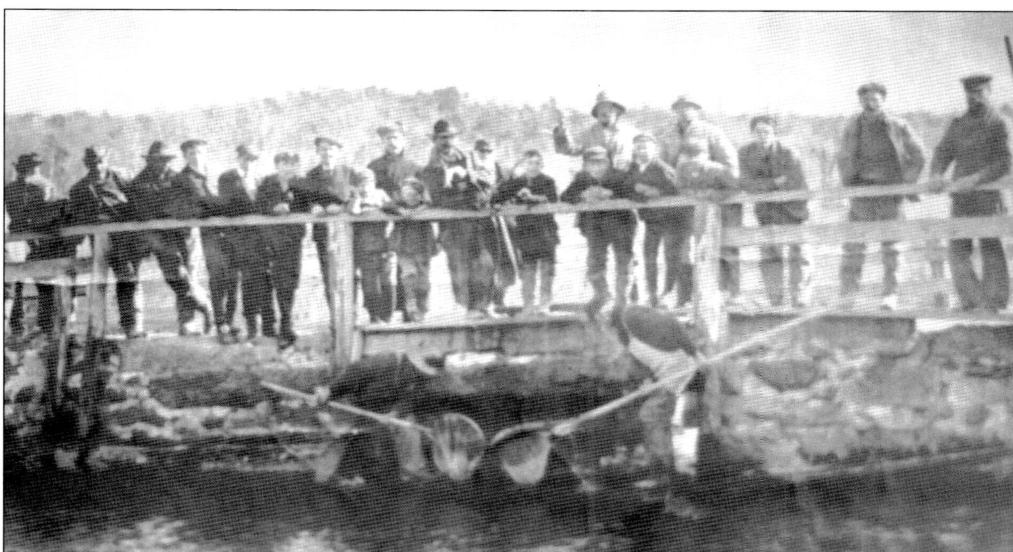

Men line up along the road as two men hold their nets under the flowing water waiting for an annual herring run to begin. In the first half of the 20th century, herring at one time flowed so prolifically that they were even used for fertilizer. In the 1960s, large ships outfitted with trawling nets caught the herring in such quantities that the population collapsed. Strict offshore fishing laws caused populations to rebound in the 1980s.

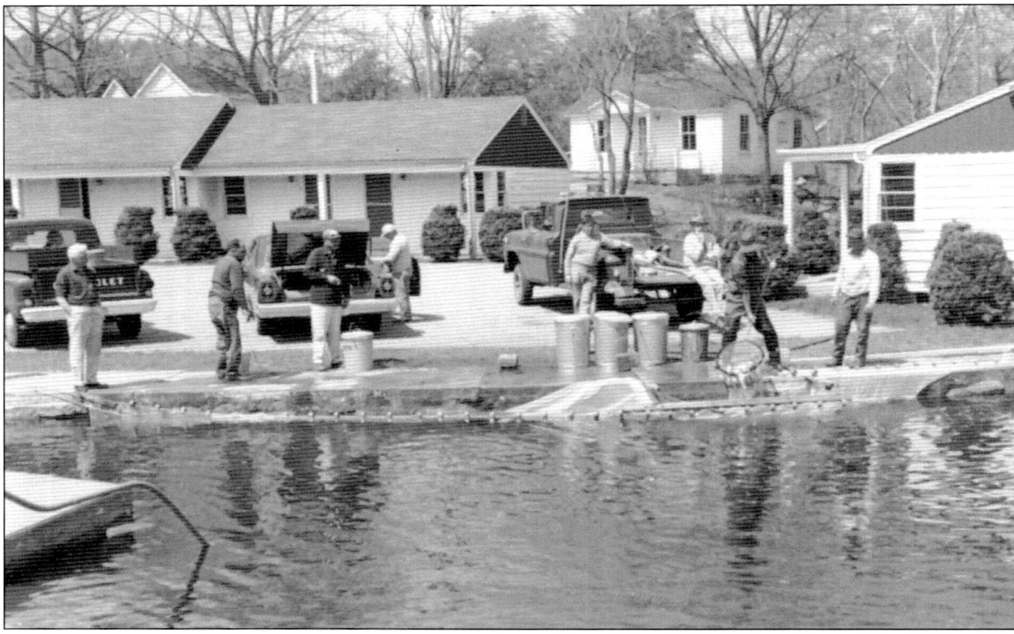

In this c. 1955 photograph, fishermen in the village of Bournedale gather enough herring with nets to fill up garbage pails. Herring was fished so extensively in the 20th century by trawlers in the Atlantic that the population collapsed. New laws resulted in the fish rebounding by the late 1980s, but the species is still threatened by commercial fishing.

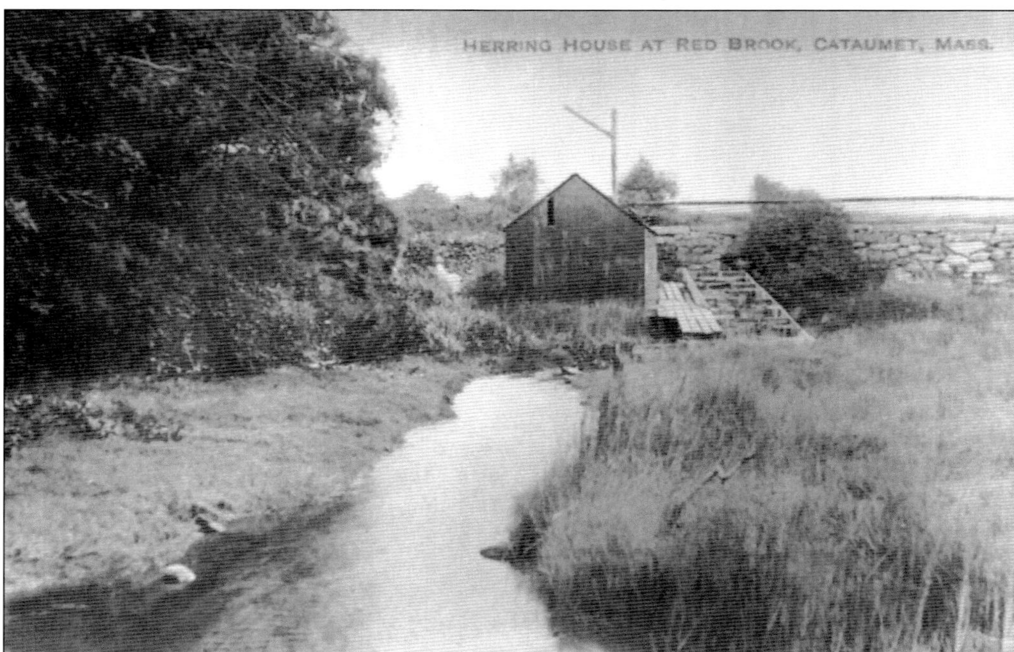

The herring house and herring run at Red Brook in Cataumet village is pictured around the 1920s. The herring run usually came in April, and people would gather to catch the fish and dry or smoke them for later use.

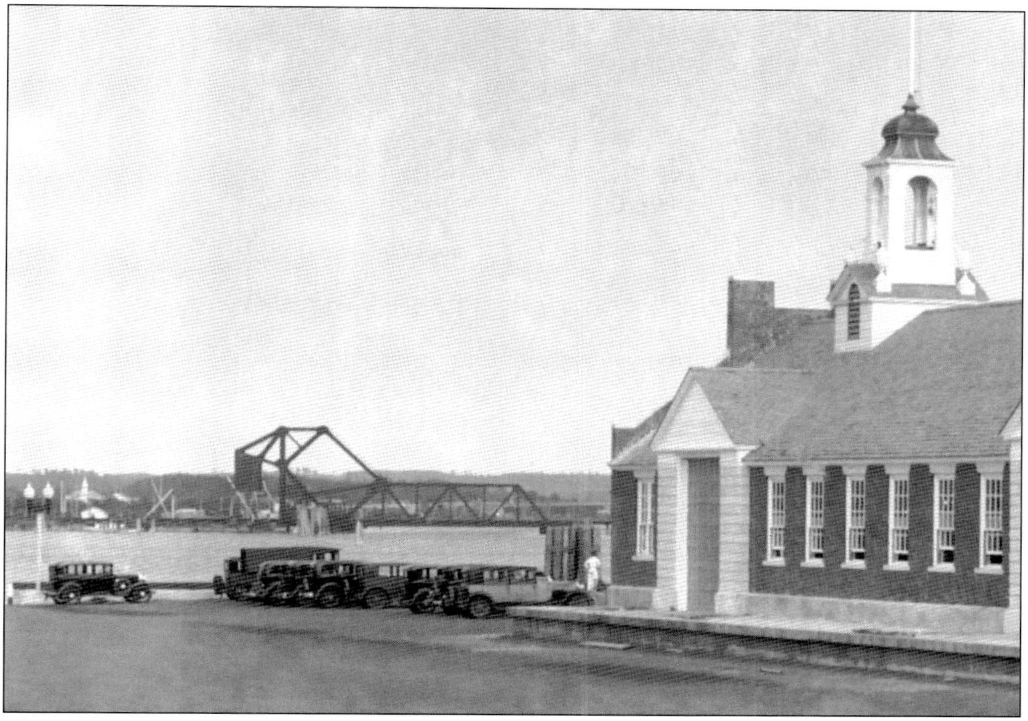

The old railroad bridge can be seen in this photograph from 1933 that shows the State Pier building (right) on Taylor's Point in Buzzards Bay Village.

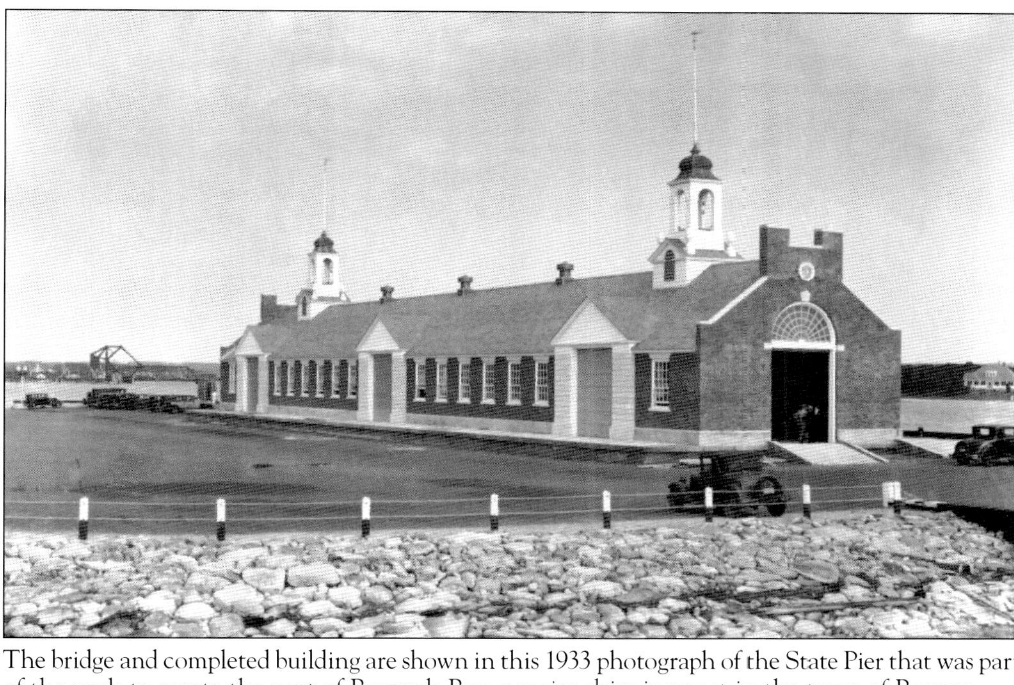

The bridge and completed building are shown in this 1933 photograph of the State Pier that was part of the push to create the port of Buzzards Bay, a major shipping port in the town of Bourne.

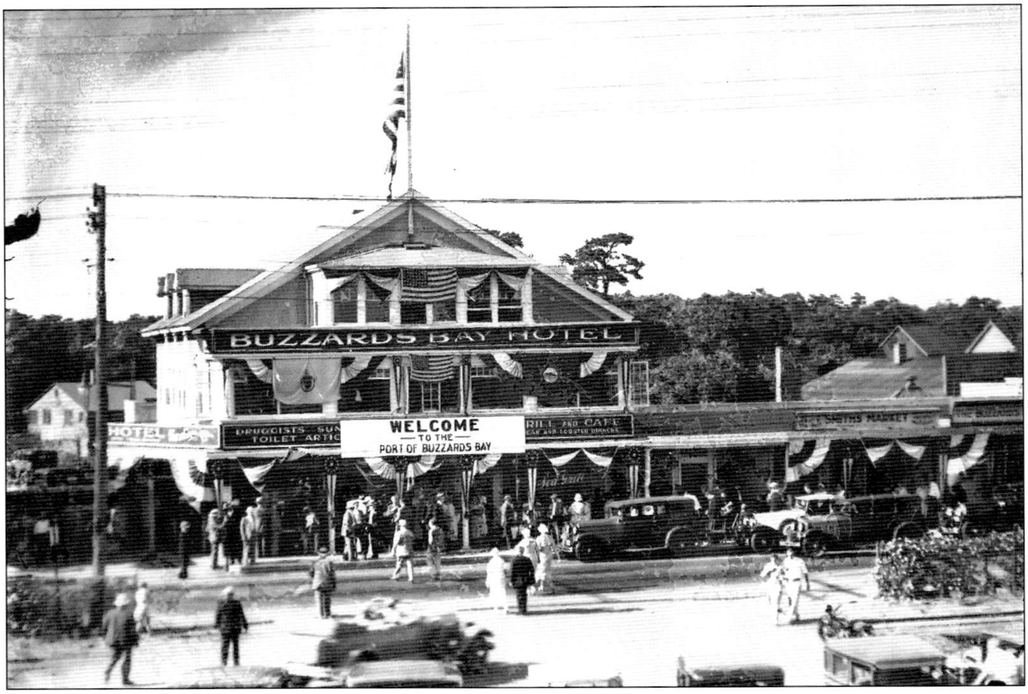

The Buzzards Bay Hotel and the village of Buzzards Bay are all dressed up for the celebration surrounding the completion of State Pier on Taylor's Point in 1933.

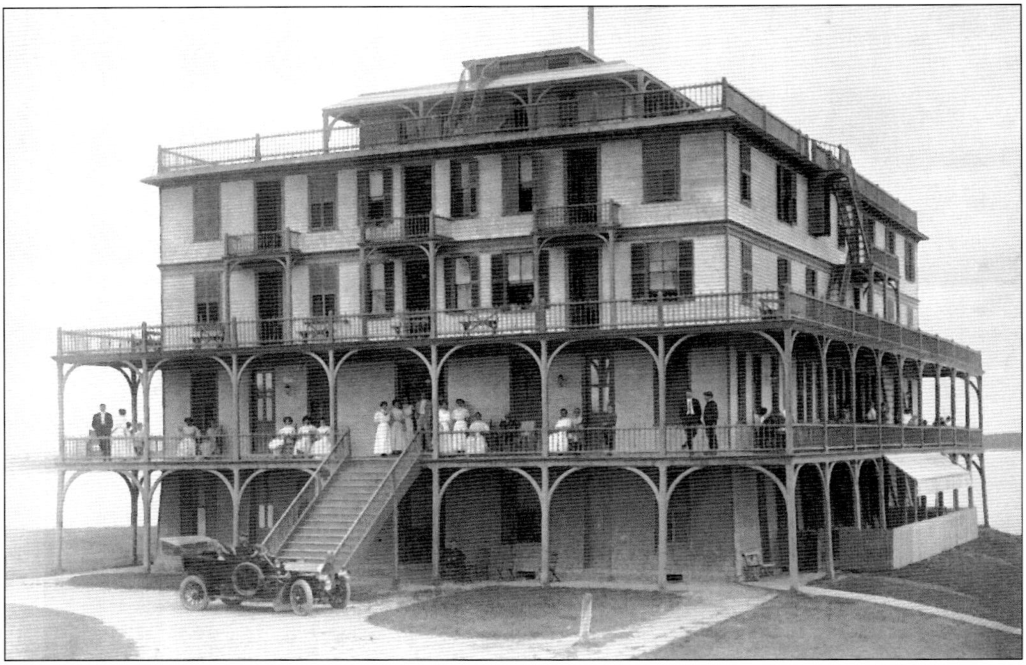

Guests around the turn of the century pose for a photograph on the porches around the Norcross Hotel in Monument Beach. The Norcross catered to the growing business of summer visitors to Cape Cod.

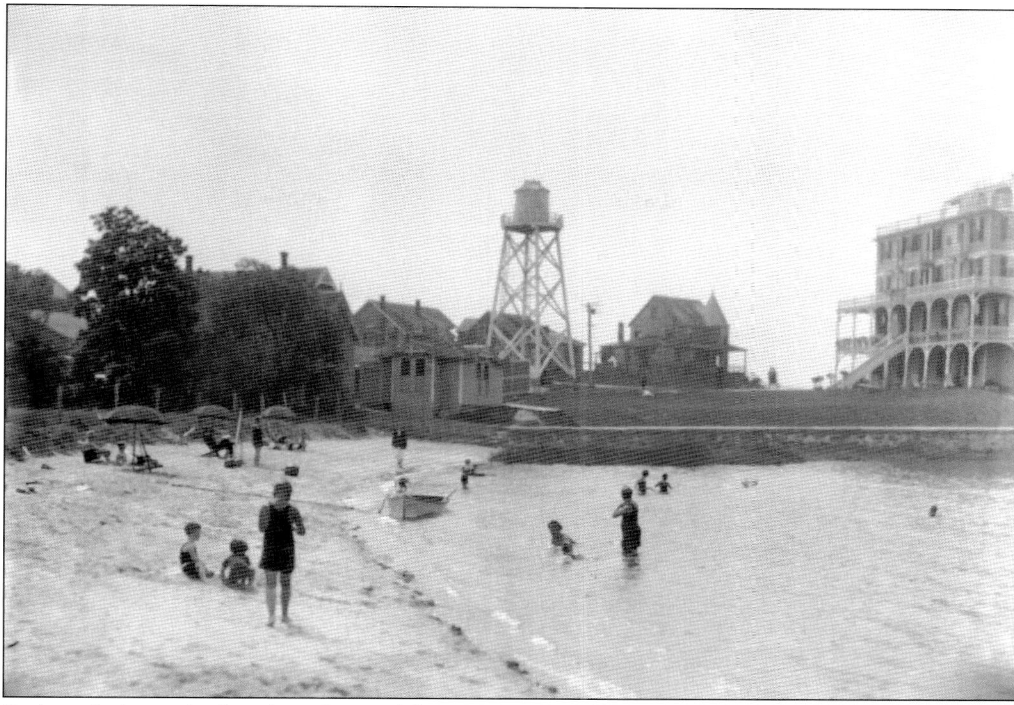

Bathers frolic at the beach in front of the Norcross Hotel around 1900. Originally known as the Stearns Hotel, it was bought and altered by James Norcross in 1890.

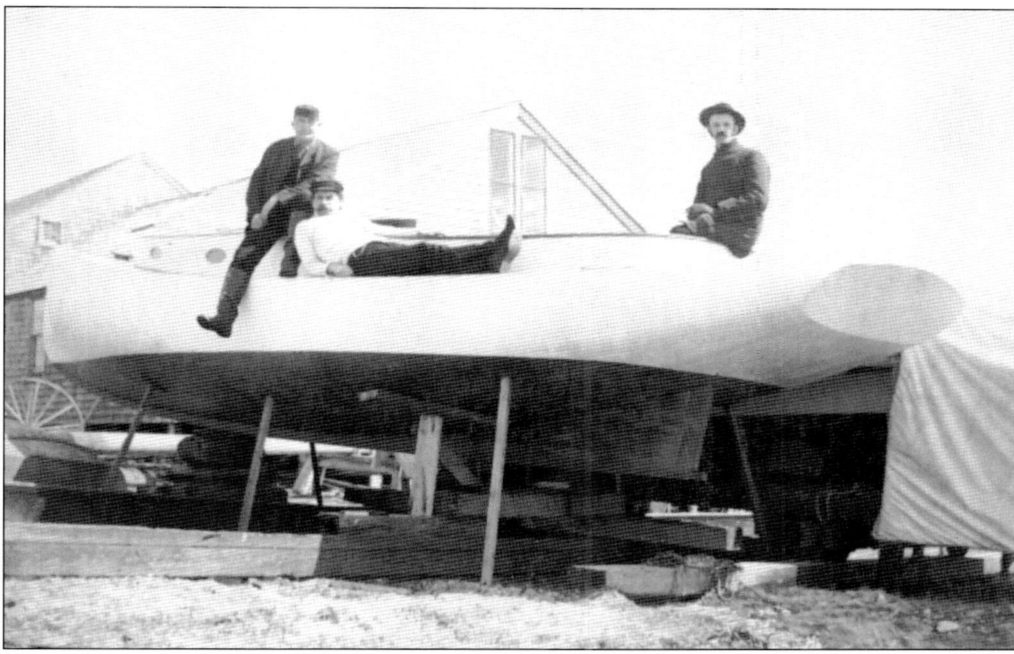

In this pre-1896 photograph, workers at Hanley's Boatyard on Back River in Monument Beach pose on one of the catboats the boatyard was famous for. The catboat was both a pleasure and a work boat. Hanley's Boatyard burned down in 1896.

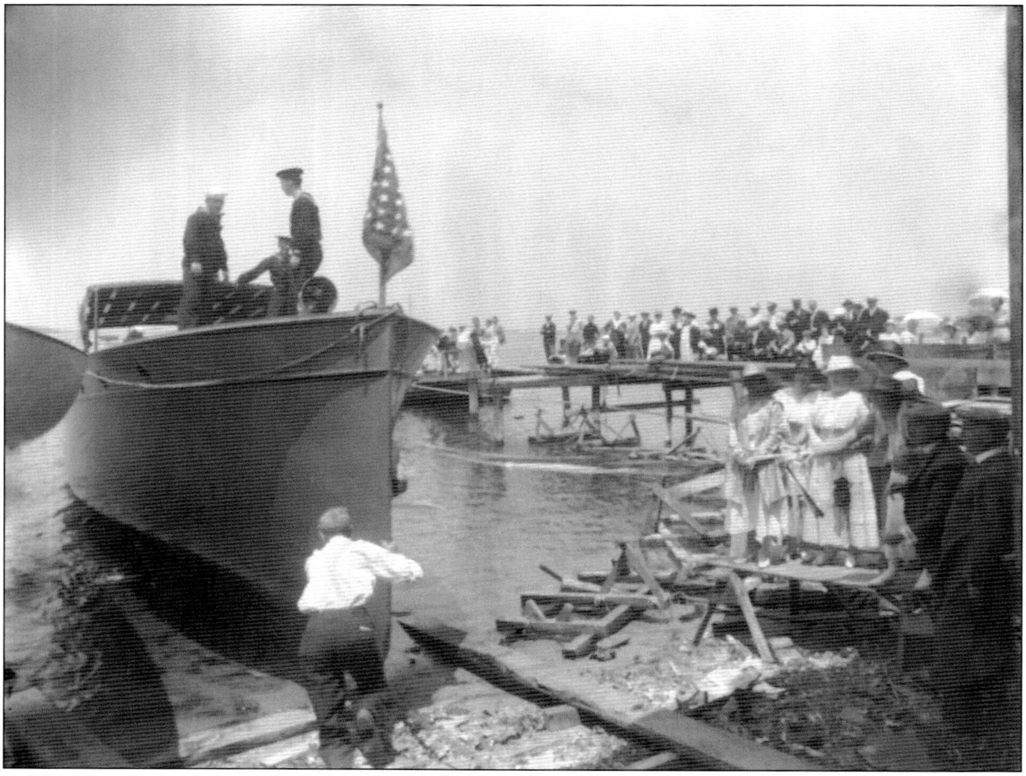

A US Navy boat is launched from a marina in Bourne in this early-20th-century photograph.

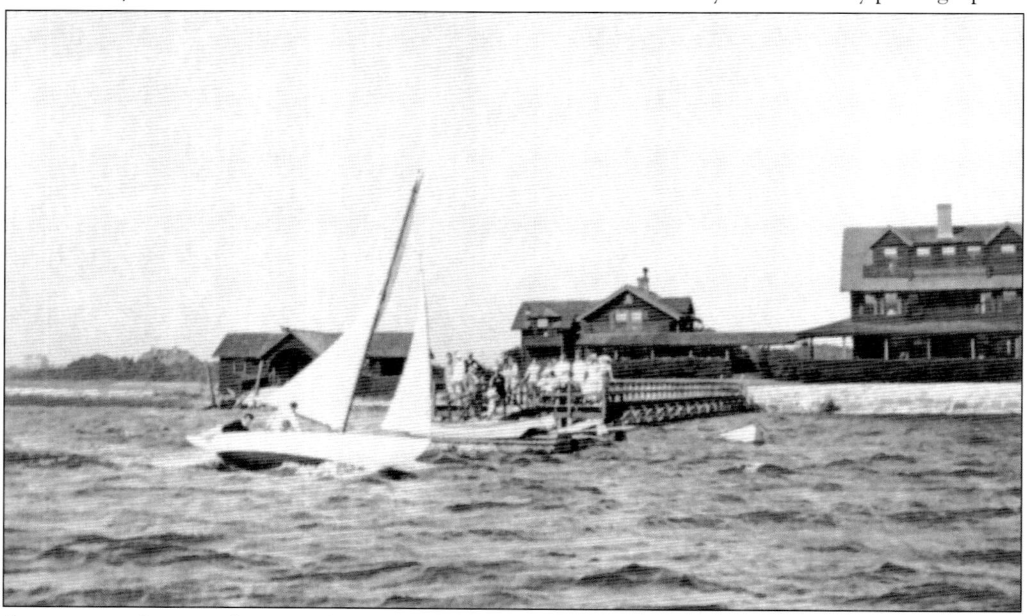

Summer revelers watch as a catboat moves sleekly through the waters in Cataumet in this c. 1900 photograph. Boating, swimming, and anything to do with the sea were the activities that drew the summertime crowds.

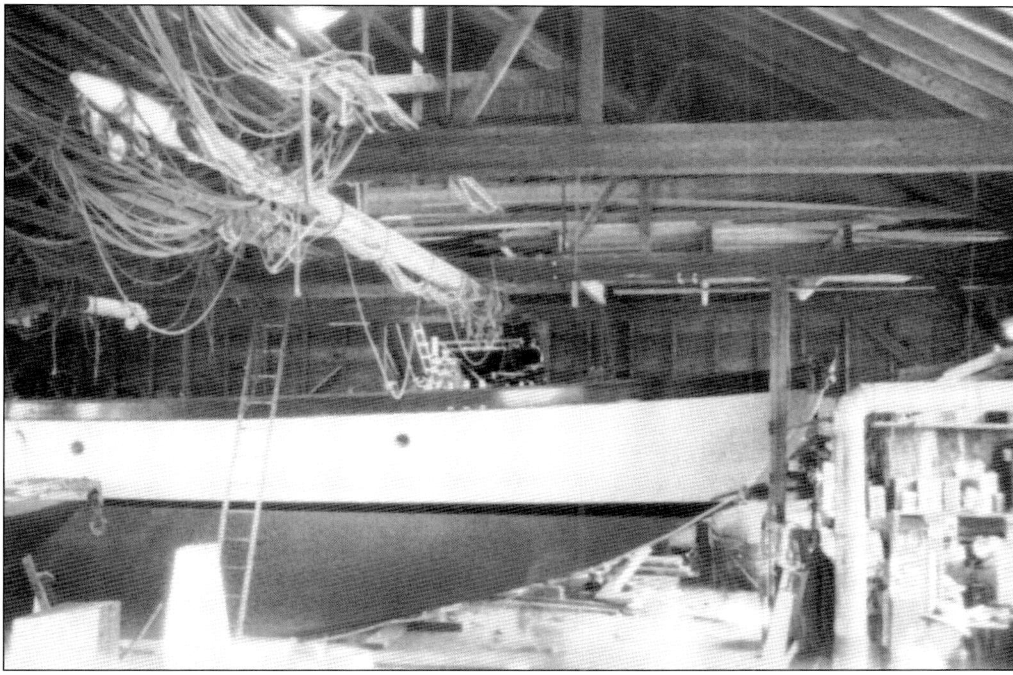

This c. 1930s photograph, taken inside of Bigelow's Boatyard in Monument Beach, shows the process of building of a sailboat.

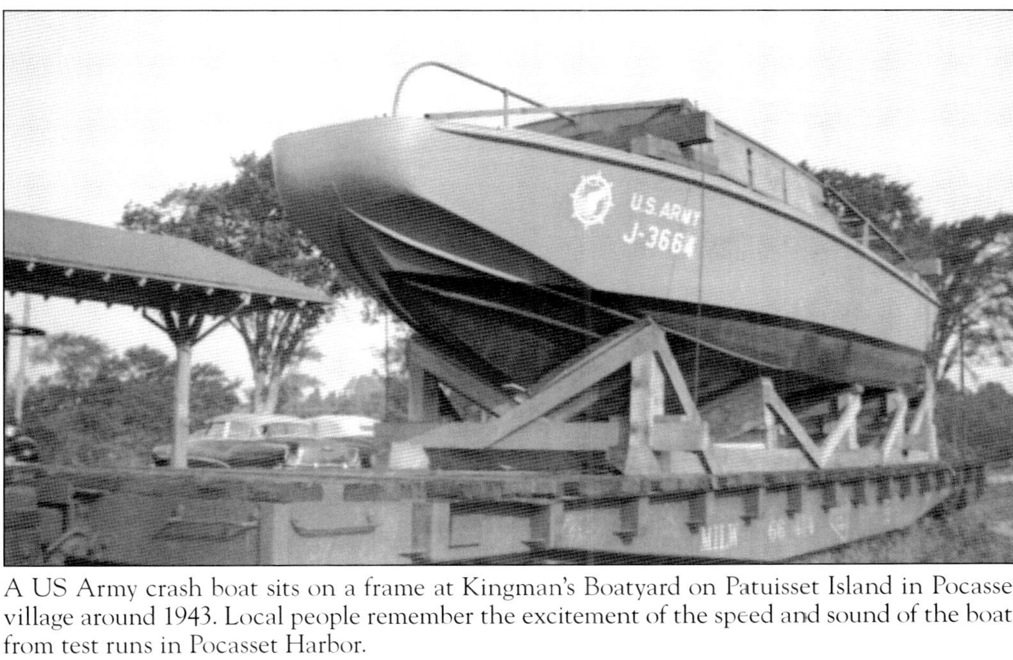

A US Army crash boat sits on a frame at Kingman's Boatyard on Patuisset Island in Pocasset village around 1943. Local people remember the excitement of the speed and sound of the boats from test runs in Pocasset Harbor.

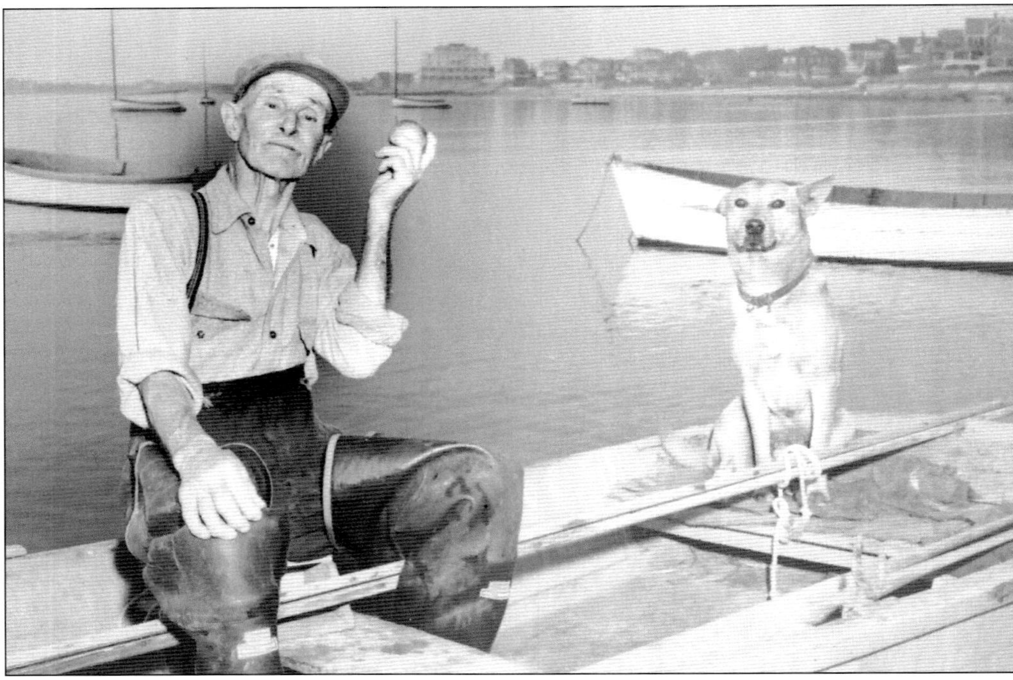

Local personality Wallace "Jet" Judson Perry holds forth in his skiff with apple in hand in this c. 1910 photograph in Monument Beach. He and his family owned oyster grants in the Monument River that were gone with the digging of the Cape Cod Canal.

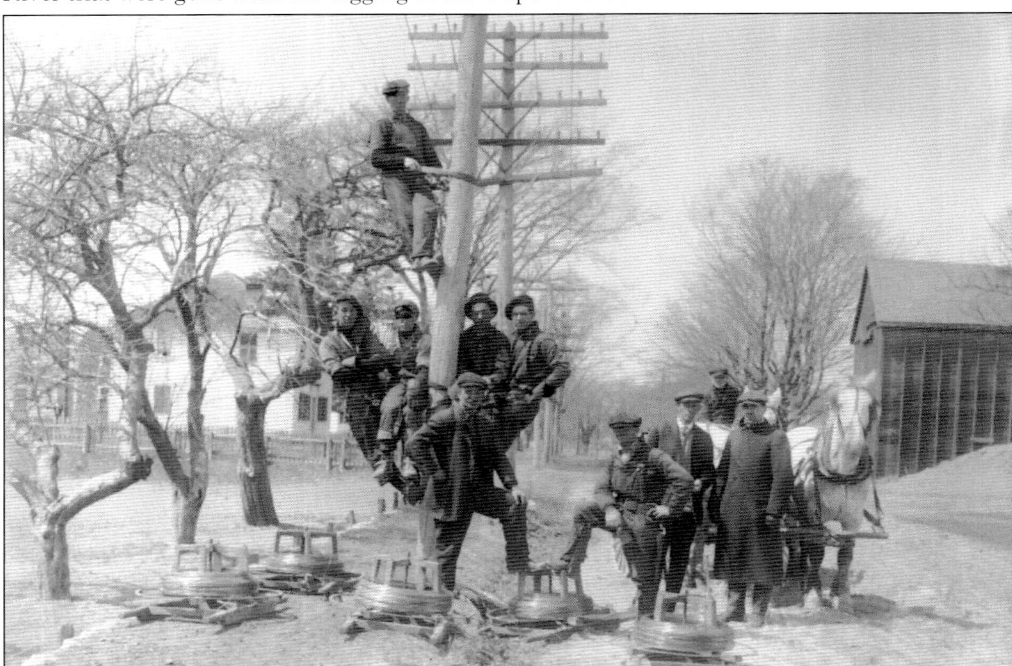

Electrical workers pose for an interesting photograph as they string lines in Bourne during the widening of the Cape Cod Canal around 1915.

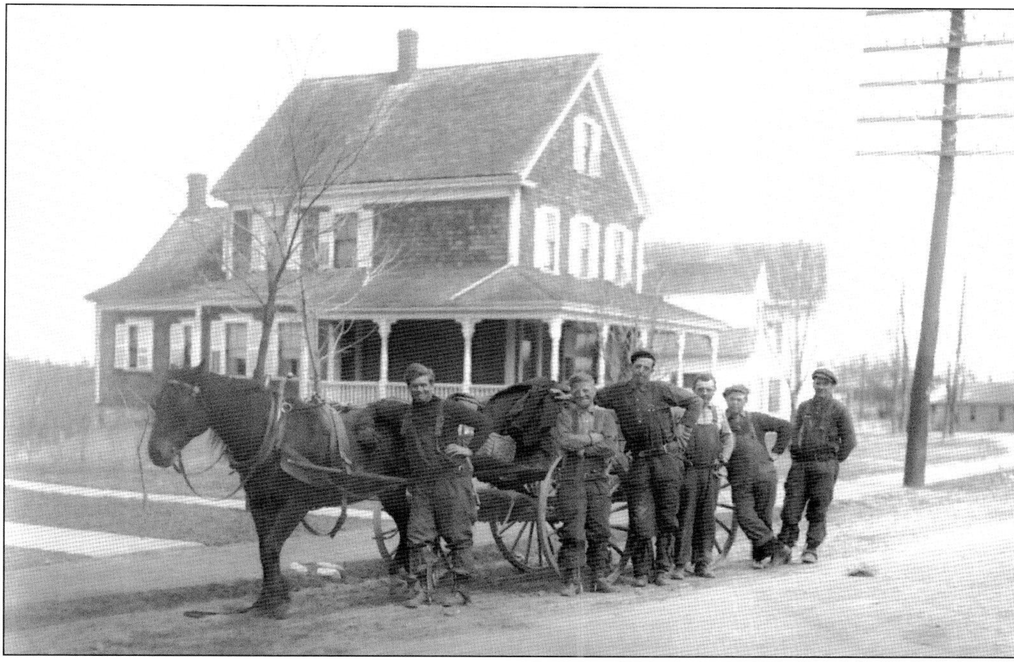

Electrical workers stand with their horse and work wagon in this c. 1918 photograph. Horse-drawn wagons were the most common means of local transportation for both electrical workers and firemen in the early 20th century.

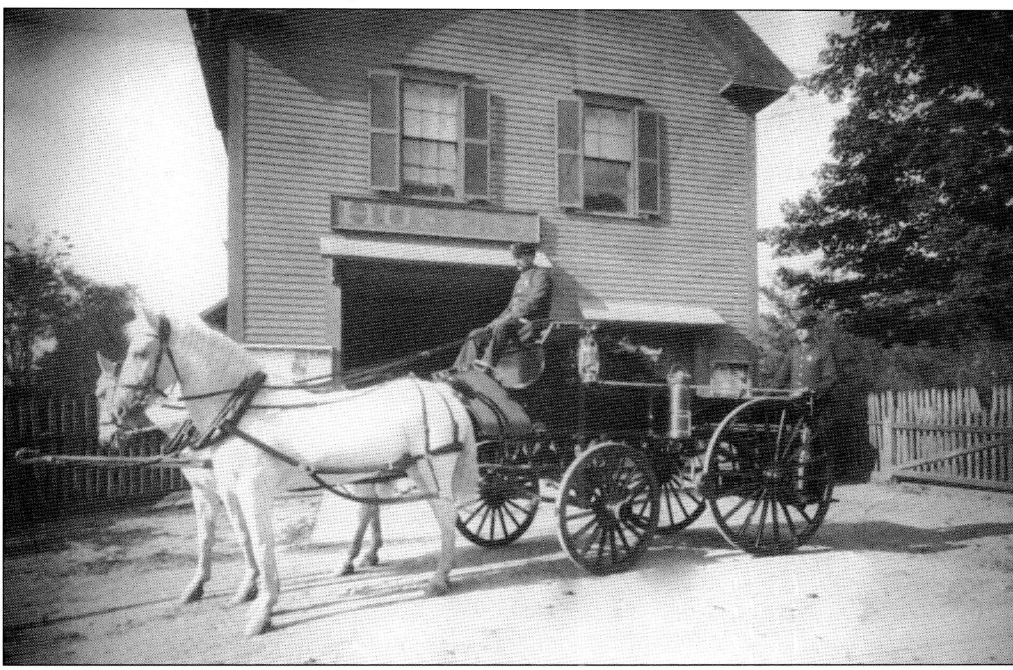

Firemen pose with their truck and horses in this c. 1910 photograph. The first firefighting wagon in Bourne was the result of a "Progressive Society" from the various villages pulling together for the good of the town and putting up the resources needed.

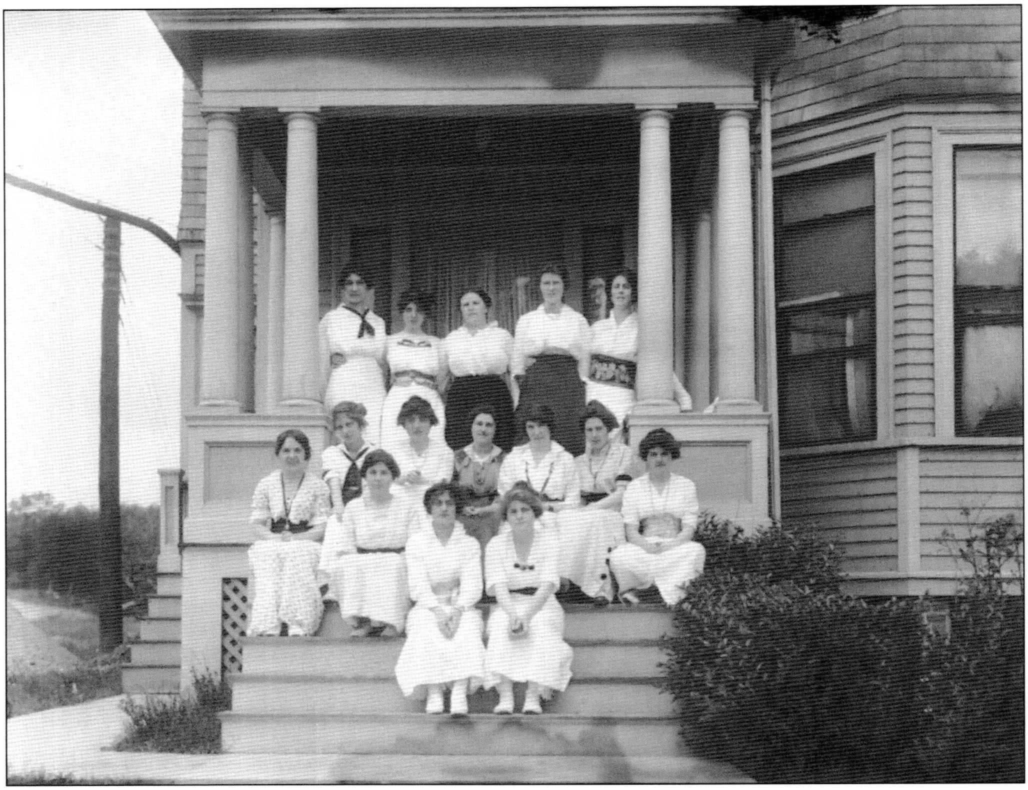

In this c. 1930s photograph, the local telephone operators sit in front of the Buzzards Bay office of the Southern Massachusetts Telephone Co.

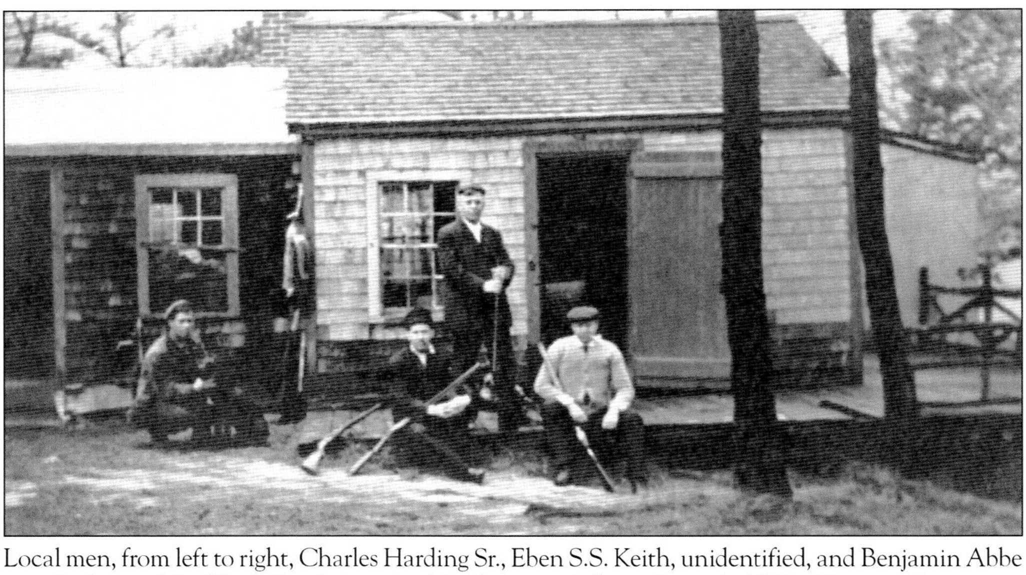

Local men, from left to right, Charles Harding Sr., Eben S.S. Keith, unidentified, and Benjamin Abbe pose in front of the Black Pond camp in this photograph from the early 1900s. The sporting camps were popular retreats for locals and visitors to fish and hunt in a more casual atmosphere.

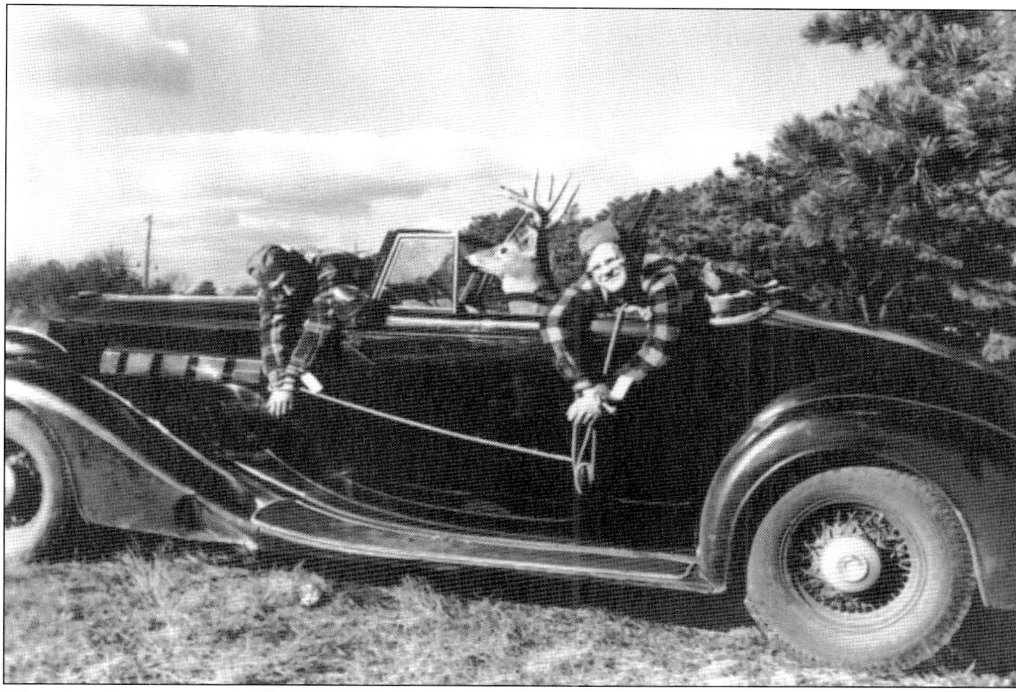

The deer has gotten the better of these two local hunters in this posed c. 1950 photograph.

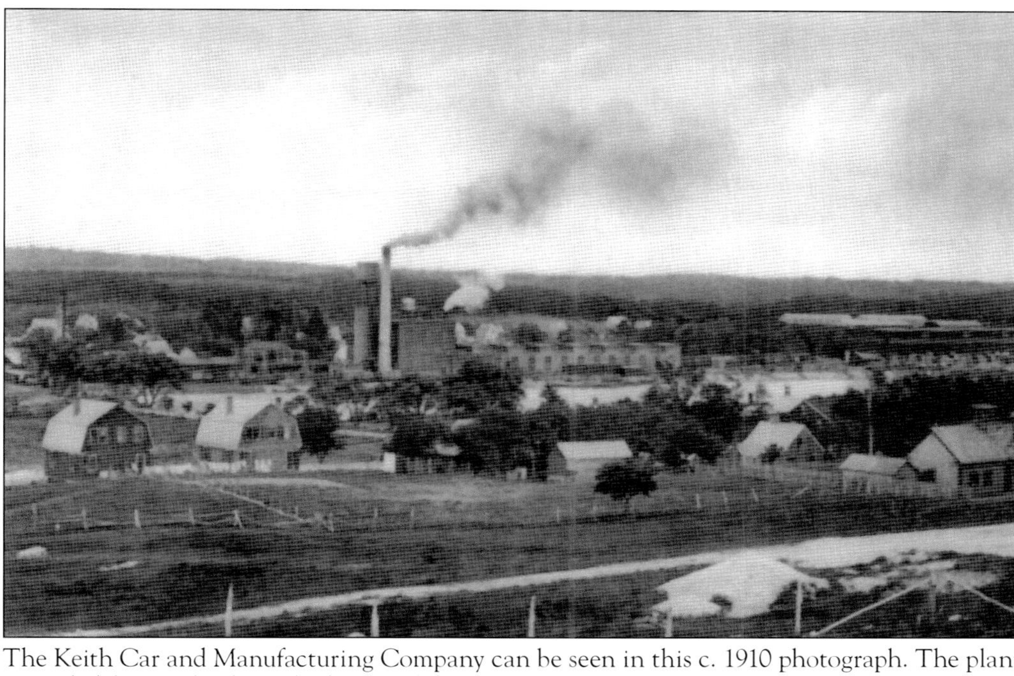

The Keith Car and Manufacturing Company can be seen in this c. 1910 photograph. The plant extended for a mile along the banks of the river that would become the Cape Cod Canal. The company began its production with the prairie wagons that took the pioneers on their journeys to settle the westward lands of North America.

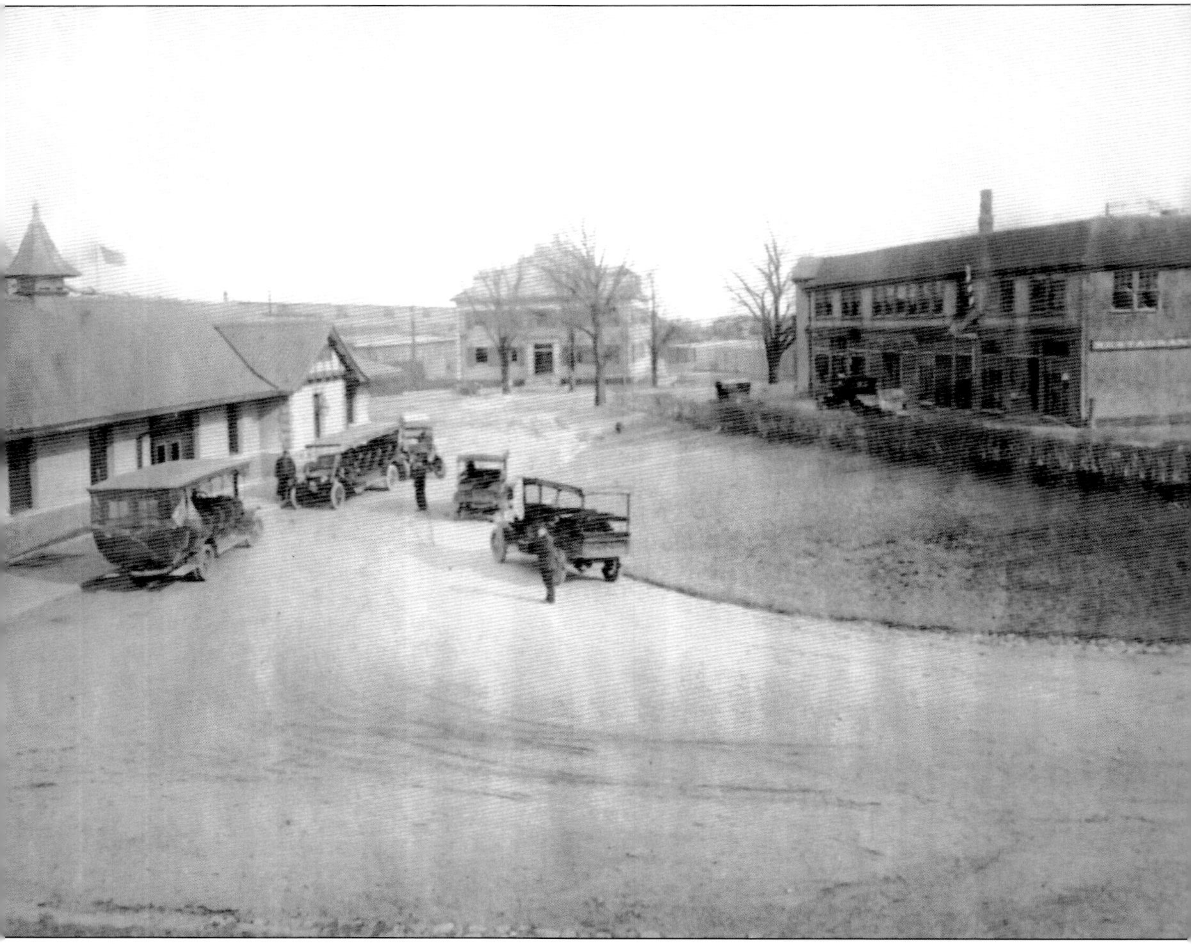

This c. 1900 photograph shows the Keith Car and Manufacturing Company plant area, which includes the railroad station (left), the offices (center), and the company store.

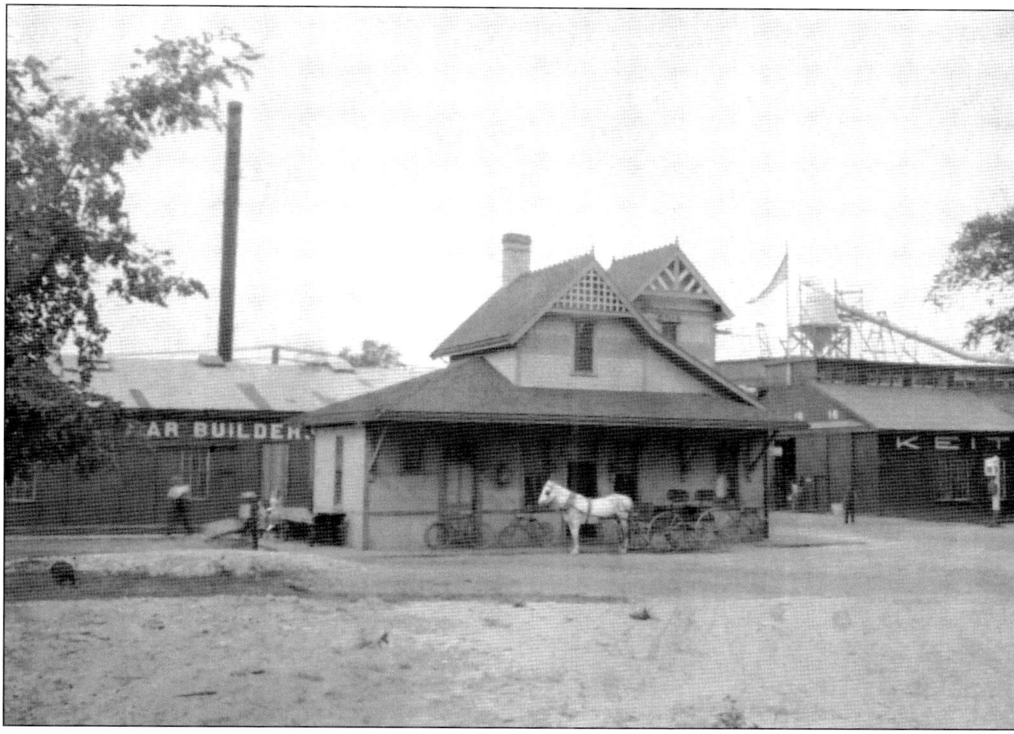

The horse and buggy of Dr. Ernest Curry waits at the Sagamore train station in front of the Keith Car and Manufacturing Company plant in this 1900 photograph.

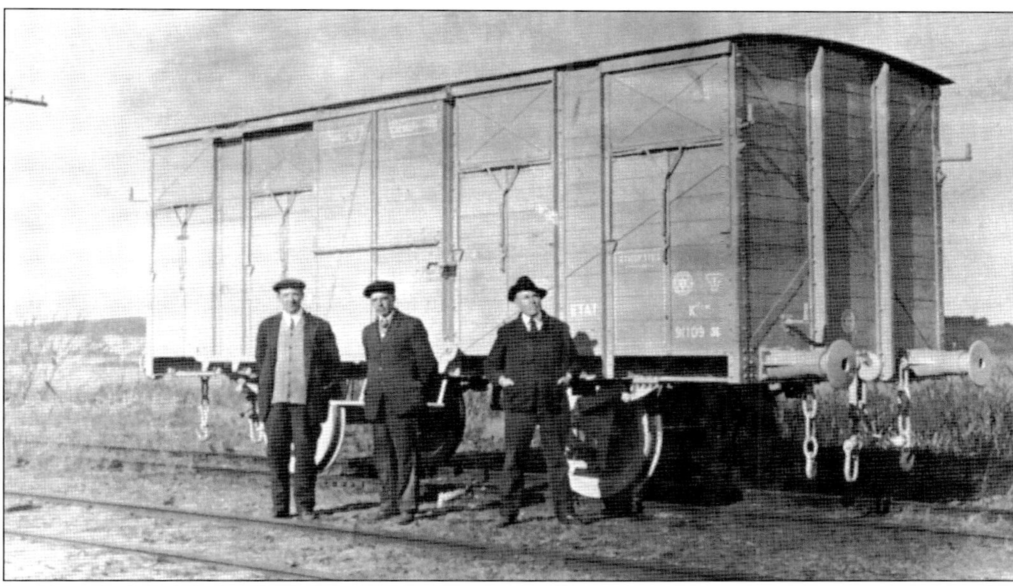

In this c. 1910 photograph, men stand in front of one of the railroad cars produced by Keith Car and Manufacturing Company. By 1910, the company was the premier maker of railroad cars.

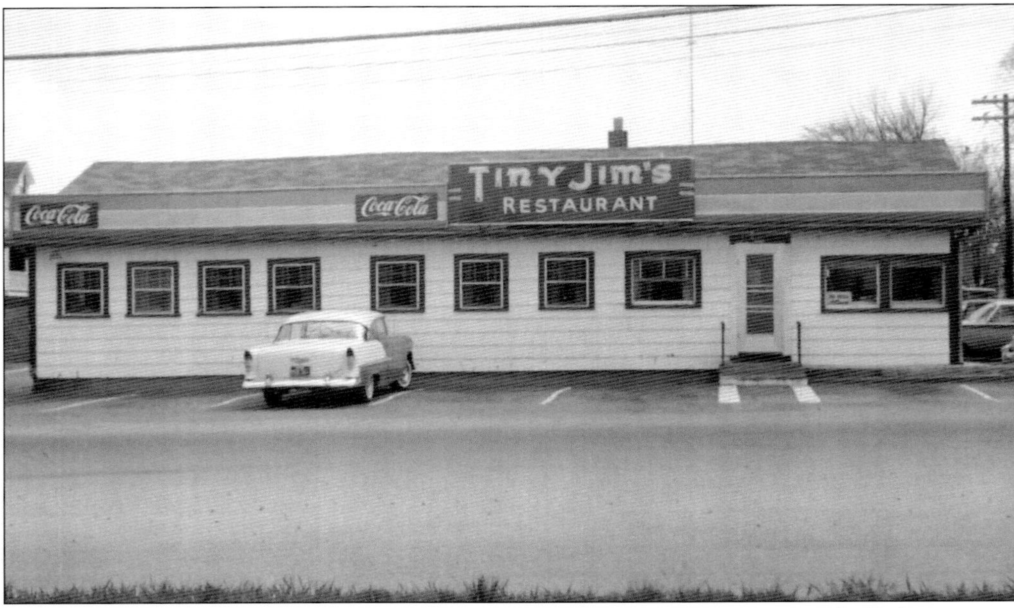

Tiny Jim's restaurant at the Belmont Rotary in Buzzards Bay was a favorite stop for locals in the 1930s.

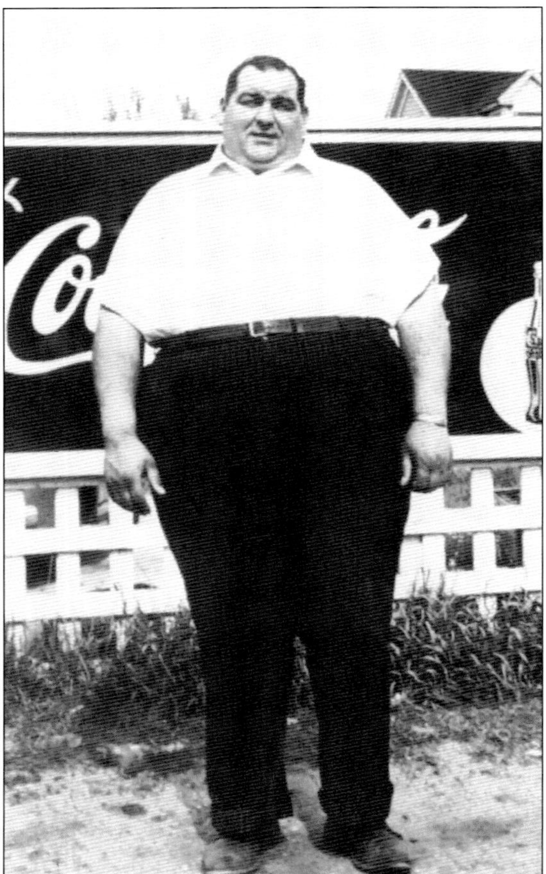

Tiny Jim's owner Jim Tamagini poses for a photograph in the 1930s.

Six

Gone but Not Forgotten

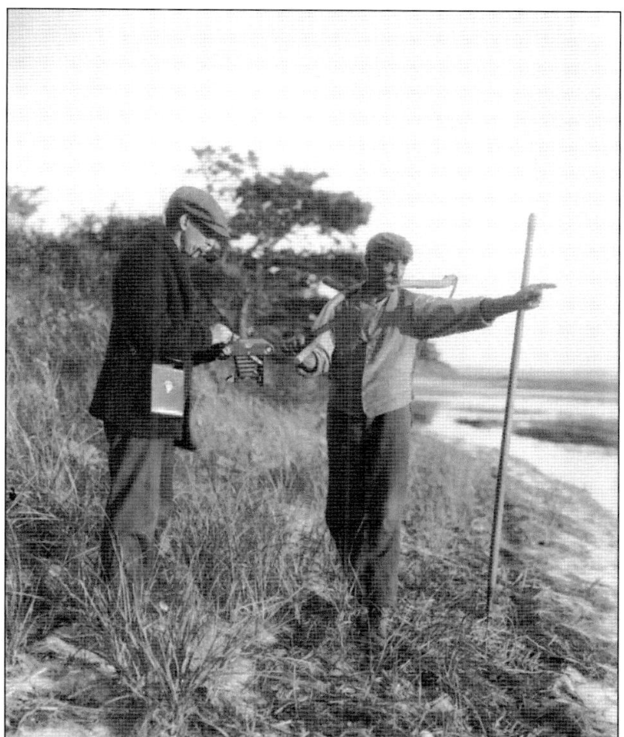

Local photographer Fred Small (left) loads his camera as an unidentified local man talks to him in this c. 1905 photograph. The man carries tools for cutting the salt hay that is used extensively all over Cape Cod as winter fodder for animals.

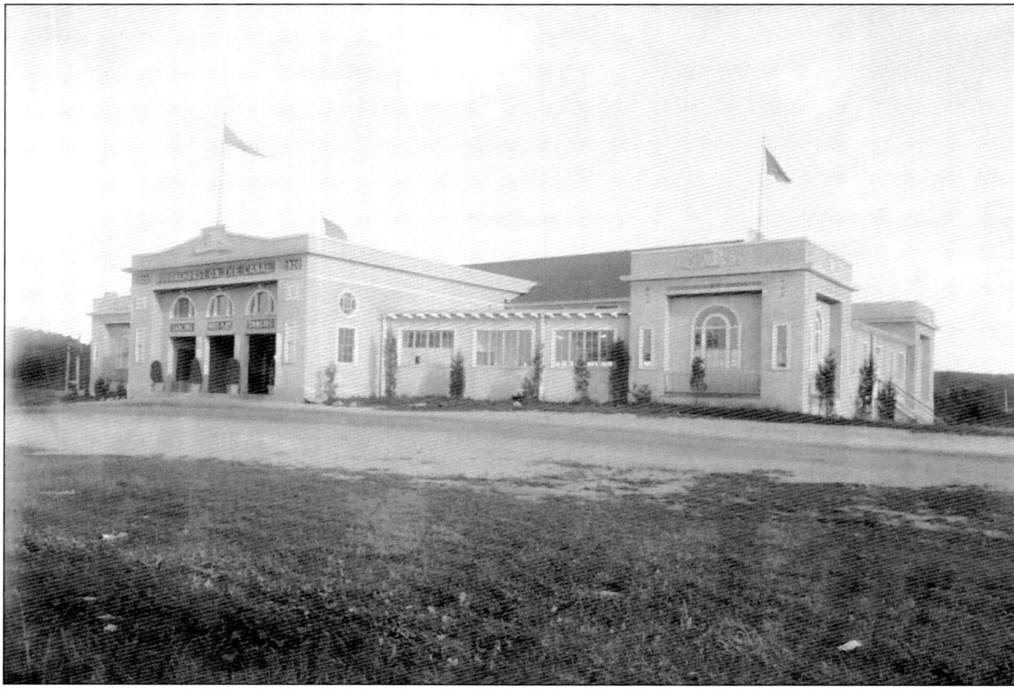

From 1920 to 1933, the Bournehurst on the Canal, located in Buzzards Bay, was a favorite dance place for locals. The club burned down in 1934.

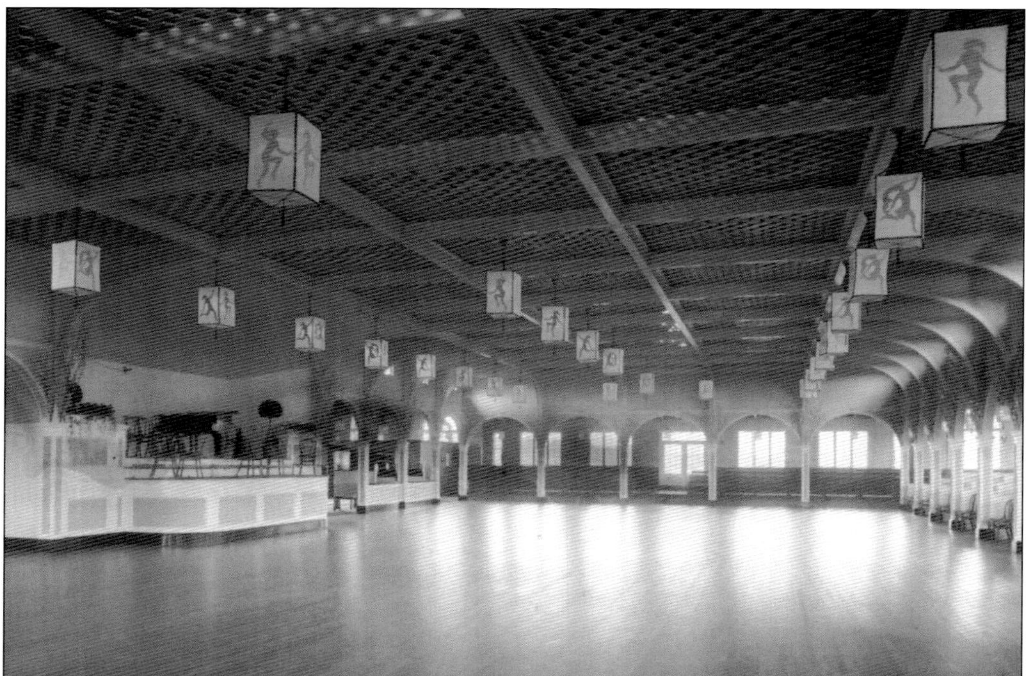

The interior of the Bournehurst on the Canal dance club shows the ballroom dance floor hung with lanterns and the stage at left.

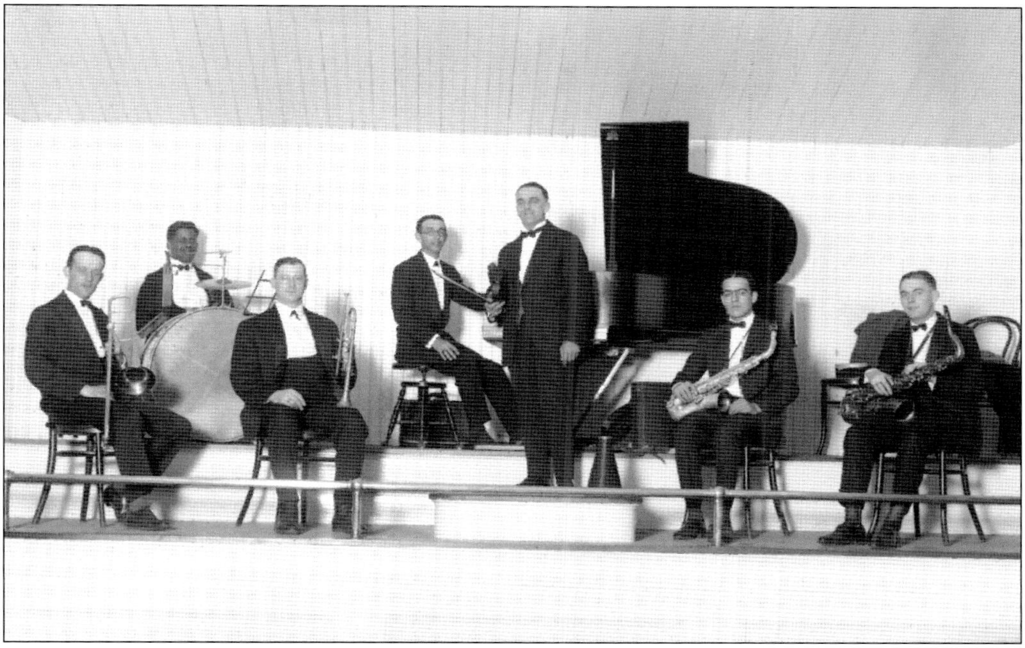

Band members sit for a photograph in the late 1920s. This is one of the bands that played at the Bournehurst.

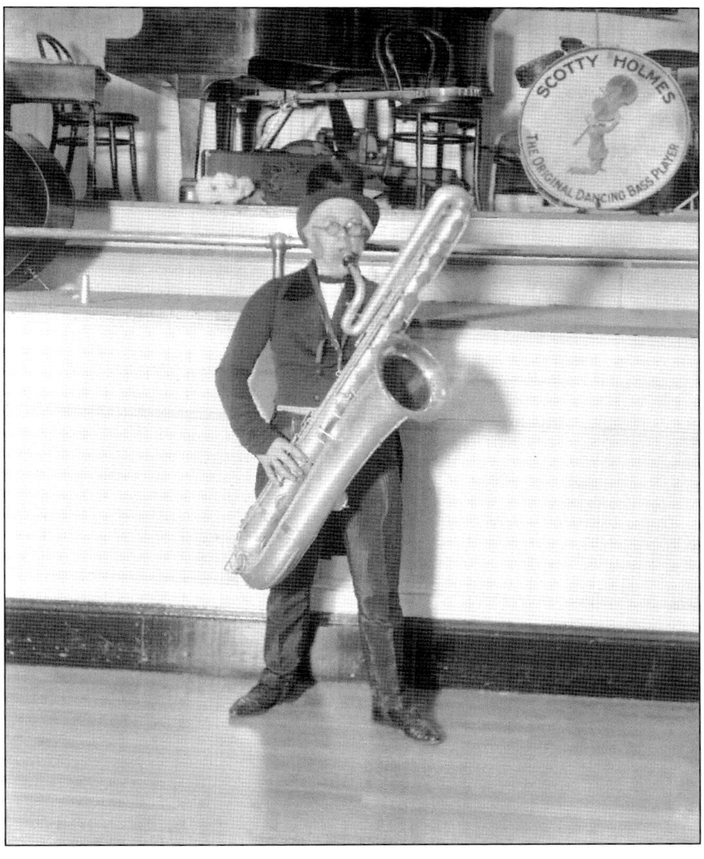

Bandleader Scotty Holmes plays the giant saxophone in front of the stage in Bournehurst in the 1920s.

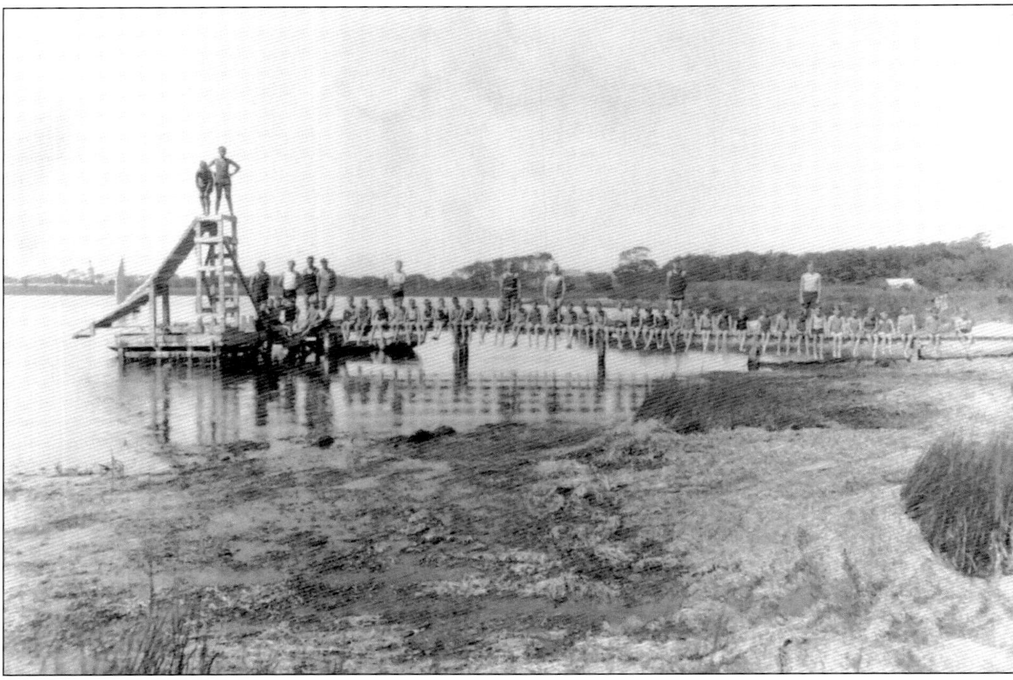

In the 1930s, campers line up on the dock at Camp Wampanoag, named after the indigenous peoples of the area. It was a summer camp for young people complete with cabins that catered to summer visitors and locals alike.

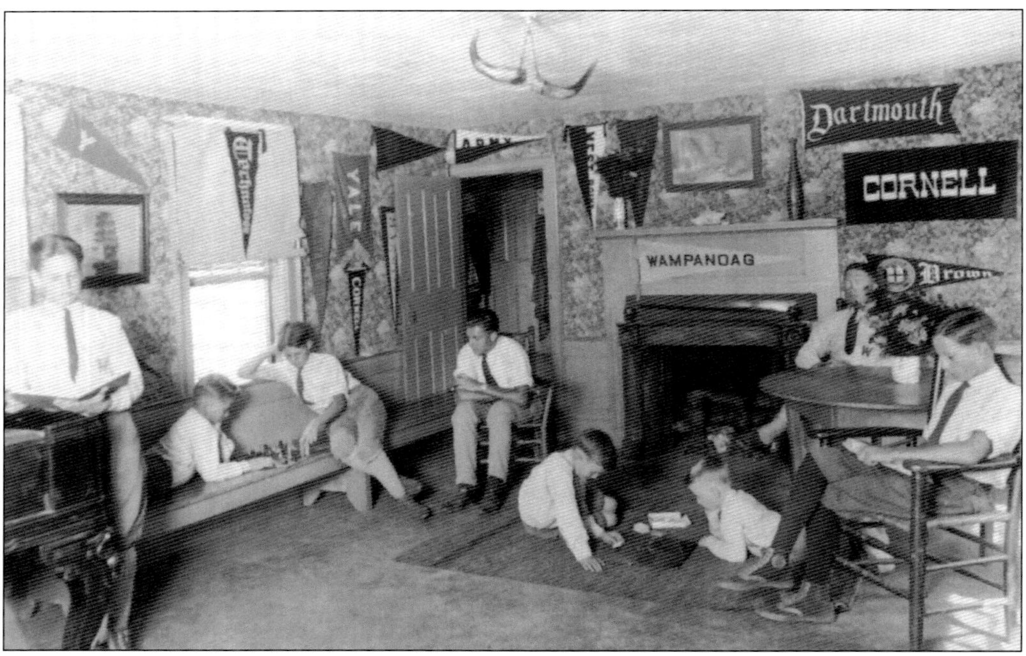

In this c. 1945 photograph, young campers keep busy in one of the cabins at Camp Wampanoag.

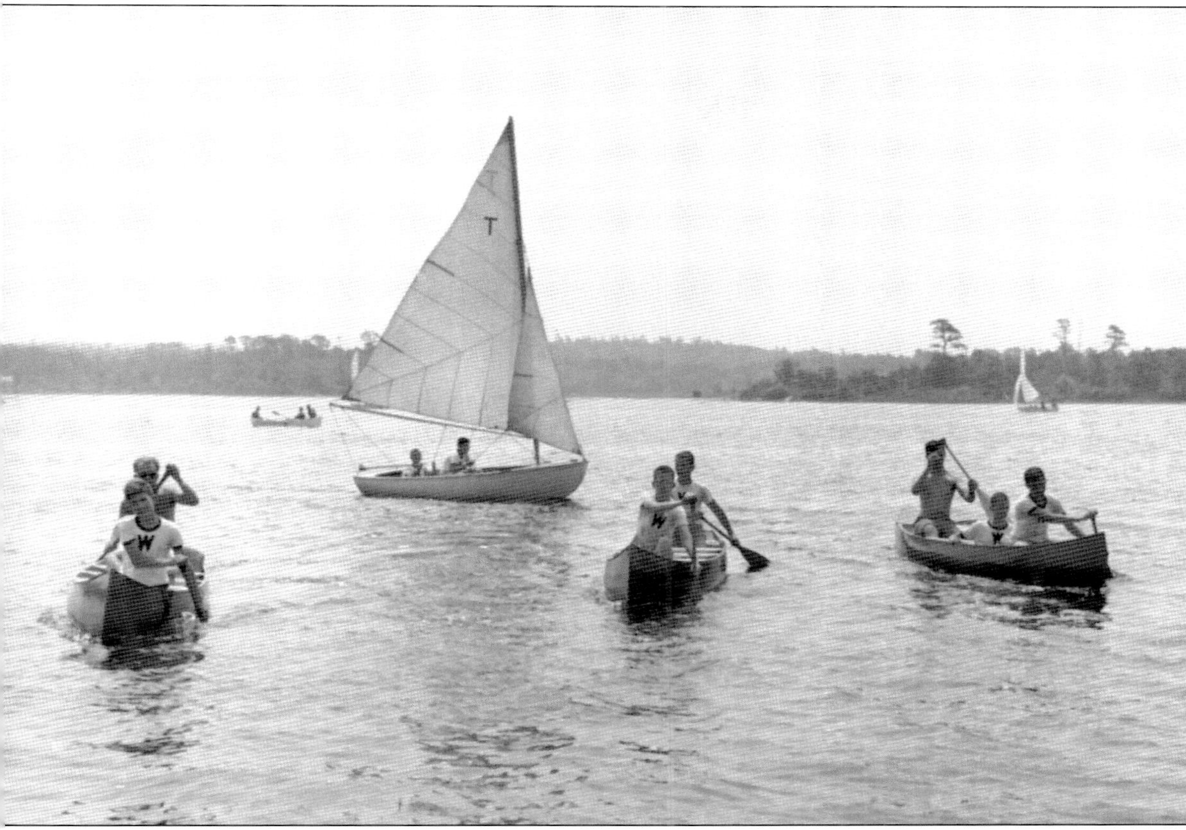

Campers paddle canoes and sail in the camp boats at Camp Wampanoag in this 1950s photograph. One of the activities at Camp Wampanoag was learning to handle sailboats, rowboats, and canoes.

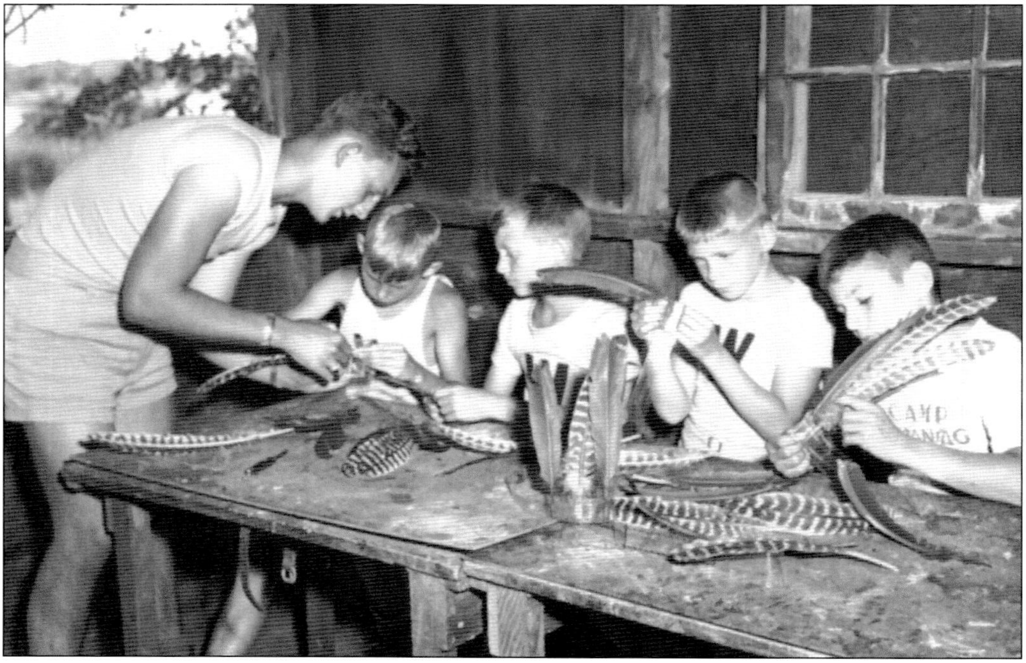

Campers create Native American headdresses with feathers at Camp Wampanoag during the 1950s. The only thing left of Camp Wampanoag is the totem pole, which can be seen today off Old Dam Road in Bourne village.

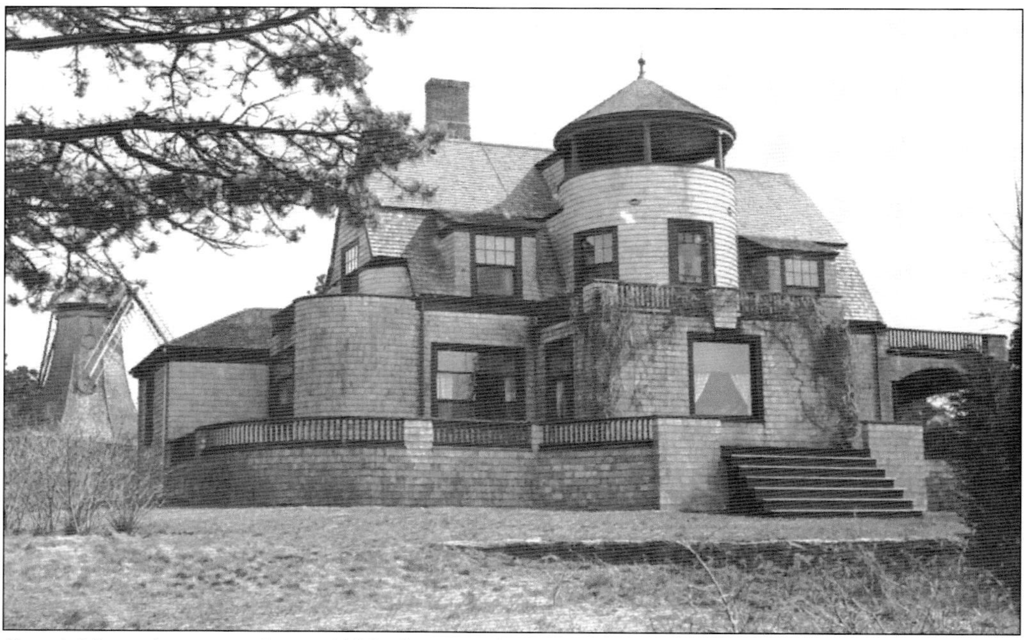

Crow's Nest, shown in this c. 1900 photograph, was the name given to the home of actor and painter Joseph Jefferson. The original home burned down, but the windmill (left), which was the actor's art studio, was donated to the Bourne Historical Society and stands today on the grounds of the Aptucxet Trading Post Museum.

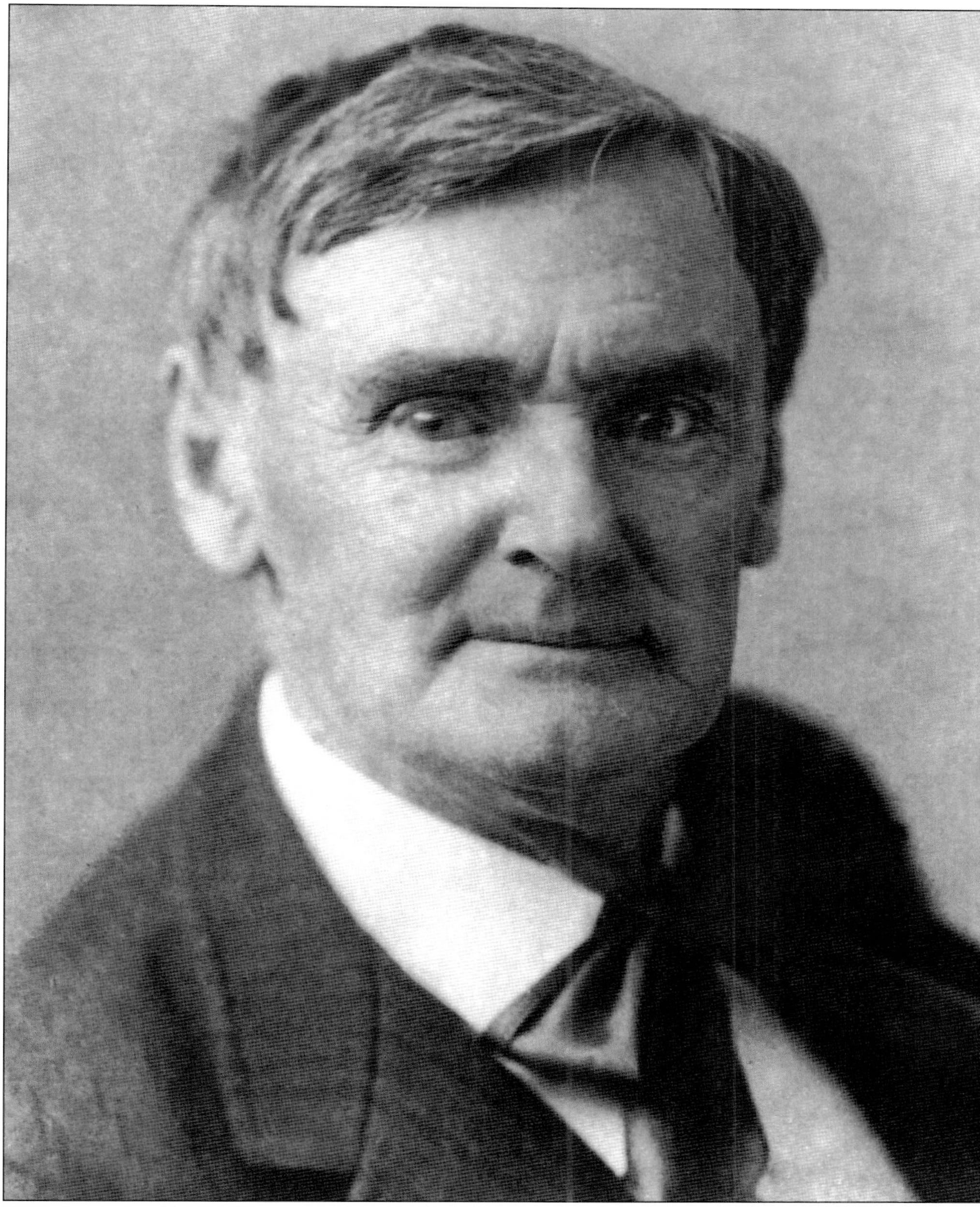

Actor Joseph Jefferson (1829–1905) poses for the photographer in the 1890s. Jefferson began acting at age four. Jefferson was an ardent fisherman and enjoyed fishing in Buzzards Bay with his friend Pres. Grover Cleveland.

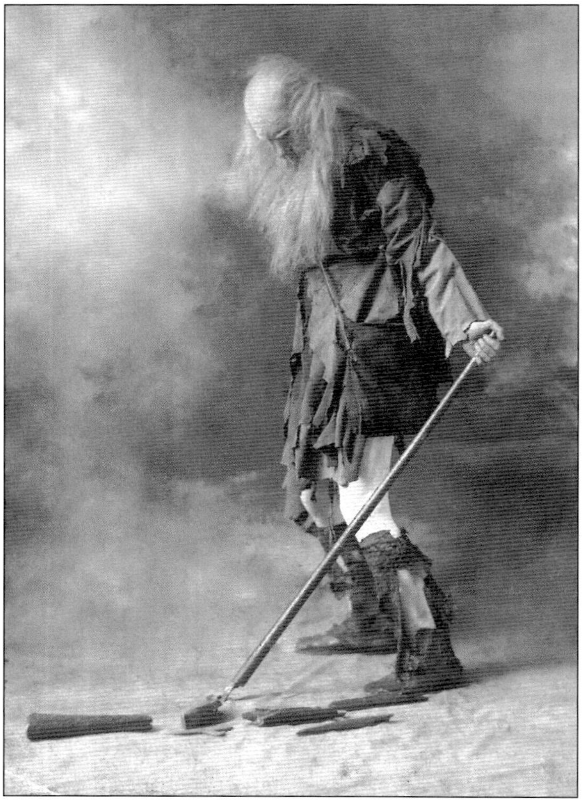

Actor Joseph Jefferson wears his costume for the role of Rip Van Winkle, his most well-known stage role, in this 1896 photograph.

The interior front hall of actor Joseph Jefferson's home, Crow's Nest, is seen here in this c. 1900 photograph.

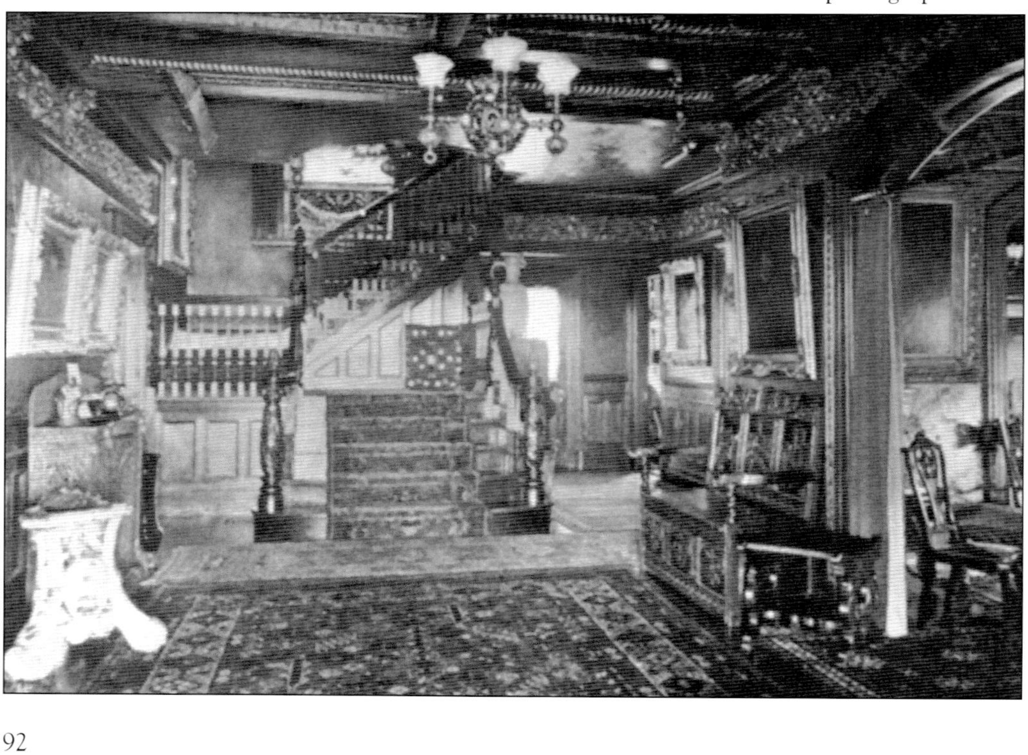

Thomas Jefferson, the son of actor Joseph Jefferson and who was also bit by the acting bug, can be seen here practicing for a role in the early 1900s in front of the family home, Crow's Nest.

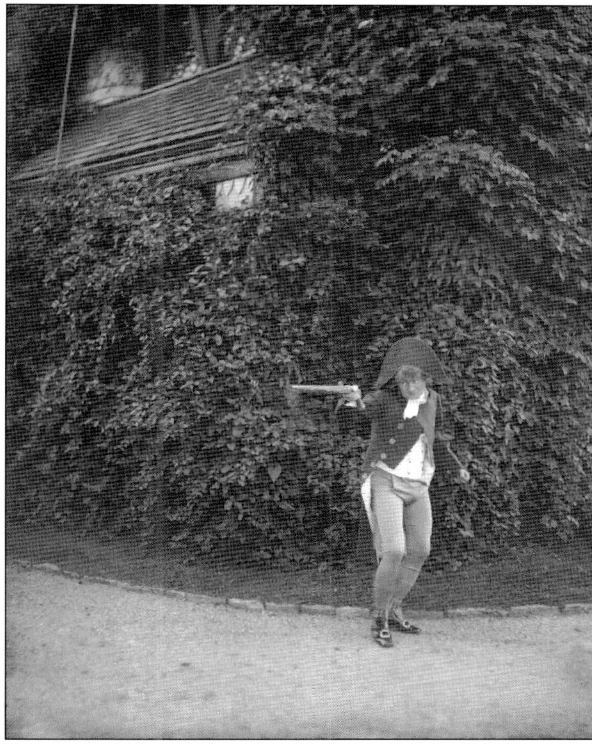

Painter Edgar Clark (1869–1944) paints in his home in Sagamore Beach. Clark was known for his paintings of clipper ships, seascapes, and Cape Cod scenes.

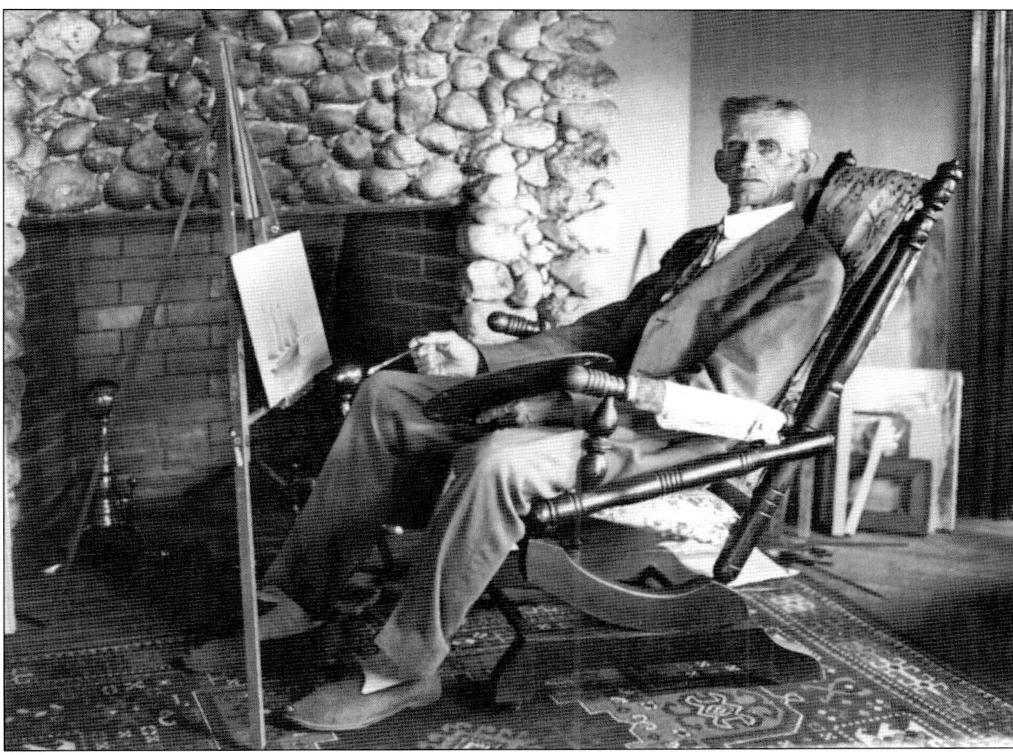

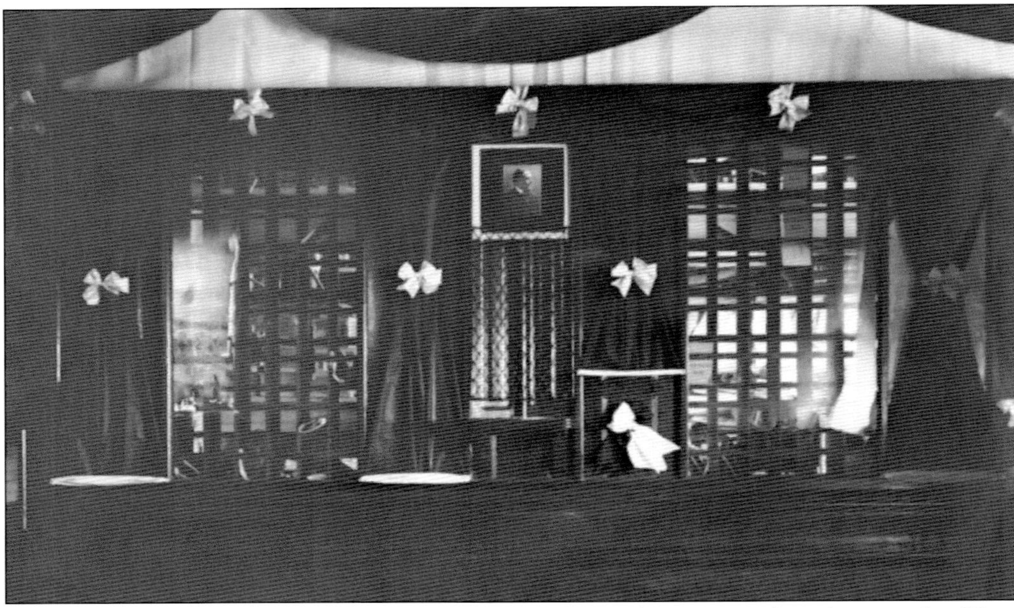

The local post office is decked out in mourning in September 1901 with a photograph of Pres. William McKinley hanging in the center. McKinley, the 25th president, was shot on September 6, 1901, on the grounds of the Pan-American Exposition in Buffalo, New York. He was greeting the public when he was shot by anarchist Leon Czolgosz. The president died from his wounds eight days later, on September 14.

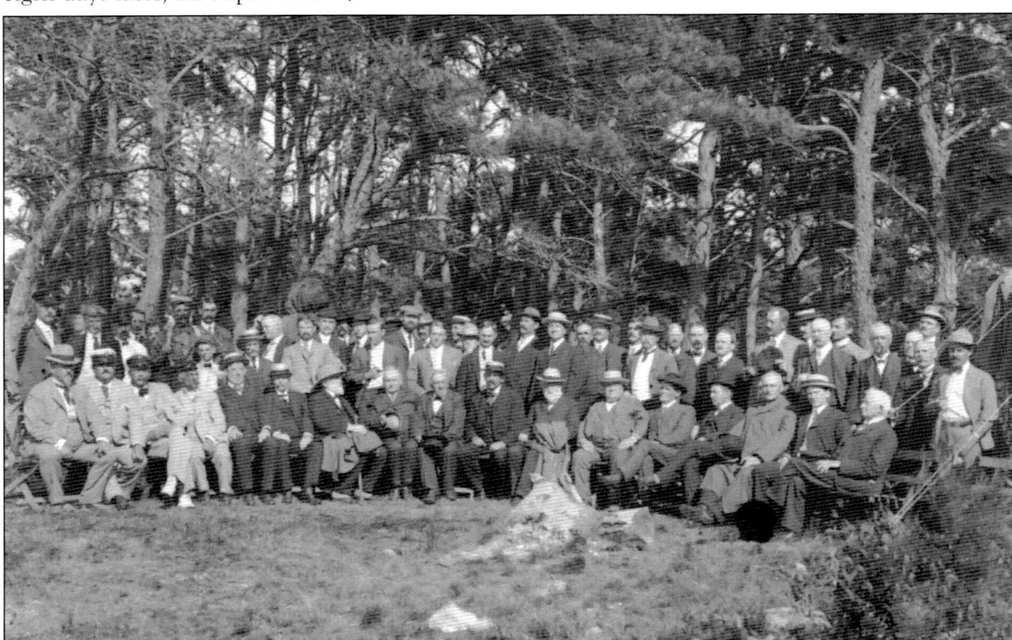

Members of the Old Colony Club of Sagamore Beach assemble for a portrait during one of their gatherings in this c. 1900 photograph. Actor Joseph Jefferson served for many years as president of the men's social club, whose annual seafood dinners were a highlight of the summer season.

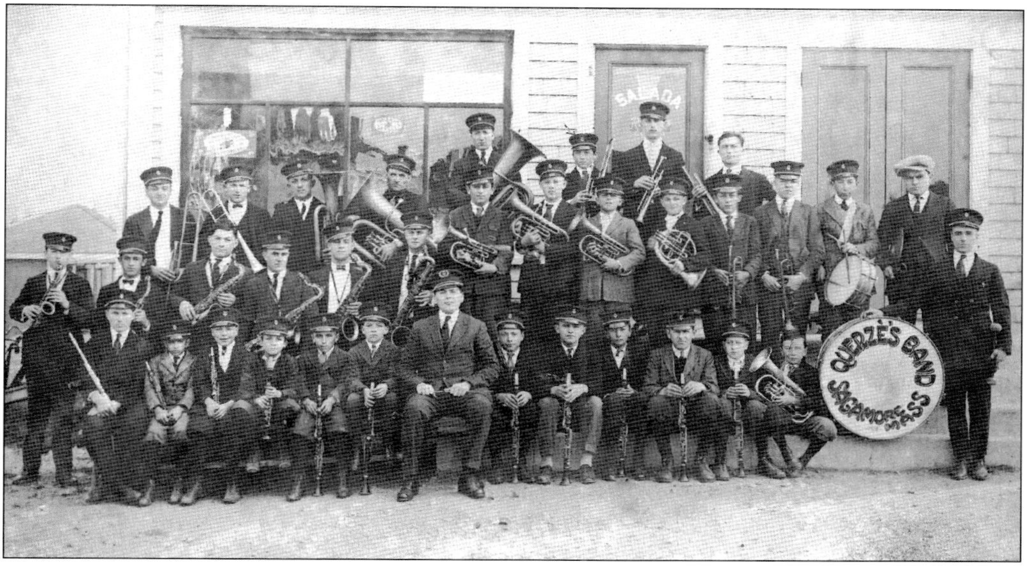

In this c. 1920s photograph, Querze's Band leader Adolfo Querze is seated front and center in front of the L. Cremonini and Son local store in Sagamore village. A large population of Italian immigrants settled in Sagamore as part of the workforce of the Keith Car and Manufacturing Company.

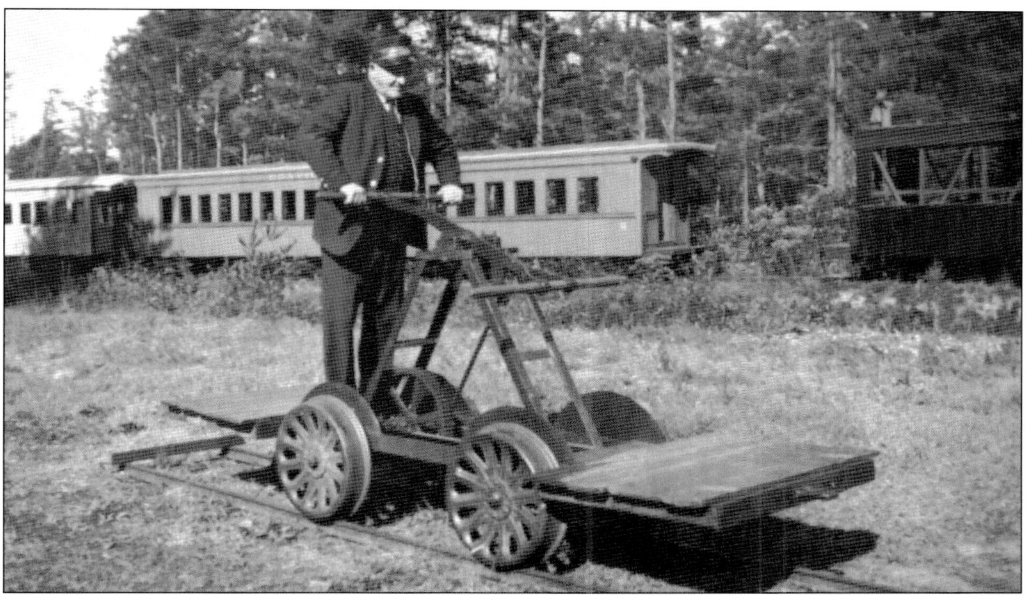

Local Roswell Phinney poses for a photograph in the early 1960s. Roswell was the conductor of the Edaville Railroad for many years.

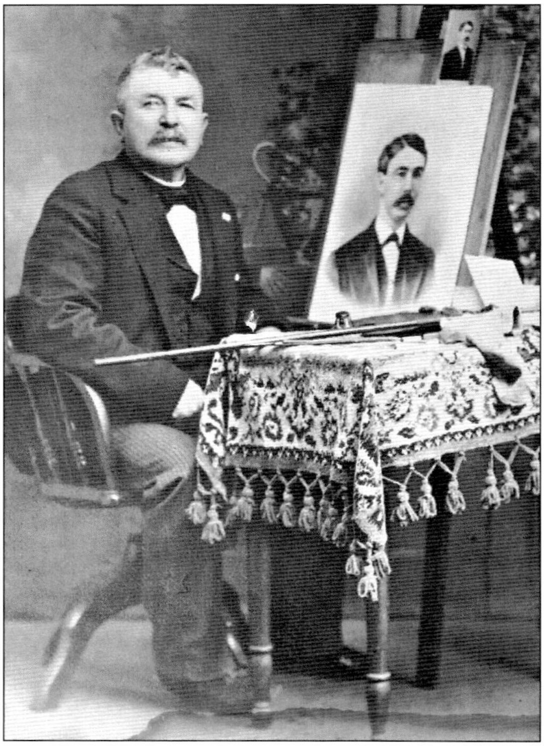

Charles Sydney Raleigh (1830–1925) is shown in this c. 1915 photograph. Raleigh is credited with some 1,100 paintings of the sea, including whaling ships, lighthouses, polar bears, and shipwrecks. Although in his lifetime his paintings did not command high prices, they are now highly prized and found in museums and private collections. (Courtesy of the Wareham Historical Society.)

Decorative paintings by Charles Raleigh inside of the Bourne United Methodist Church are pictured in this c. 1900 photograph. The Raleigh artwork inside the church was later painted over.

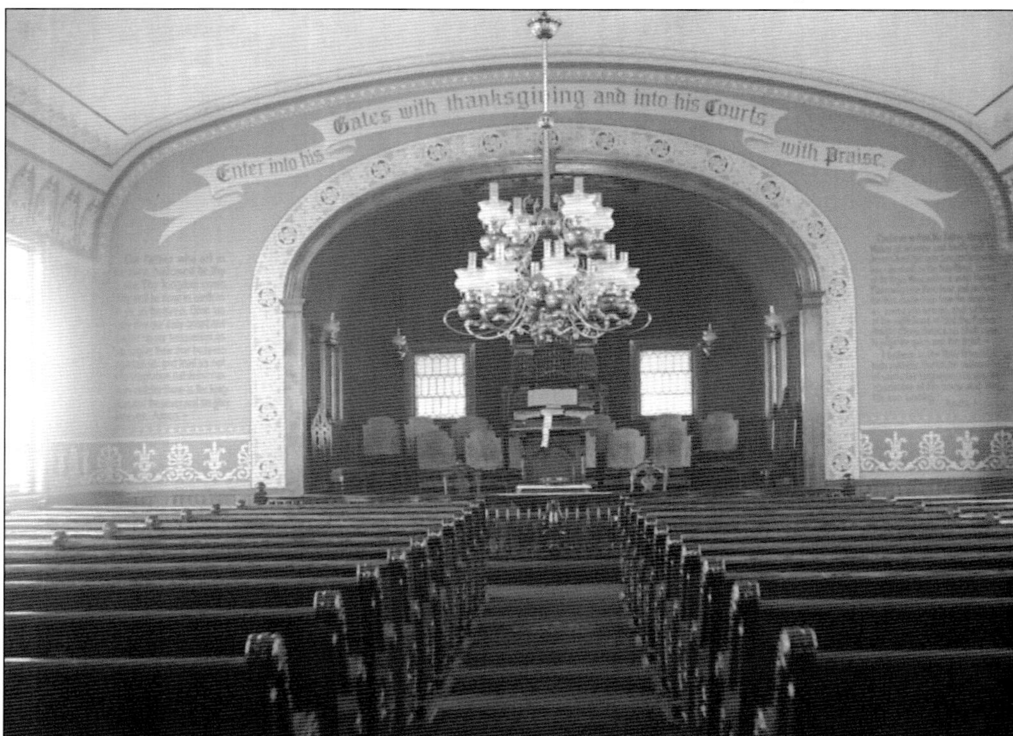

Art conservator Benjamin Lanza does restoration work in 1961 on an 1879 painting by Bourne artist Charles Raleigh (1830–1925) for the Old Dartmouth Historical Society in New Bedford, Massachusetts.

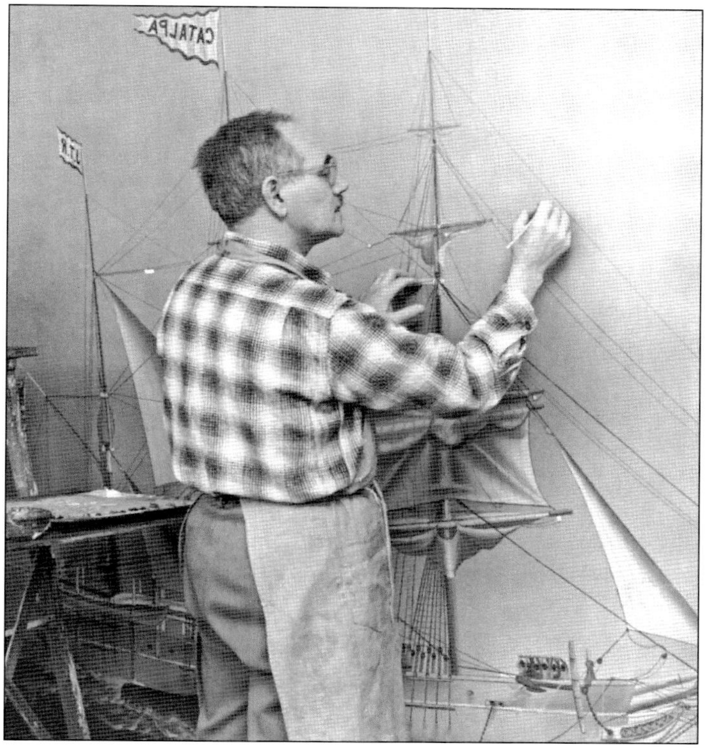

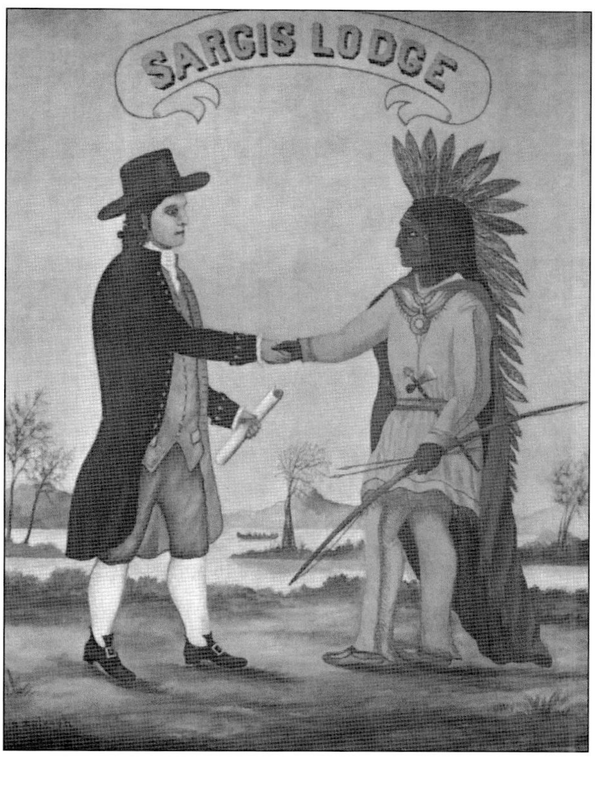

One of the illustrations done by Charles Raleigh during his lifetime is the emblem for the Sargis Lodge, a local club, which he painted in 1885. As an early painter making a living in Bourne, Raleigh painted signs. However, he is known for his decorative ceilings, some of which are still intact, including the one in the Briggs-McDermott House in Bourne village.

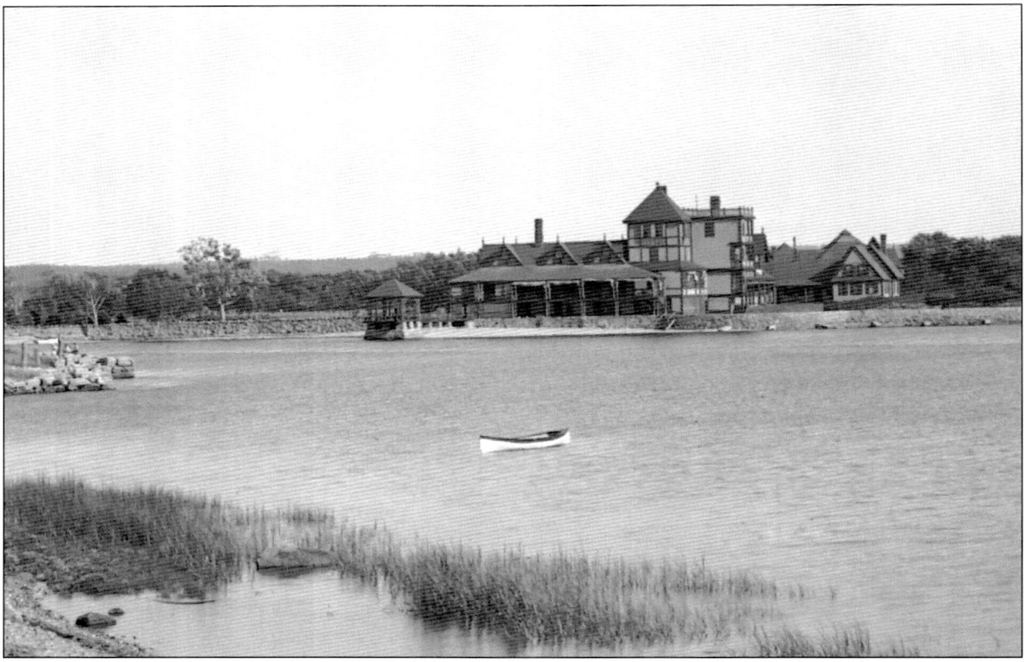

The Taylor's Point homestead, shown here around the 1920s, took up all the land that is now the Massachusetts Maritime Academy and was the home of Boston Globe owner Gen. Charles Taylor.

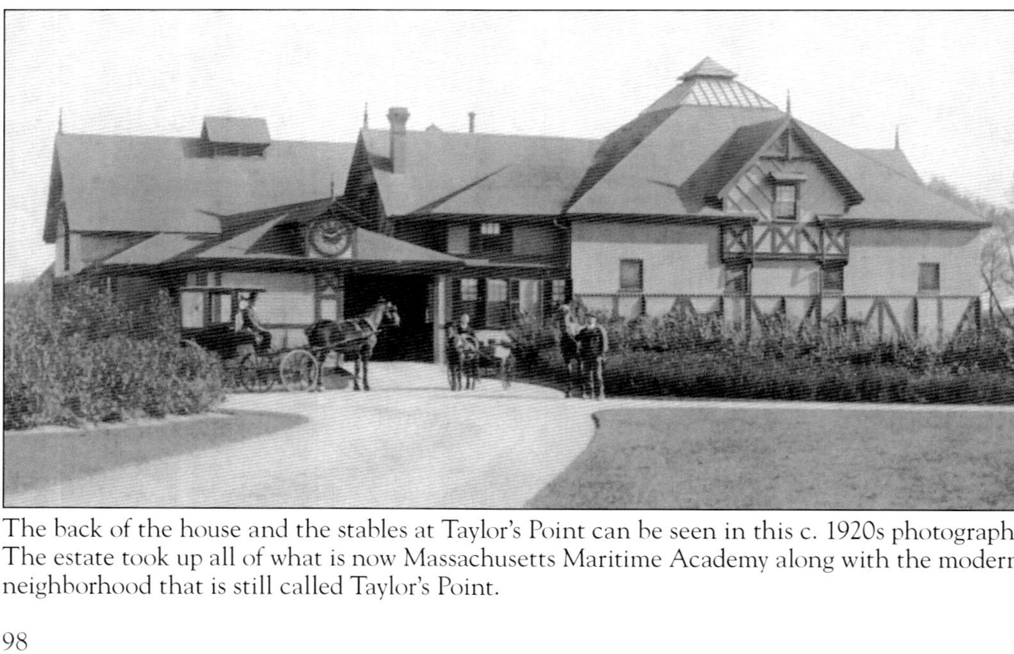

The back of the house and the stables at Taylor's Point can be seen in this c. 1920s photograph. The estate took up all of what is now Massachusetts Maritime Academy along with the modern neighborhood that is still called Taylor's Point.

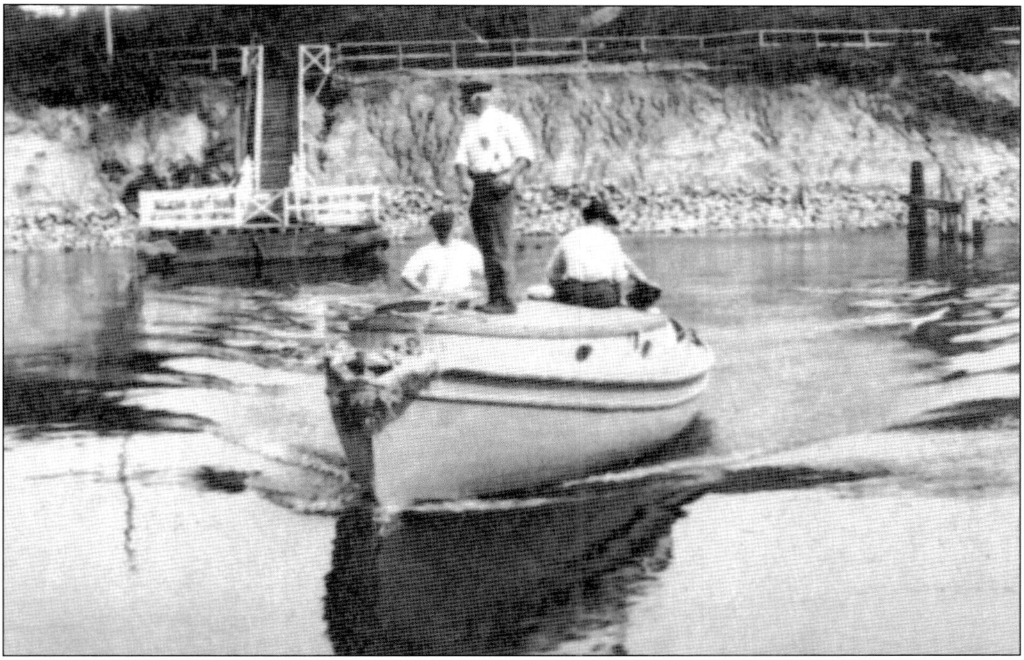

The late Donald Jacobs, former chairman of the Bourne Historical Commission and longtime historical activist in Bourne, stands in the bow of a boat during a ride on the Back River in Bourne.

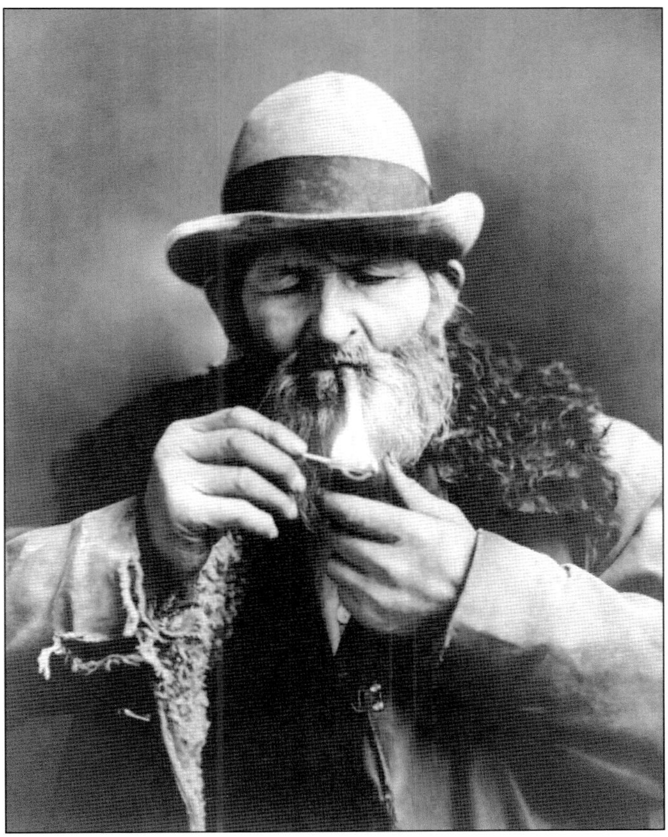

This undated portrait of local denizen Grandpa Avery looks like a composite of all the old "salts" that were common among Cape Cod folks.

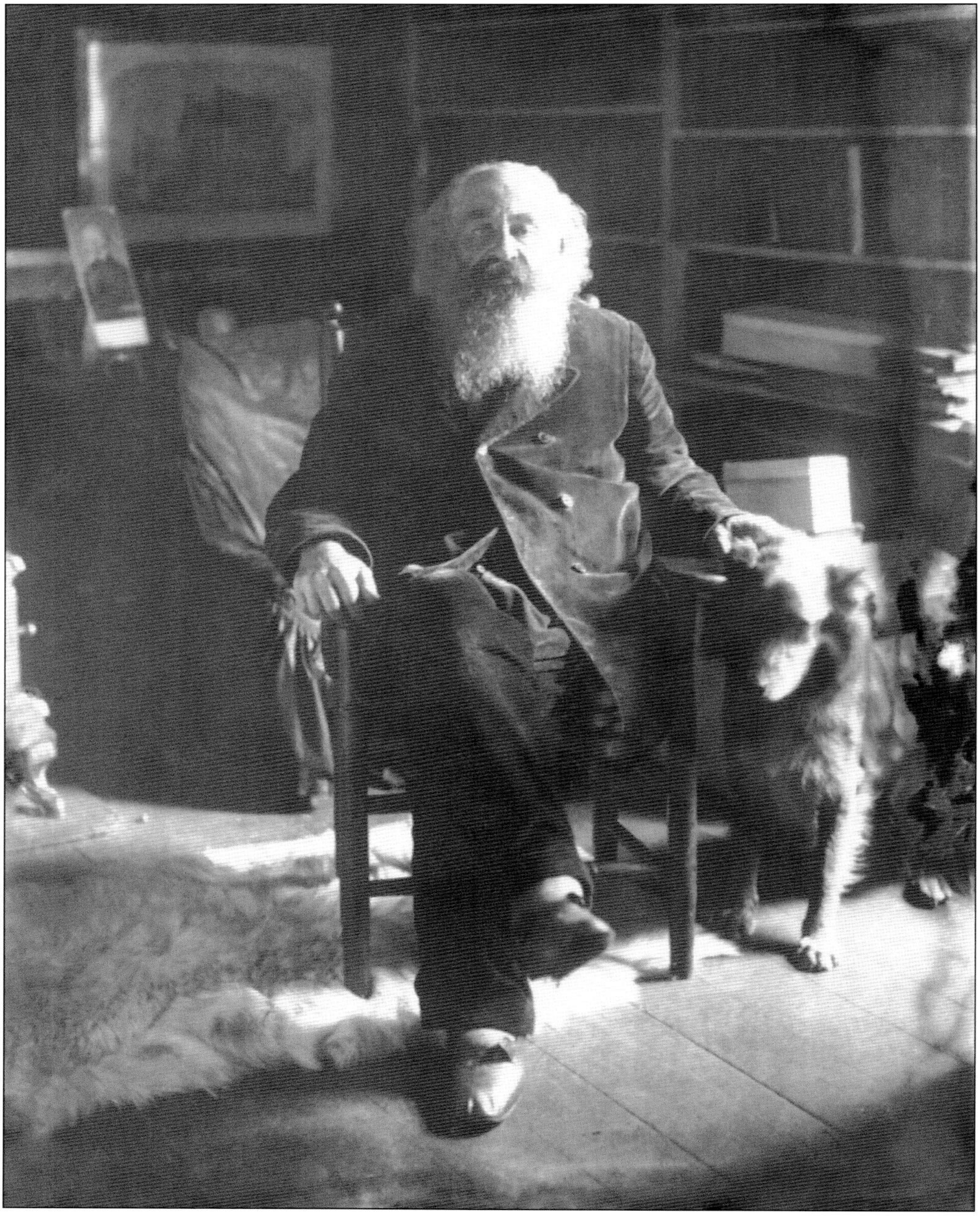

The Reverend Nathaniel Henry Chamberlayne (d. 1901) sits for a c. 1895 portrait with his dog Foxy in the study of his home on Old Dam Road in Bourne village. Chamberlayne was a fishing companion of Grover Cleveland and Joseph Jefferson and was reportedly a noticeable figure about town at six feet two inches tall.

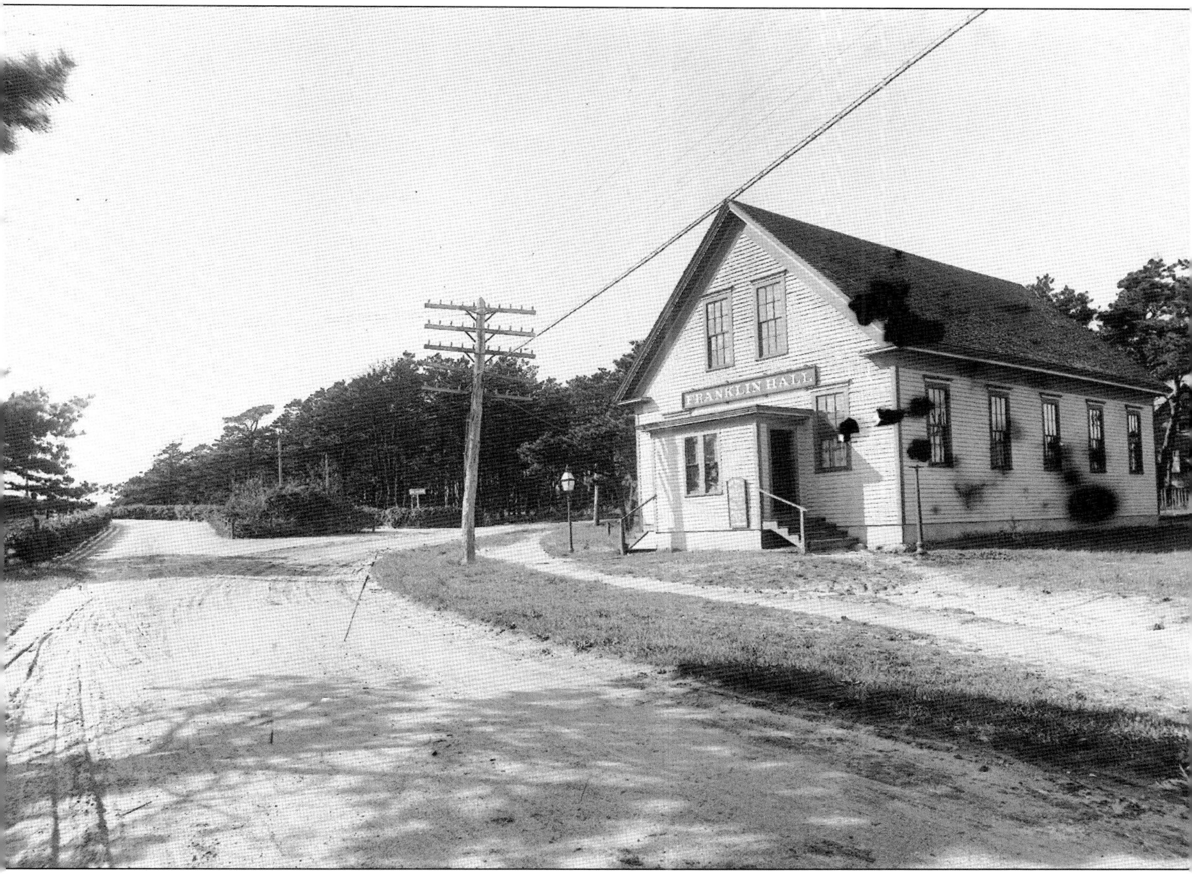

Franklin Hall in Buzzards Bay, where Bourne's first town meeting was held, is pictured here around 1920. The building was used for many community activities after that first town meeting on April 12, 1884, including old-time medicine shows, the annual Christmas tree lighting, and the annual New Year's Ball.

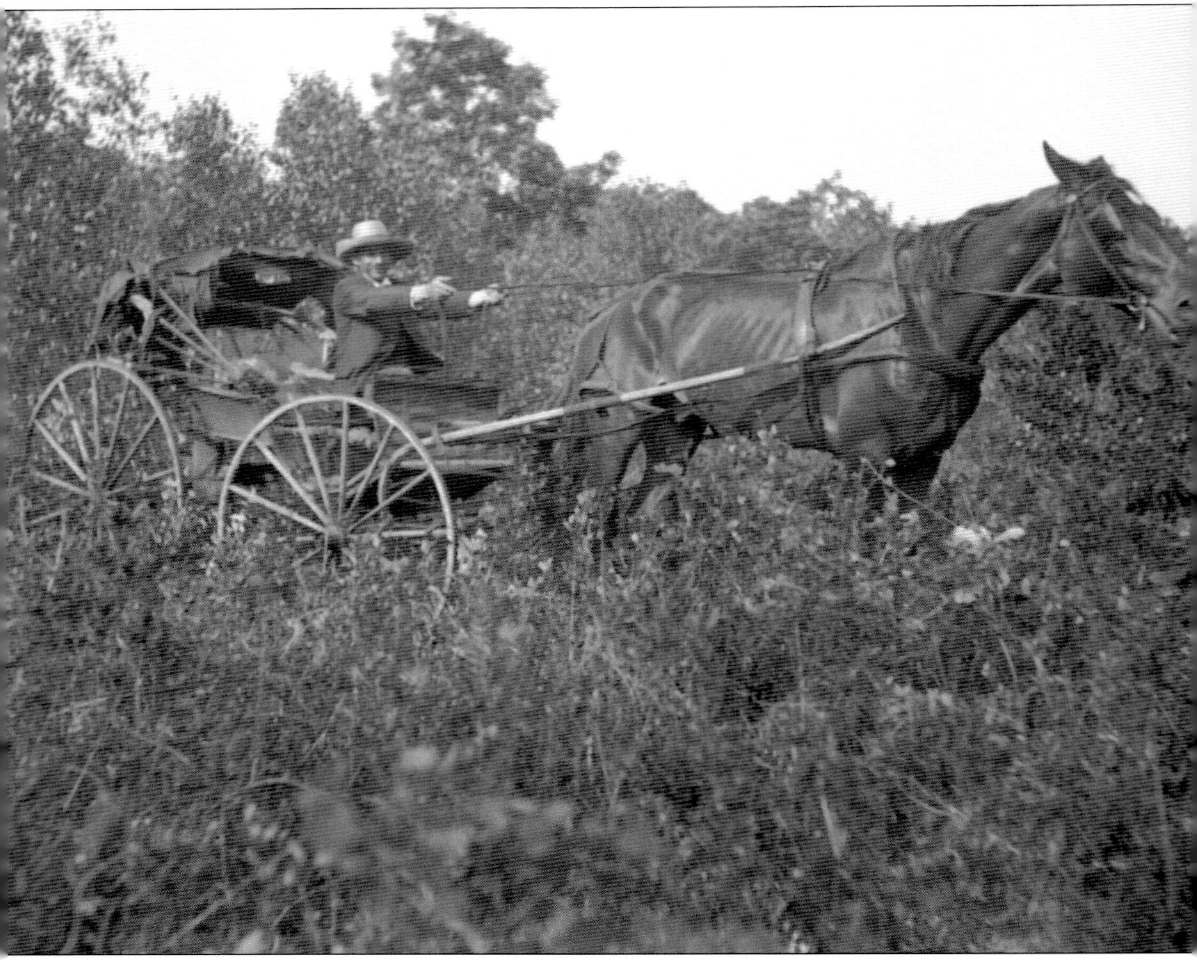

An unidentified local man poses with his horse and buggy around 1920. Horse-drawn conveyances were the most common means of local transportation between 1815 and 1915, until mass production brought the price of automobiles within the reach of most people.

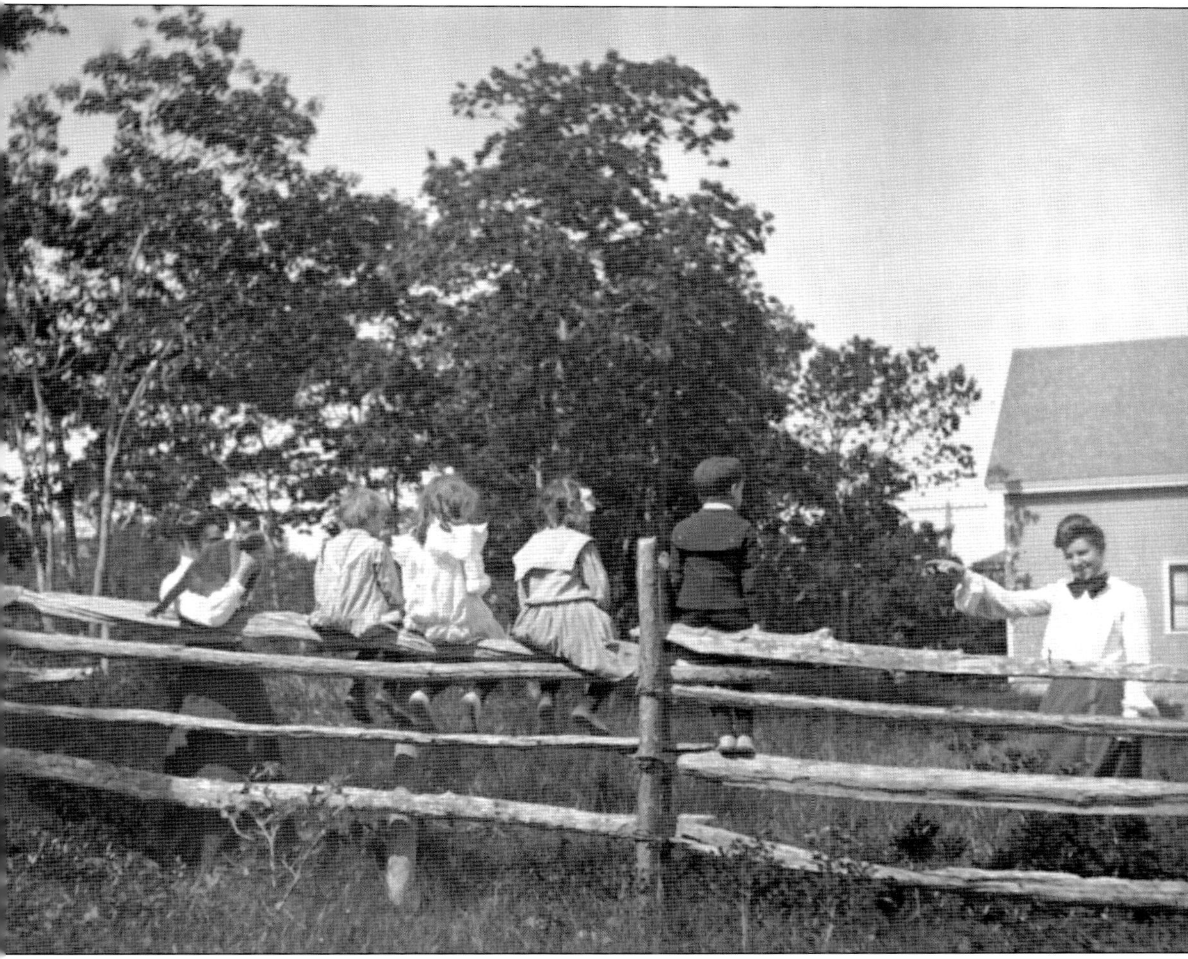

Miss Sweeney (right) gives a lesson to (from right on fence) Kenneth, Shirley, Doris, and Myra Keene as Betsey Keene and her cat look on in this c. 1920 photograph.

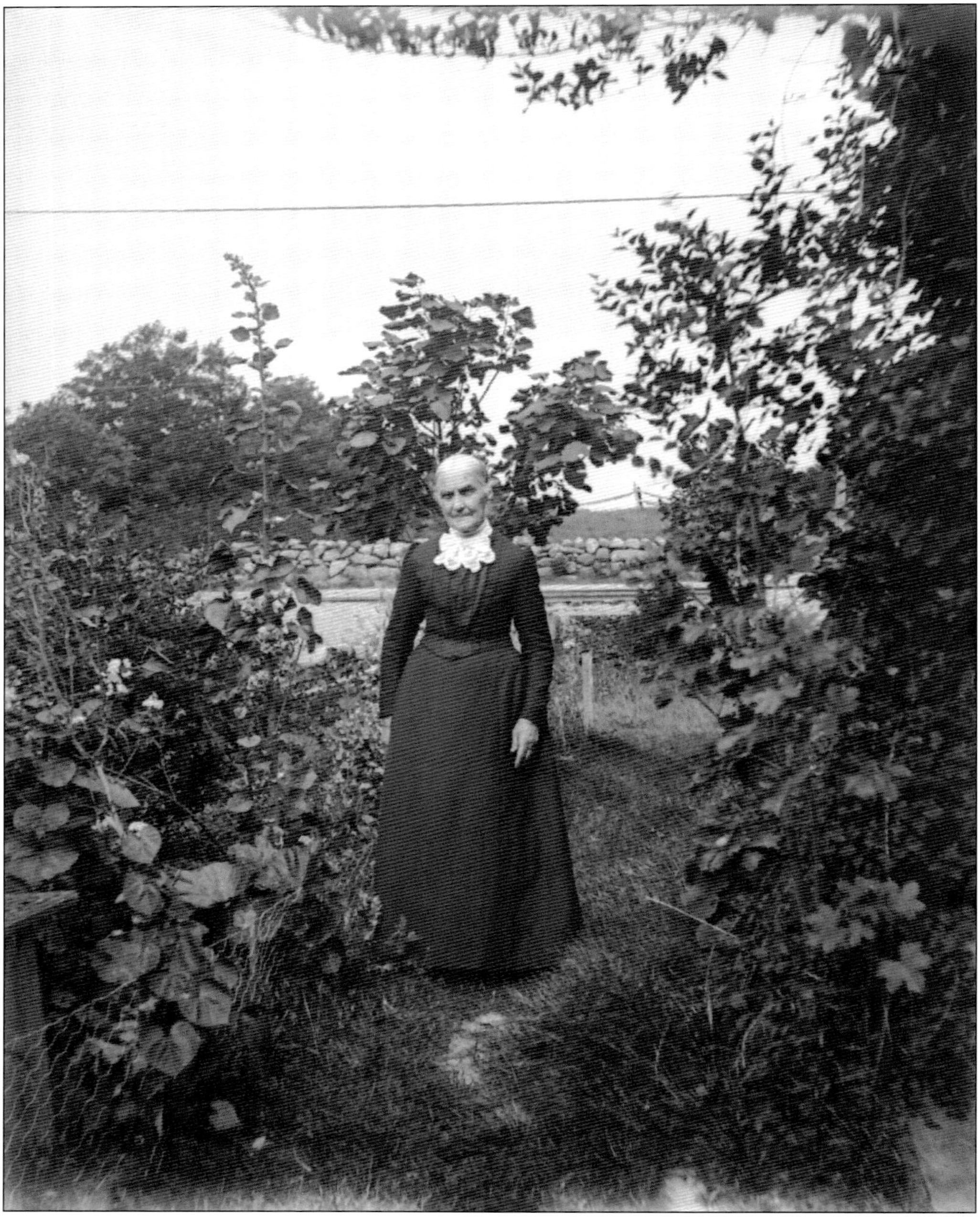

Local Emily Gibbs poses in this severe-looking photograph taken around 1920. In the days of only black-and-white photography, her beautiful garden, with hollyhocks at left and green everywhere, seems bleak and almost sinister.

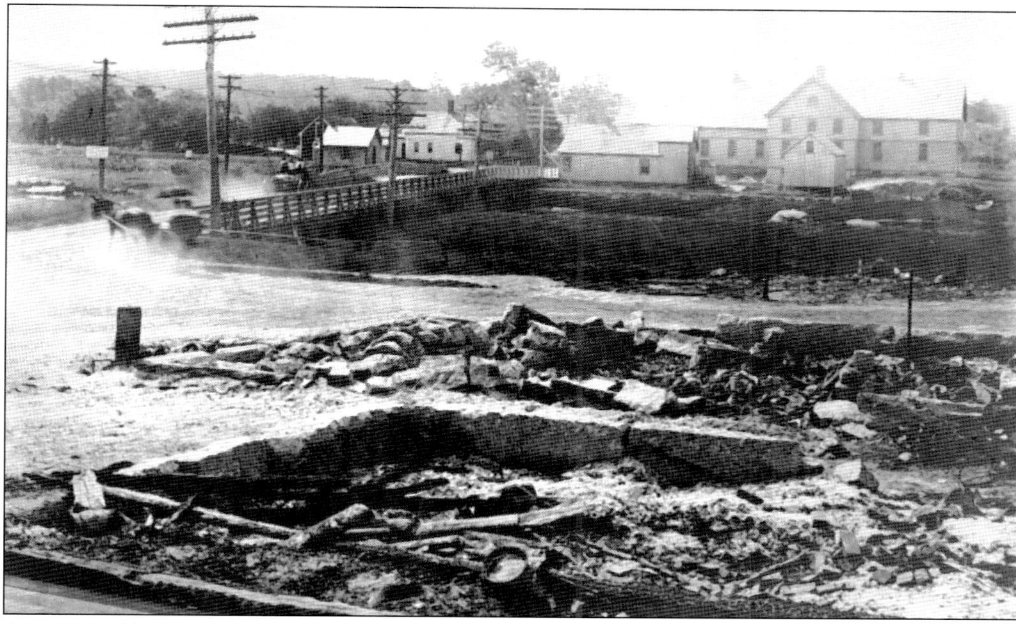

A man and his horse and buggy are about to cross the bridge over the Monument River prior to 1912 in front of the remains of the Eldridge and Keene Store that burned down that same year in a fire. Across the river are the Welcome Hall (right) and Bumpus Market.

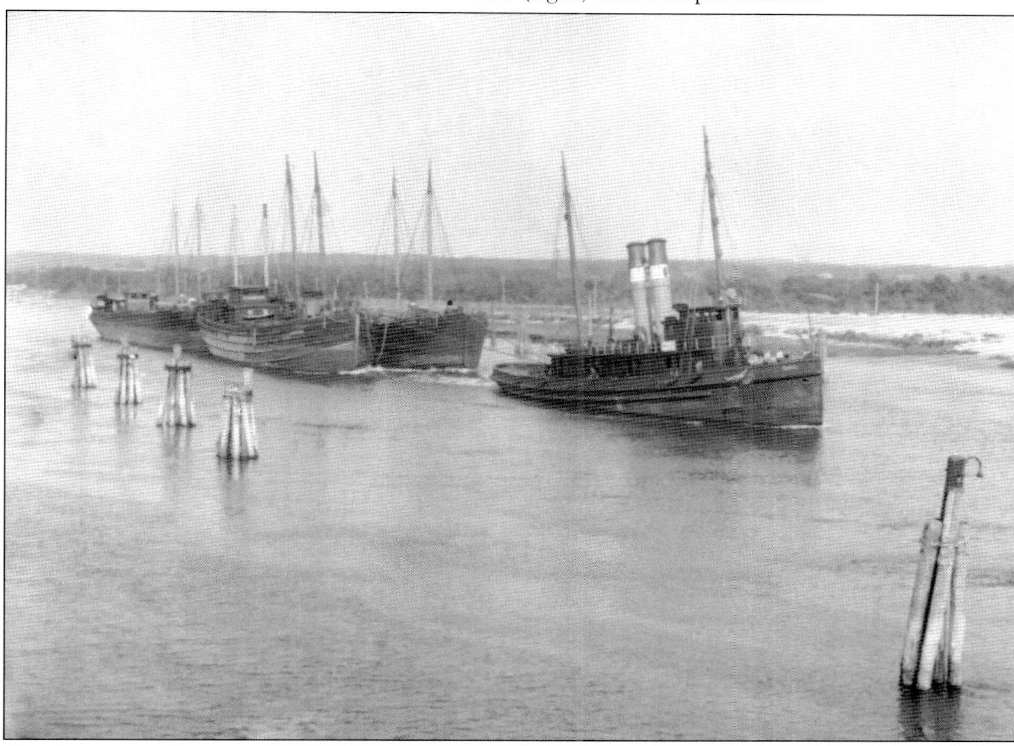

A tugboat tows decommissioned coastal schooners, with masts still intact, through the Cape Cod Canal in 1914. The schooners would be refitted for use as barges.

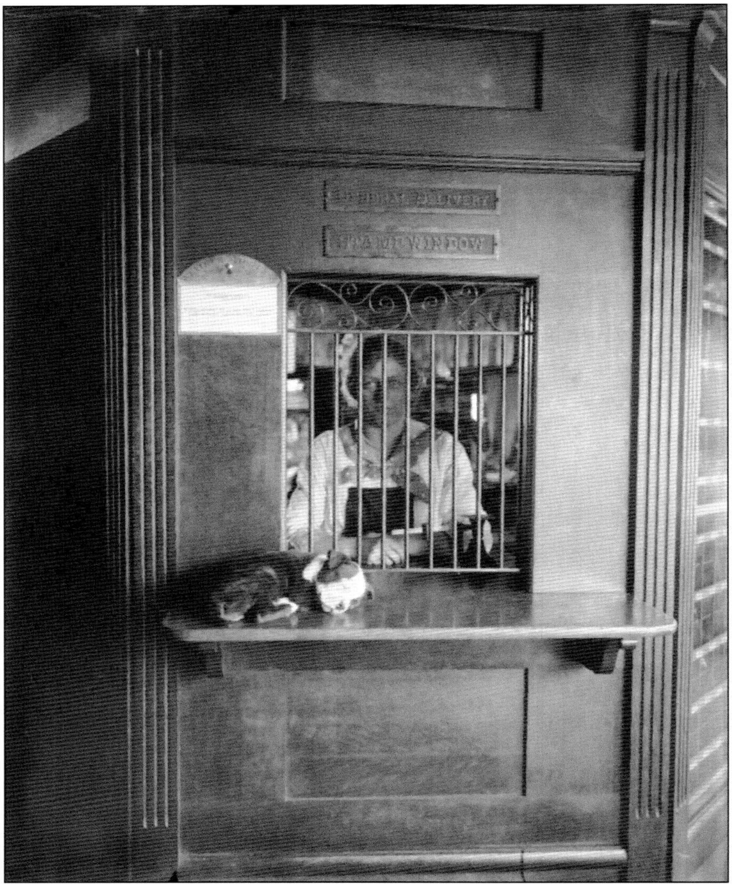

Local postmistress Cornelia Baker (1891–1992) sits at the general delivery window at the Buzzards Bay post office. Baker served as postmistress in Buzzards Bay from 1912 to 1926. Note the little dog asleep on the window shelf.

A steam shovel fills a dump truck with debris during the process of building the abutments for the highway bridges over the Cape Cod Canal in 1933.

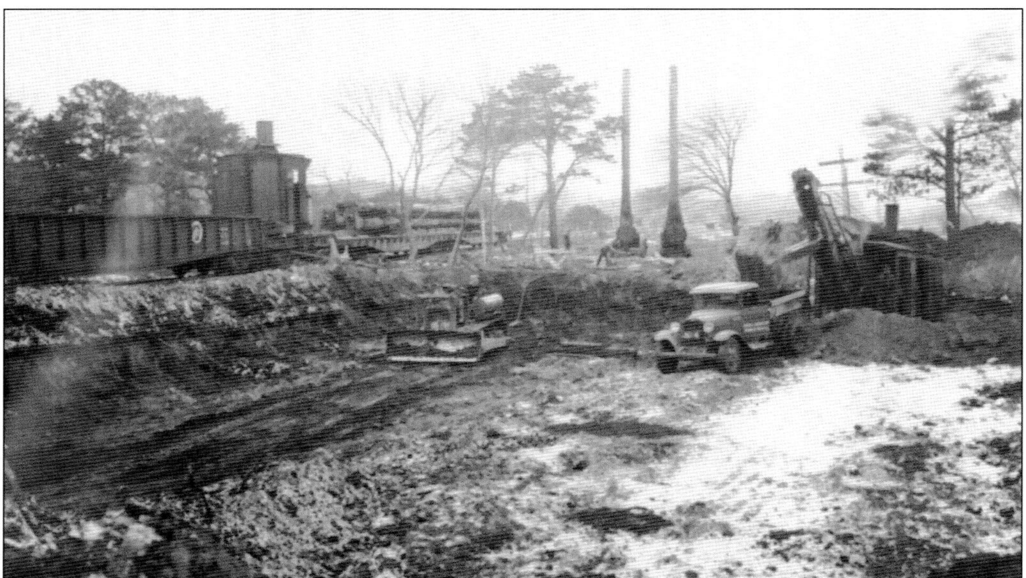

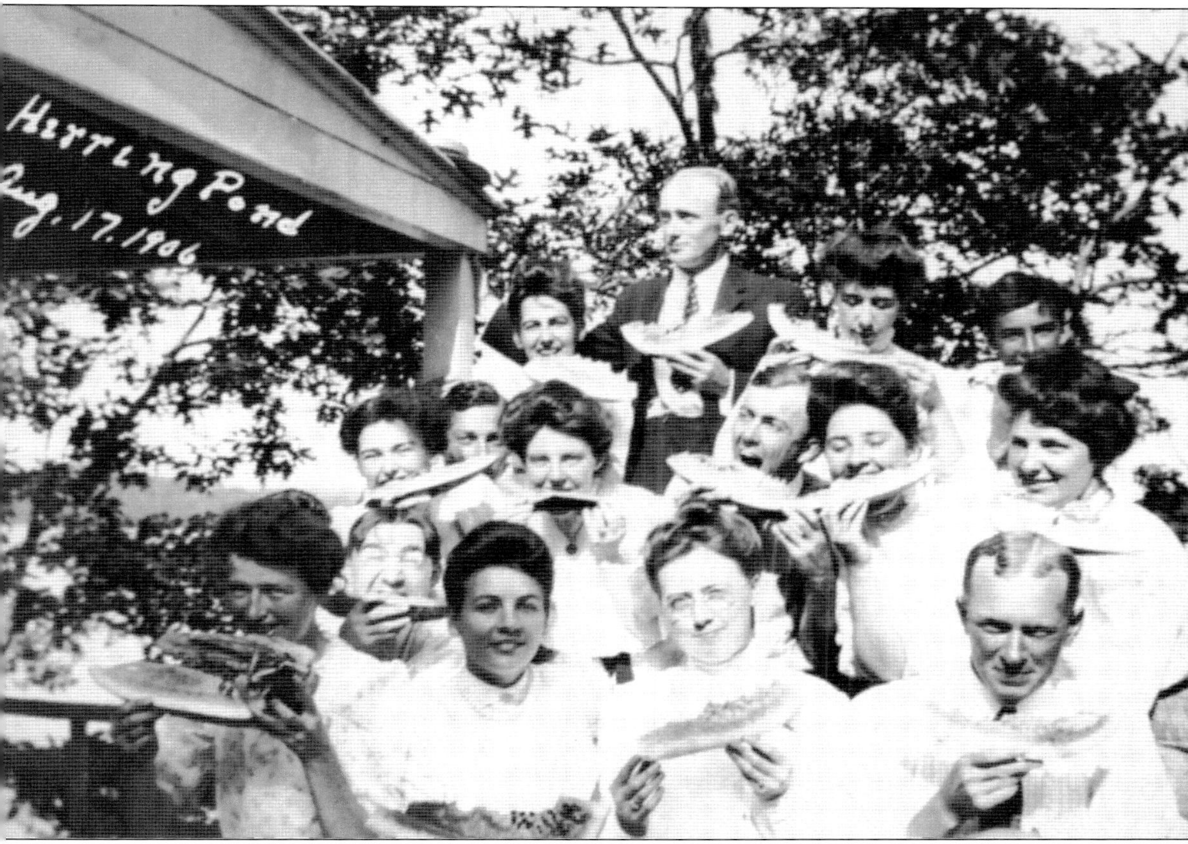

This 1907 photograph shows a picnicking group of summer visitors enjoying watermelon during an outing on Herring Pond in the village of Bournedale. Bourne, and Cape Cod in general, became a summer haven for city folks beginning in the late 1890s with the advent of railroads.

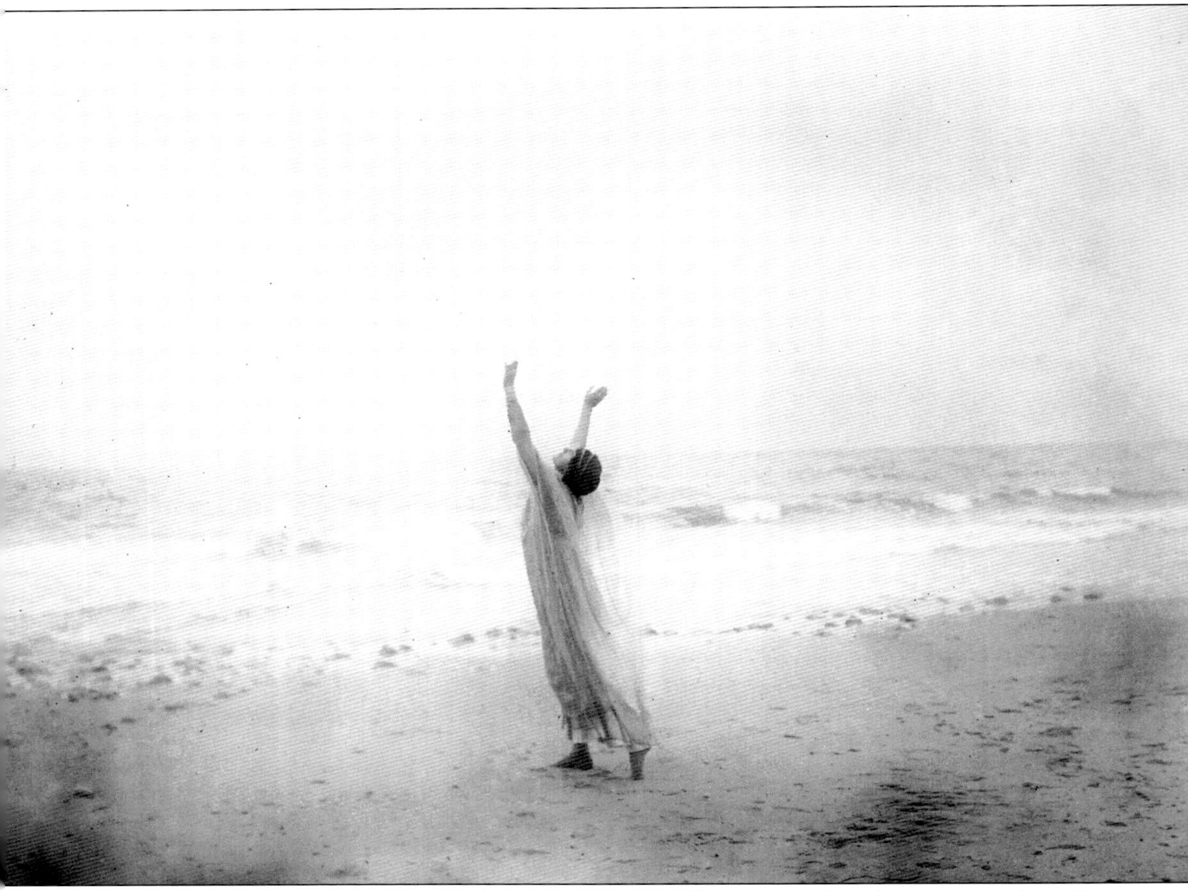

The wife of local photographer Fred Small, Daisy Small poses for this photograph, which her husband titled *The Spirit of Cape Cod*, around 1910. He took many of the iconic early photographs of Cape Cod and the Cape Cod Canal construction, but also took many of his family and friends.

Seven

When Bad Things Happen to Good Towns

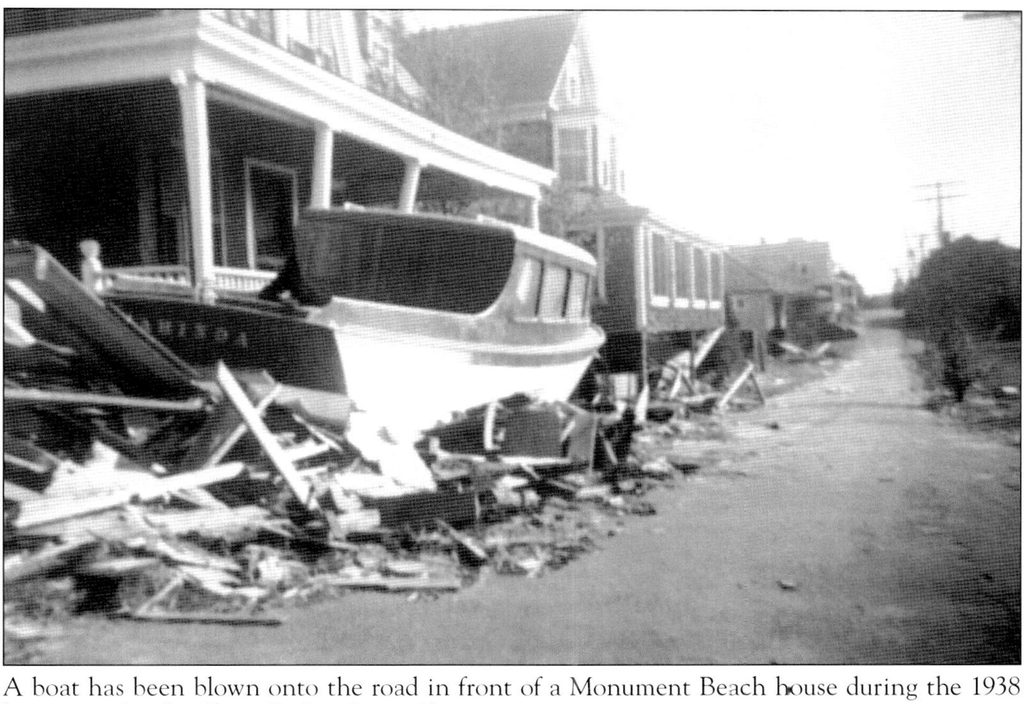

A boat has been blown onto the road in front of a Monument Beach house during the 1938 hurricane that hit Cape Cod with a wallop.

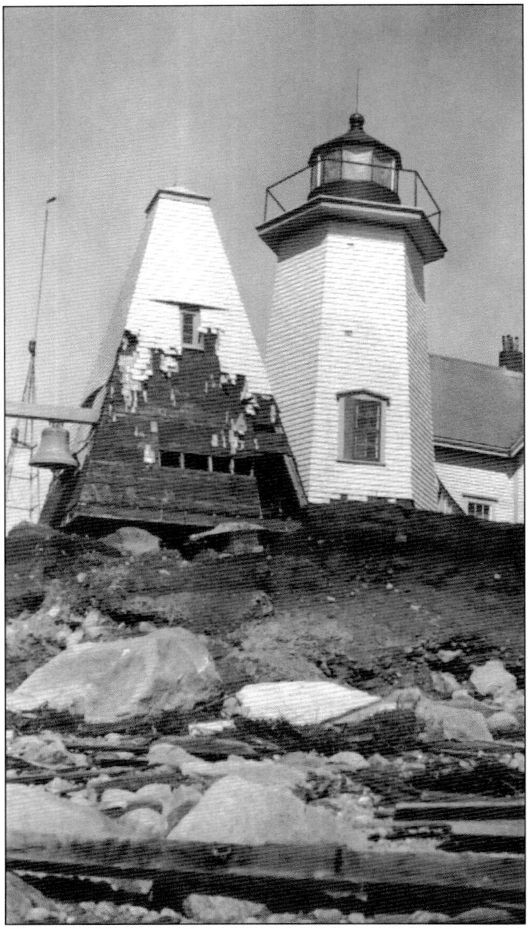

Damage to the Wing's Neck lighthouse can be seen in this 1938 photograph. The lighthouse was built in 1849 to aid traffic in and out of Buzzards Bay.

A boat and debris lie on the shore after the 1938 hurricane hit the town of Bourne. Hundreds of homes and cottages were swept away and 26 people were reported dead in what was called the storm of the century.

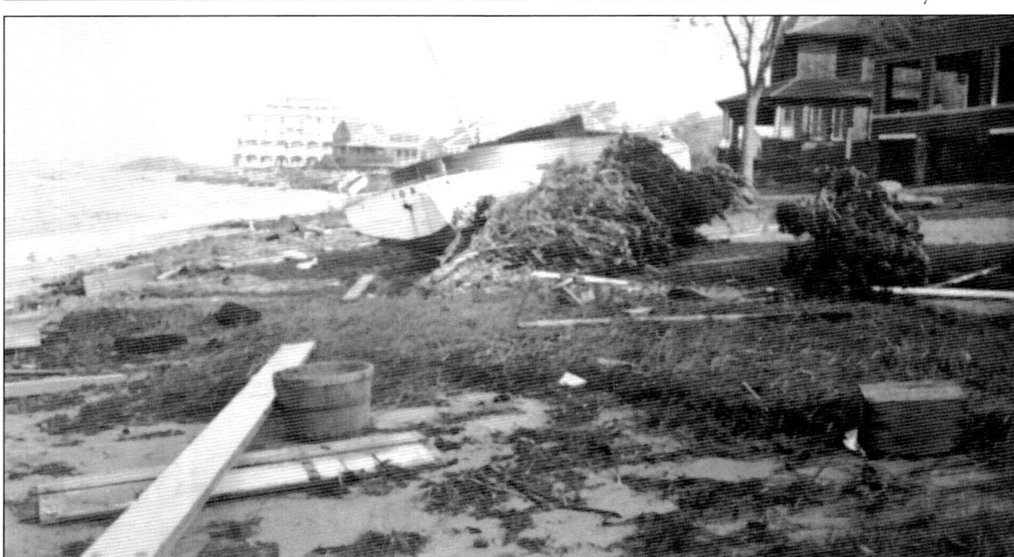

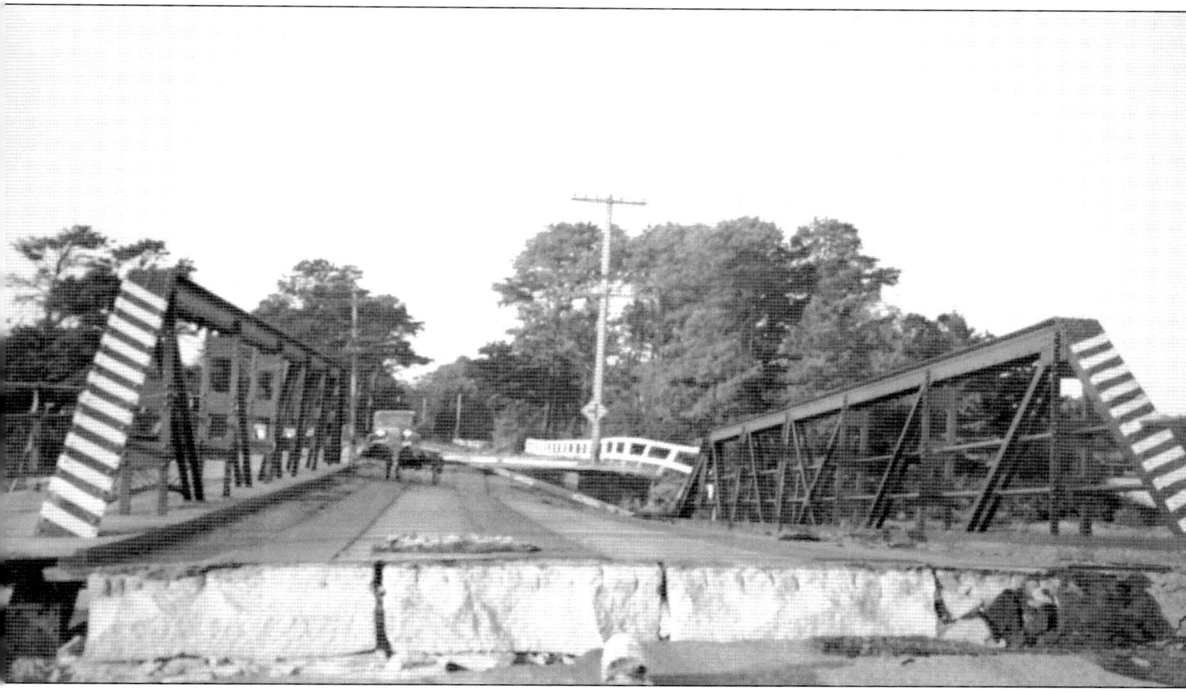

The "Singing Bridge" in Pocasset is in pieces after being damaged by the 1938 hurricane. Some 50 cottages in the village of Pocasset were either wrecked or badly damaged by the hurricane and the high tides associated with it.

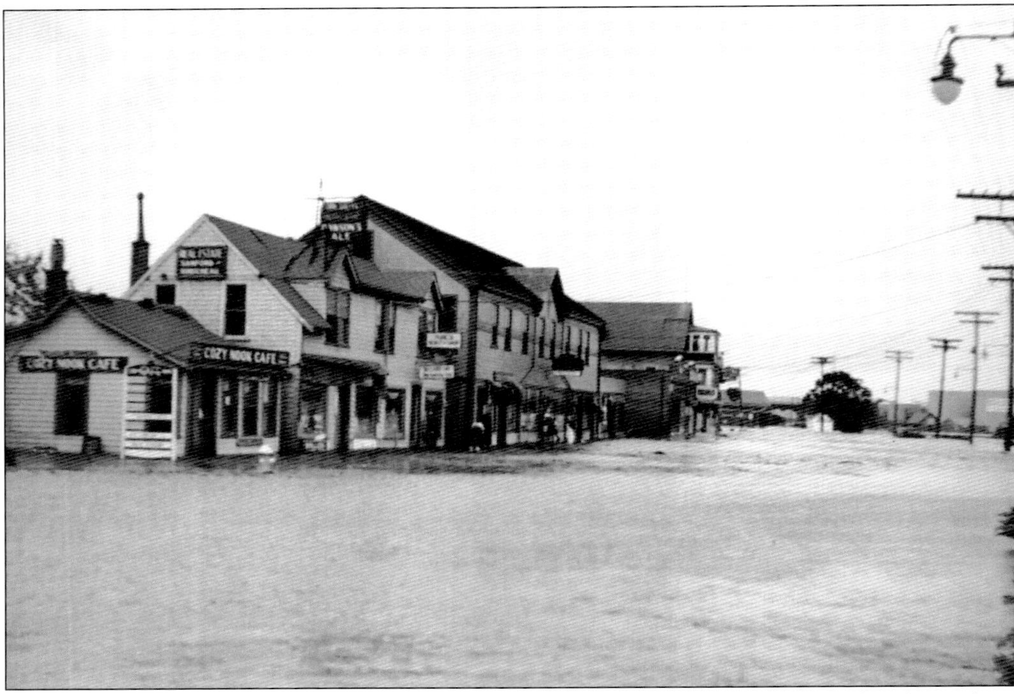

Main Street in the village of Buzzards Bay is inundated in this 1938 photograph. The railroad tracks were washed out in the storm that killed some 26 people and left countless others without homes.

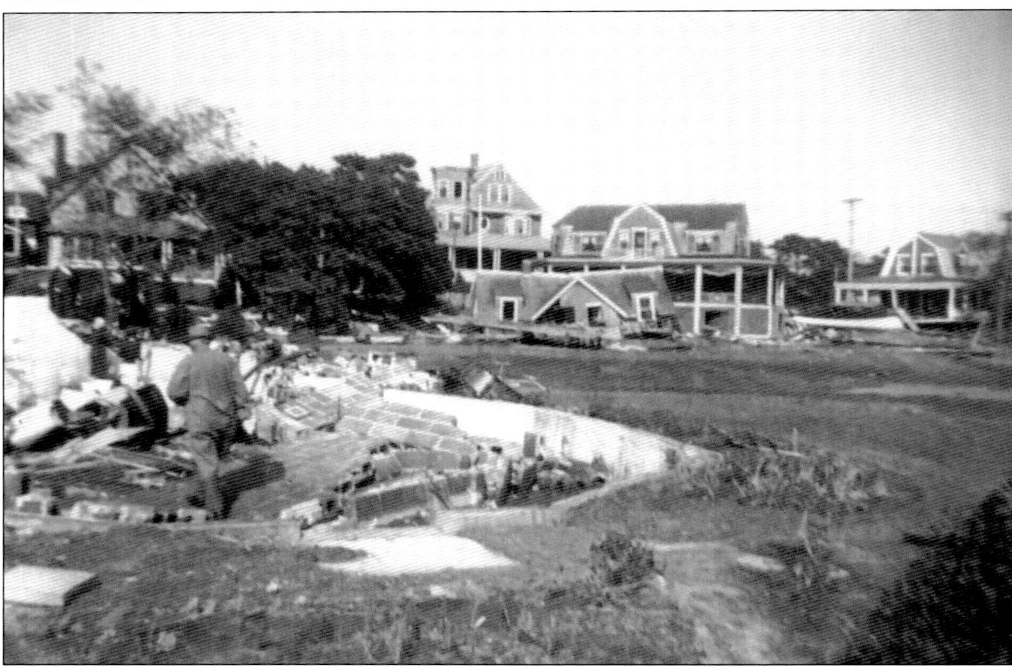

The gazebo at Monument Beach was blown down during the Hurricane of 1938. More damage is seen in the background.

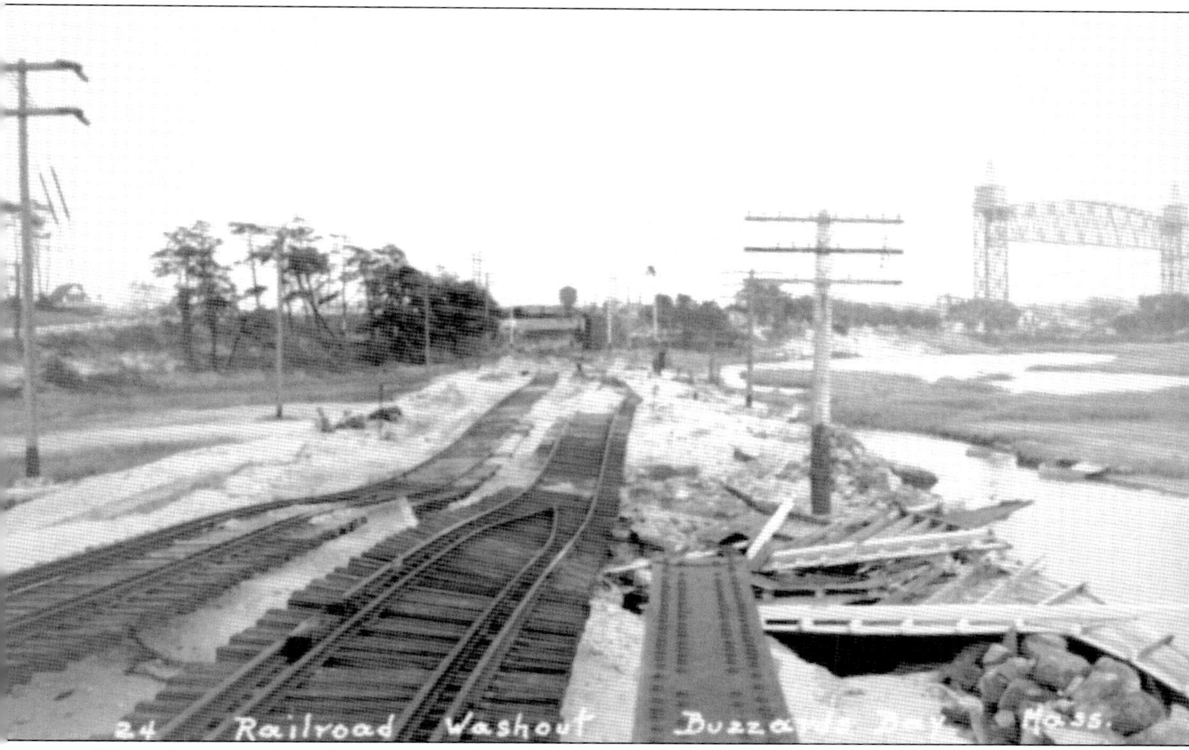

The railroad tracks in Buzzards Bay have been washed out in this 1938 photograph. Train service to the Cape was suspended for several weeks after the storm as repairs were made to the tracks.

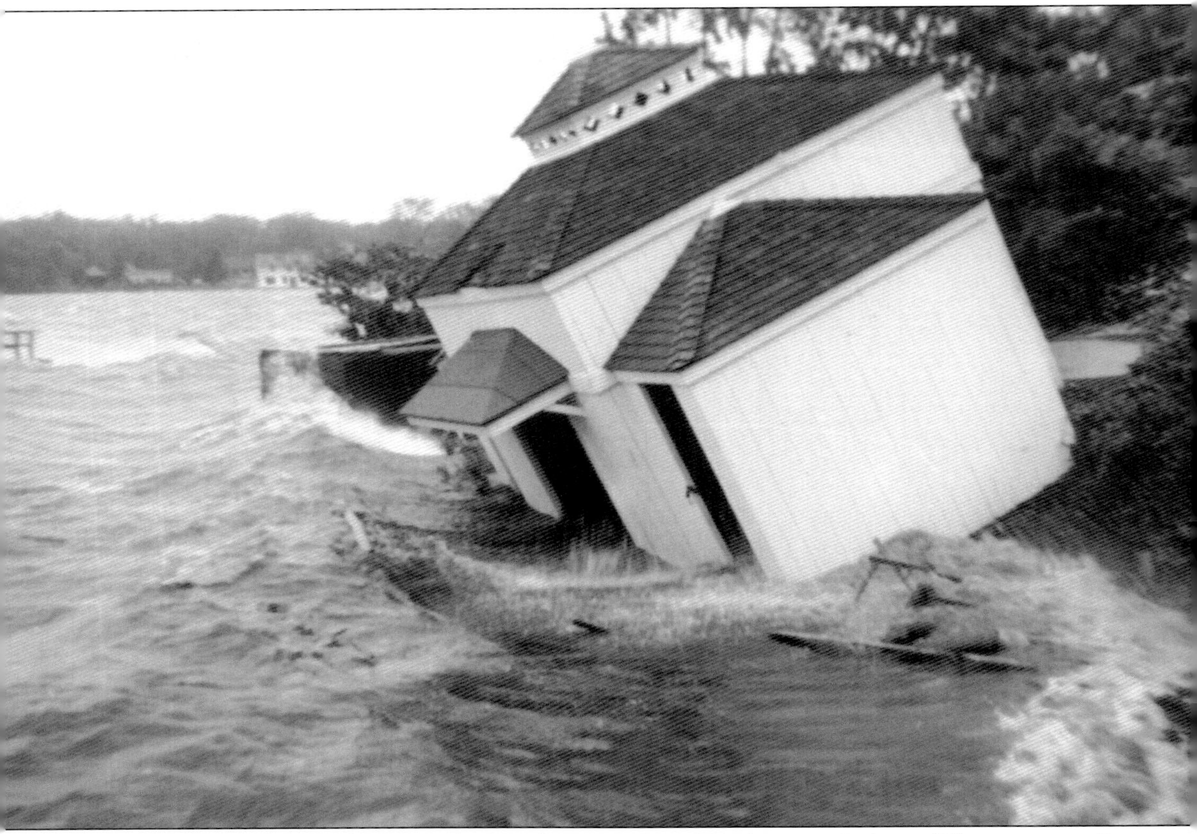

Hurricanes are always a danger in the Northeast, as this 1954 photograph shows. The seas are still roiling as the unknown photographer takes a shot of the boathouse belonging to Elmer Landers that keeled over in the 1954 hurricane.

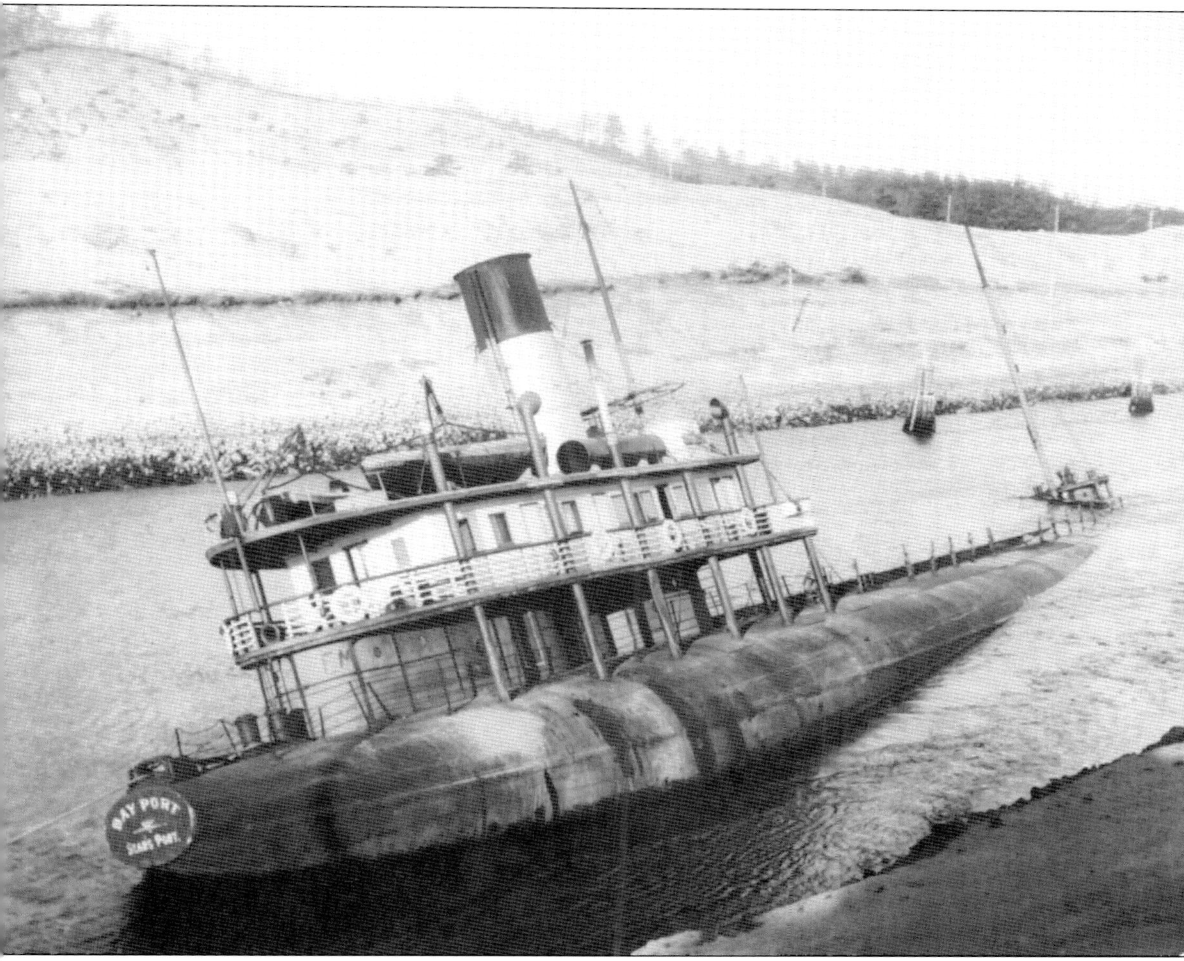

The *Bay Port*, an early tanker, sits in the Cape Cod Canal after hitting ground in Sagamore on December 16, 1916. Before the canal was widened and its sides reinforced with riprap traversing, the waterway could be a challenge.

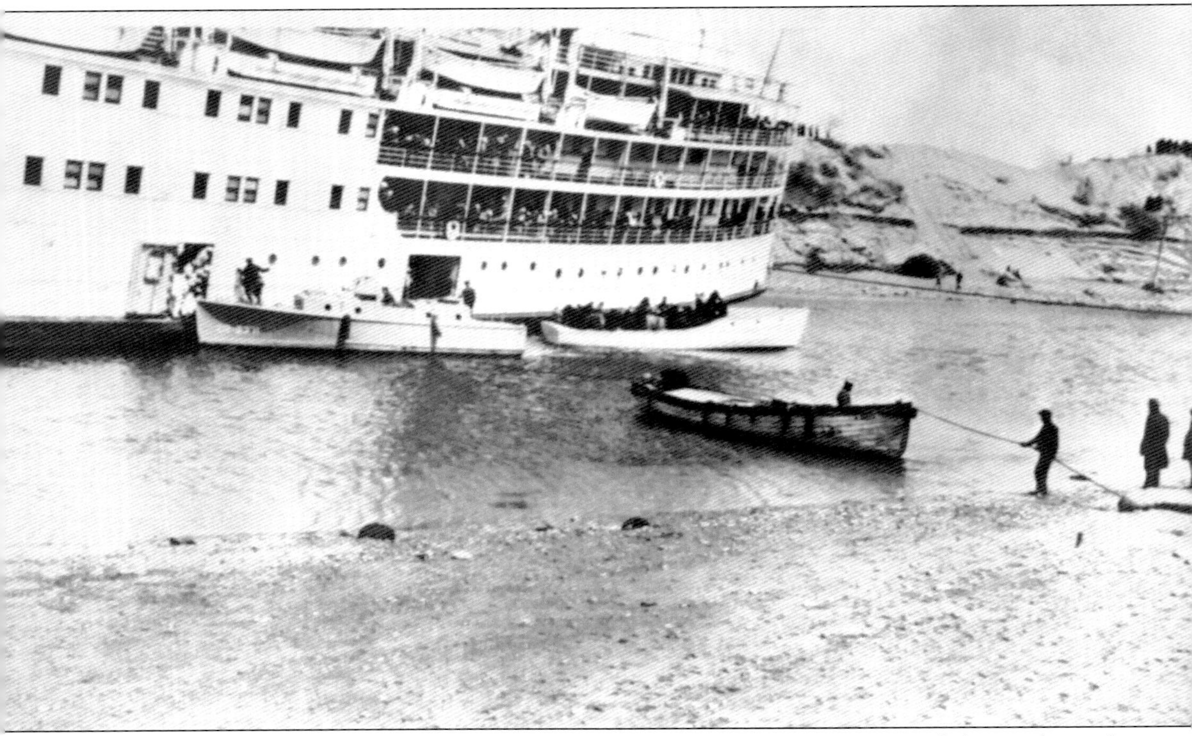

The steamship *New York* is grounded in the Cape Cod Canal near Sagamore while members of the Coast Guard evacuate the passengers on April 15, 1928.

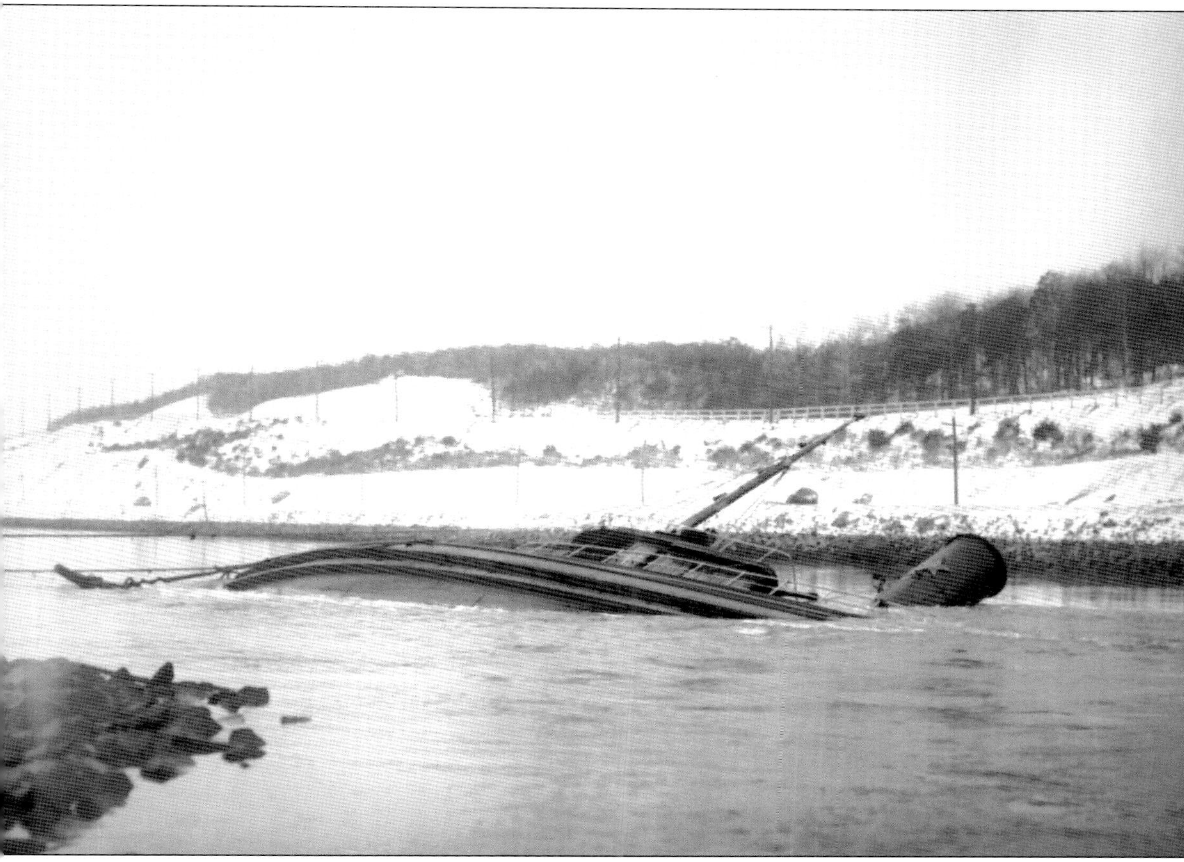

The tugboat *Watuppa* is almost submerged after going under in the Cape Cod Canal in this January 29, 1915, photograph.

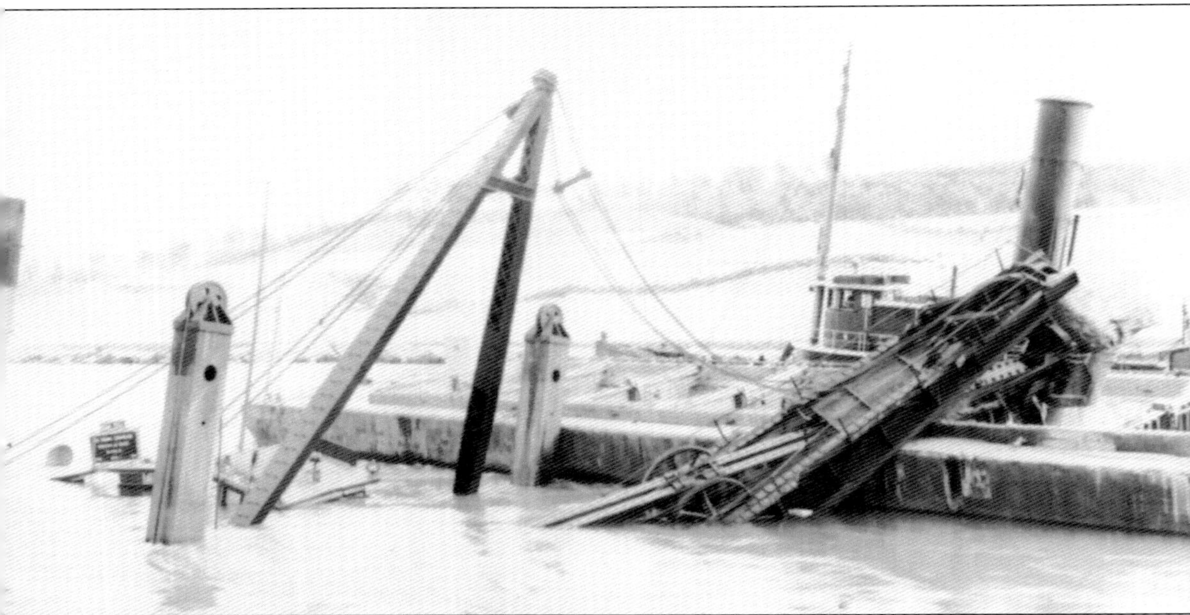

The dredge *Governor Herrick* is underwater after being bumped by another boat and tipping over in the Cape Cod Canal in January 1937. The vessel sprang a leak while digging out a boulder.

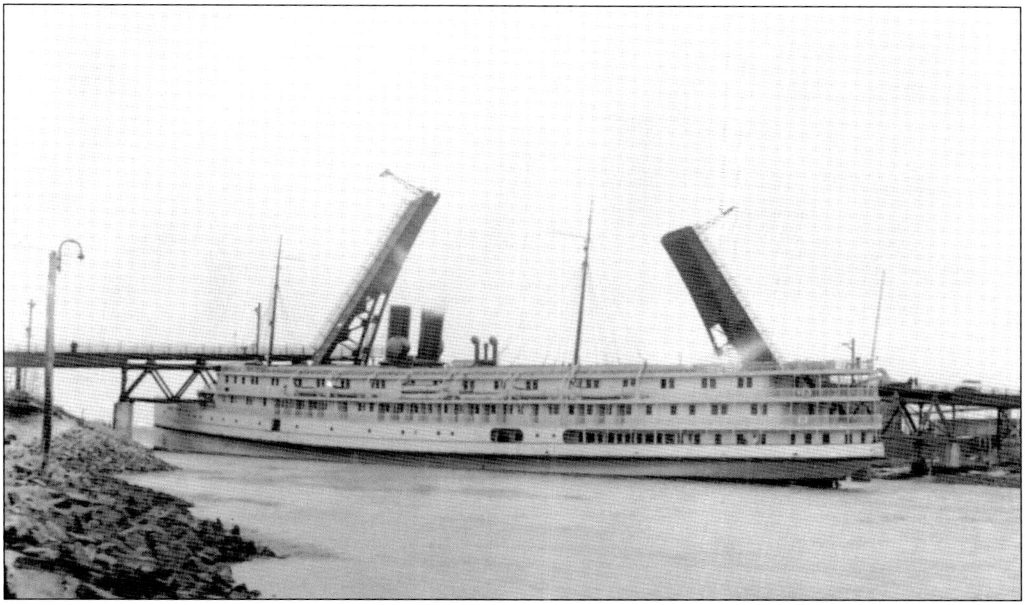

The *Belfast*, of the Eastern Steamship Lines, was caught in a stiff wind and a cross-current on its first trip of the season, missed the opening, and hit the Sagamore Bridge over the Cape Cod Canal on April 16, 1919. Three people were injured and canal traffic was blocked for over a day.

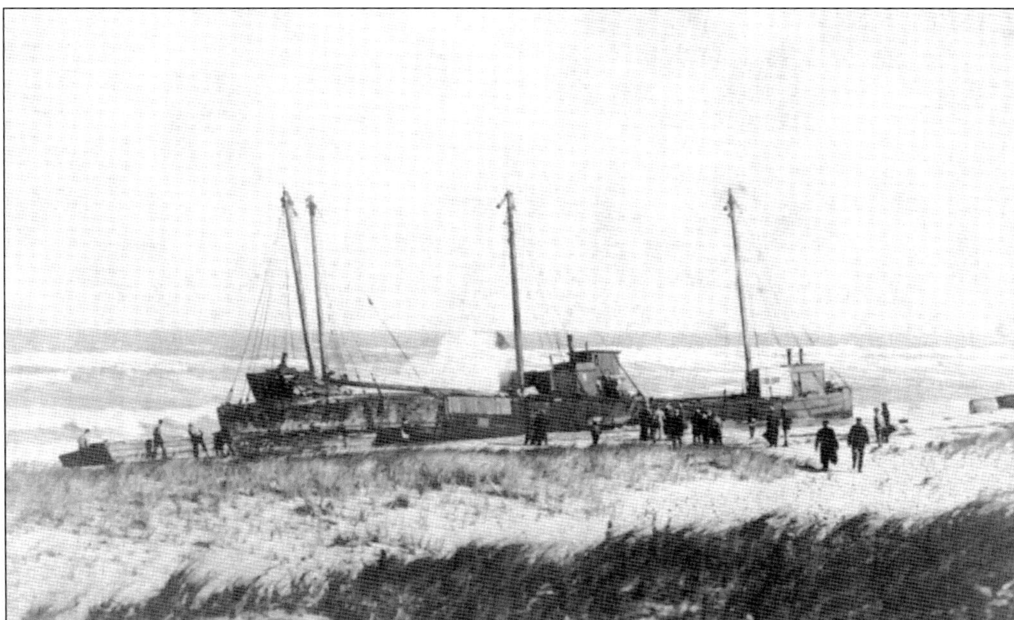

People gather on the beach to look over and salvage from the wreck of a barge that ran ashore in heavy seas in Buzzards Bay.

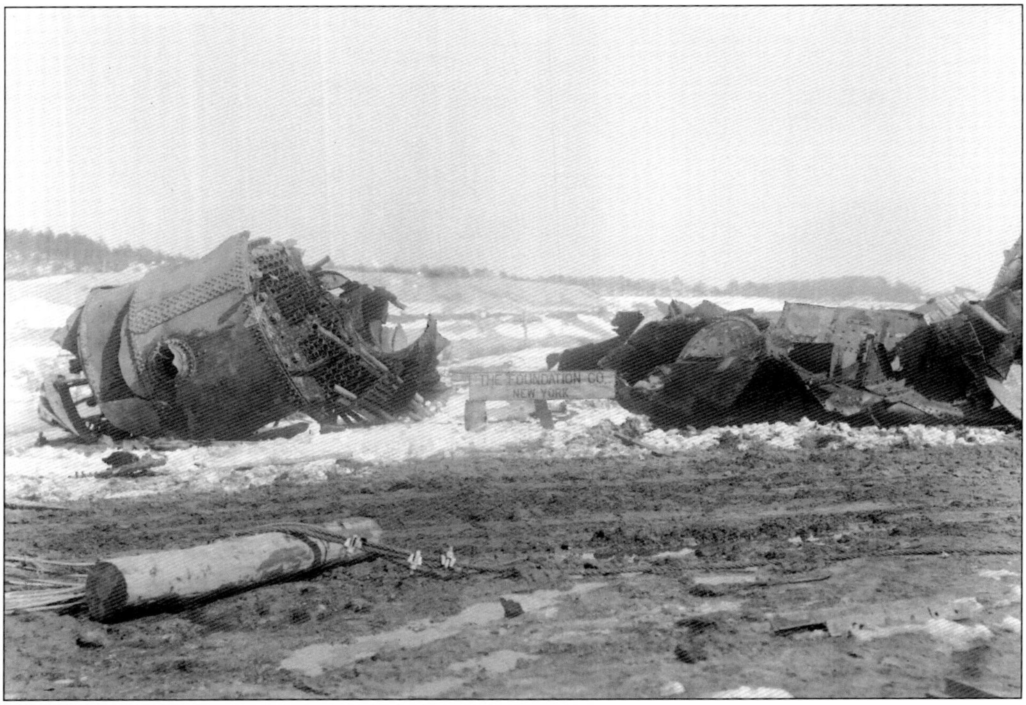

A boiler is in pieces after an explosion in one of the machine shops that was utilized during construction of the Cape Cod Canal. The machine shops, though unsightly, were a necessary component of the construction.

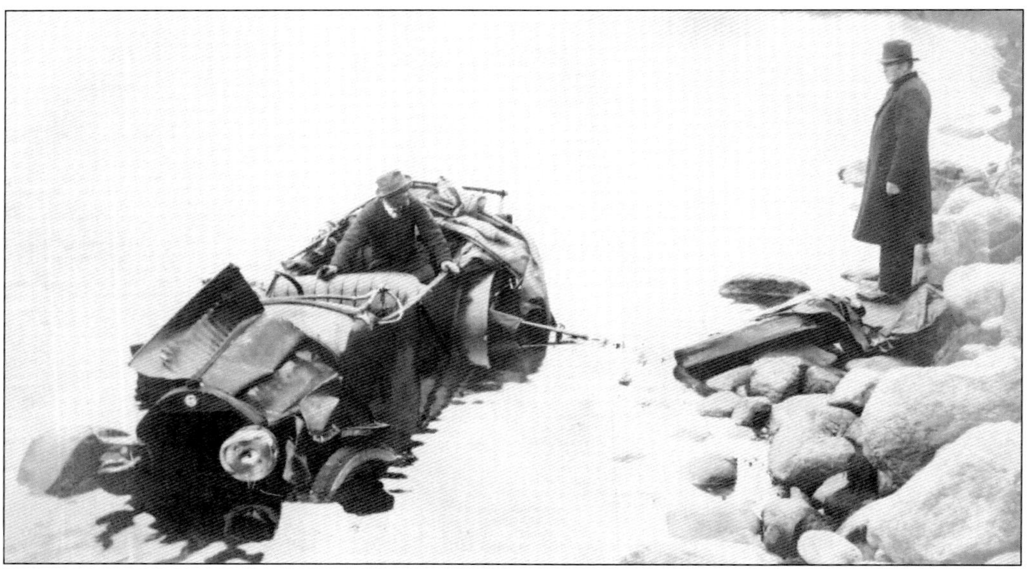

In the early years of automobile travel across the bridges spanning the Cape Cod Canal, a car ending up in the water was not an uncommon sight.

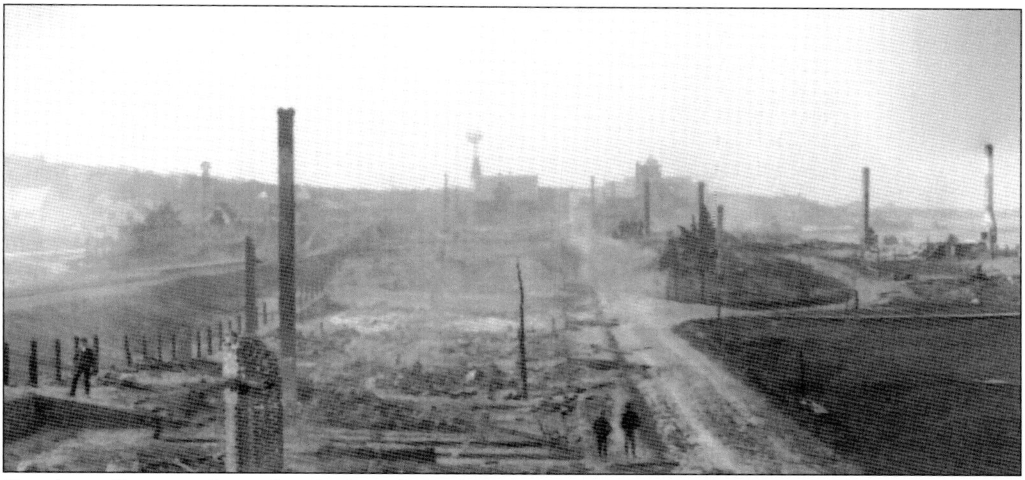

People walk around in what little is left after the 1906 great fire in Monument Beach village, which left huge swathes of land and cottages in ashes.

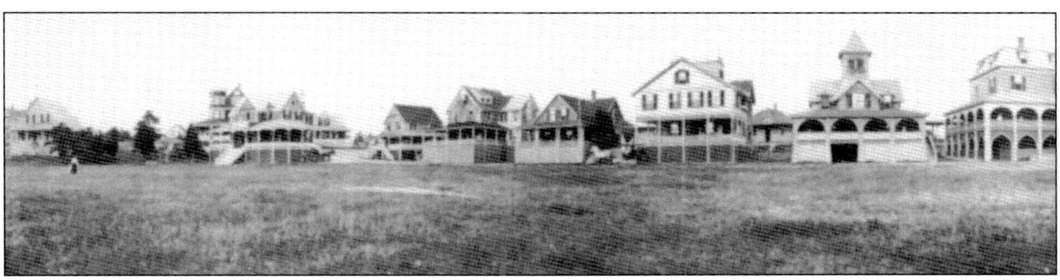

This photograph shows the line of cottages that were destroyed in the fire of 1906. Some 25 cottages were lost in the fire that raged through the village on May 17, 1906.

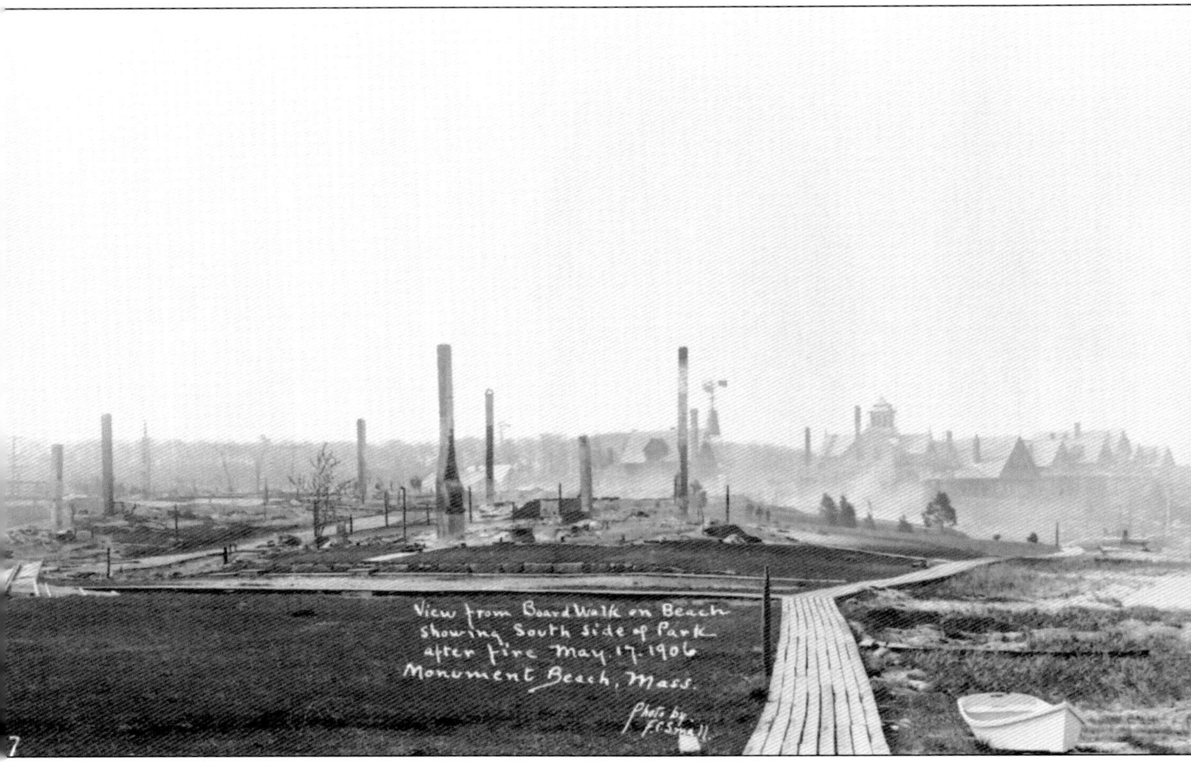

Another view of the destruction of Monument Beach in 1906 is pictured here. There is no record of how the fire started.

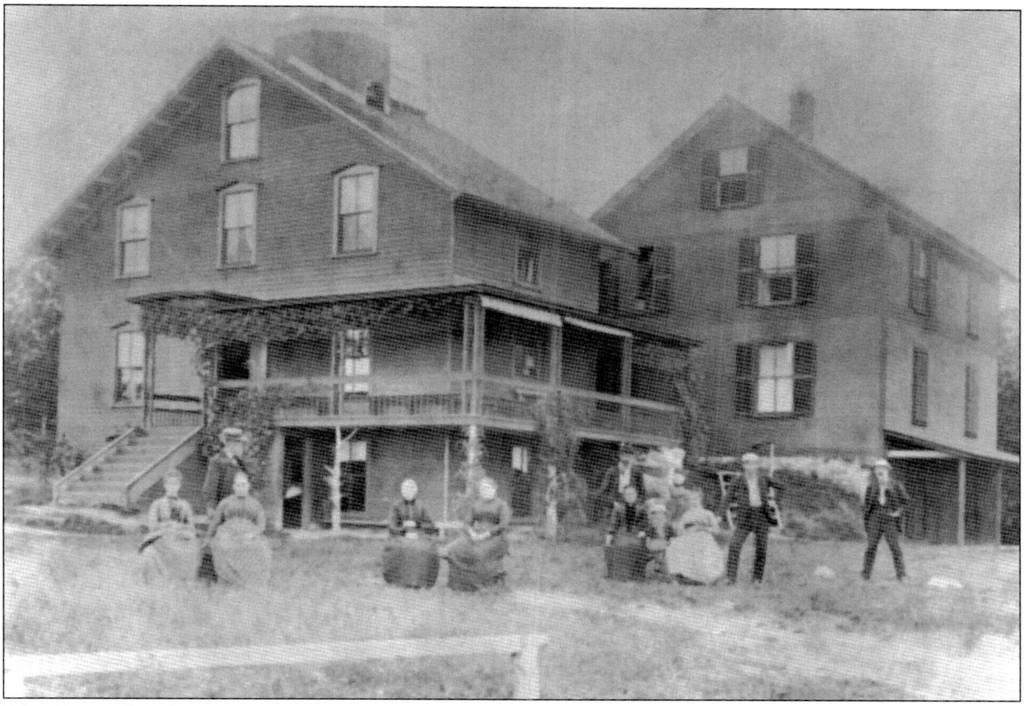

The Davis family poses in front of the Jachin Hotel in this c. 1890 photograph. Pictured, from left to right, are (seated) Mary (Davis) Gibbs, Mattie Davis (mother), Eliza Stebbins, Mrs. Bates, Edward Jones, Mrs. W.P. Hill, Philip Hill, and Genevieve (Davis) Gordon; (standing) Alden Davis (father), Charles Hobbs, and a Mr. Bates. The man at far right is unidentified. The Alden Davis house, shown below in 1890, is the family home where the murders took place.

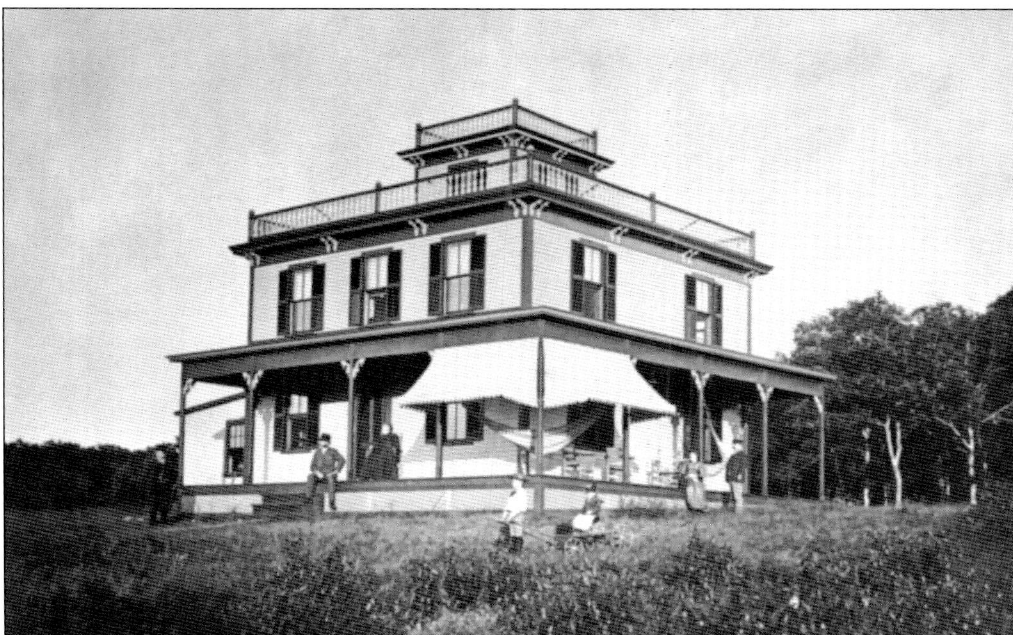

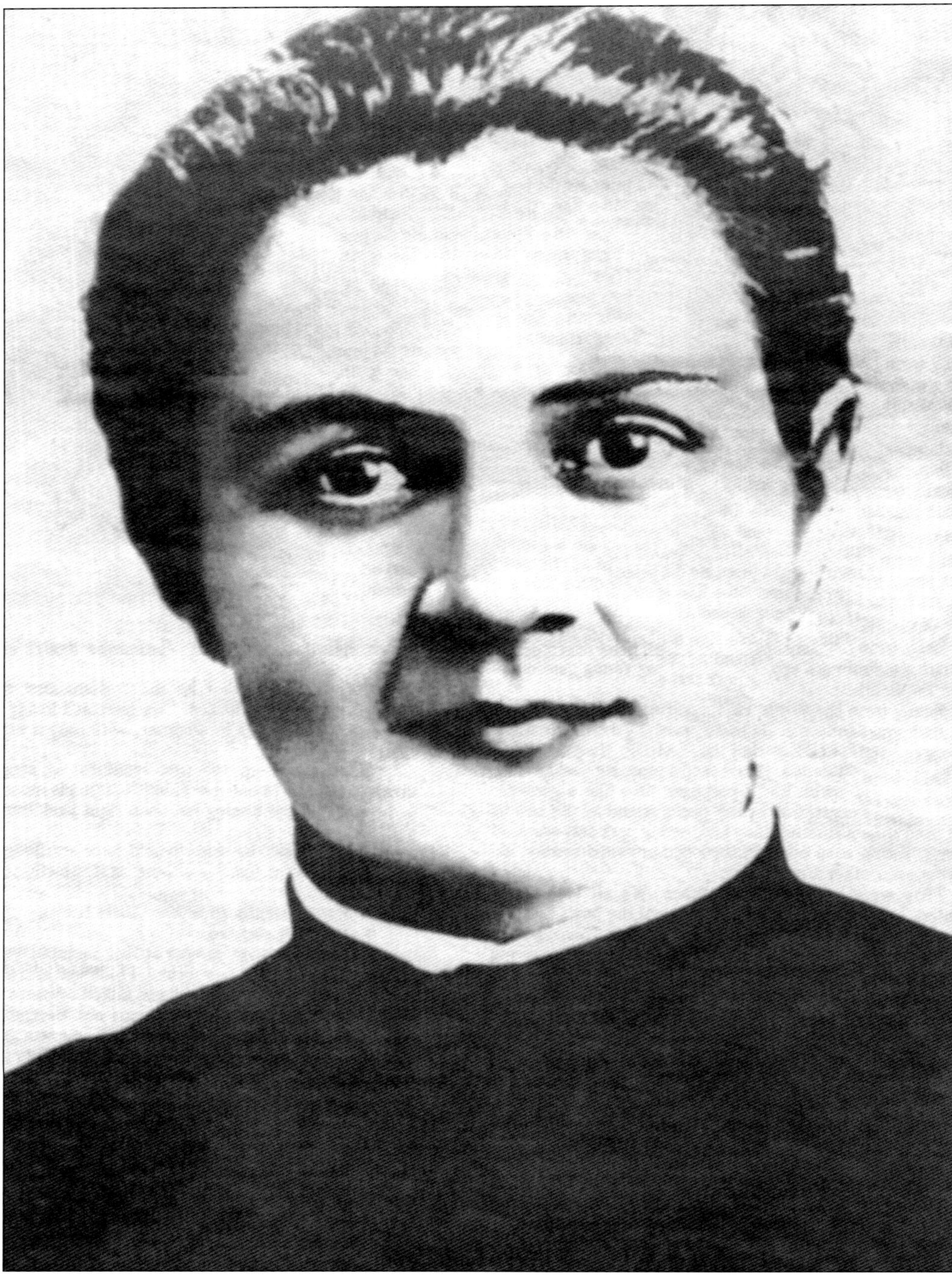

Nurse "Jolly Jane" Toppan is shown in this c. 1900 newspaper photograph. The Davis family killings were the undoing of Toppan. After four Davis family deaths in a short amount of time, all under the watchful eye of Toppan, suspicions were raised that eventually led to her confession to killing the Davis family and some 31 others. She was committed for life to Taunton State Mental Hospital, where she died in 1938 at age 81.

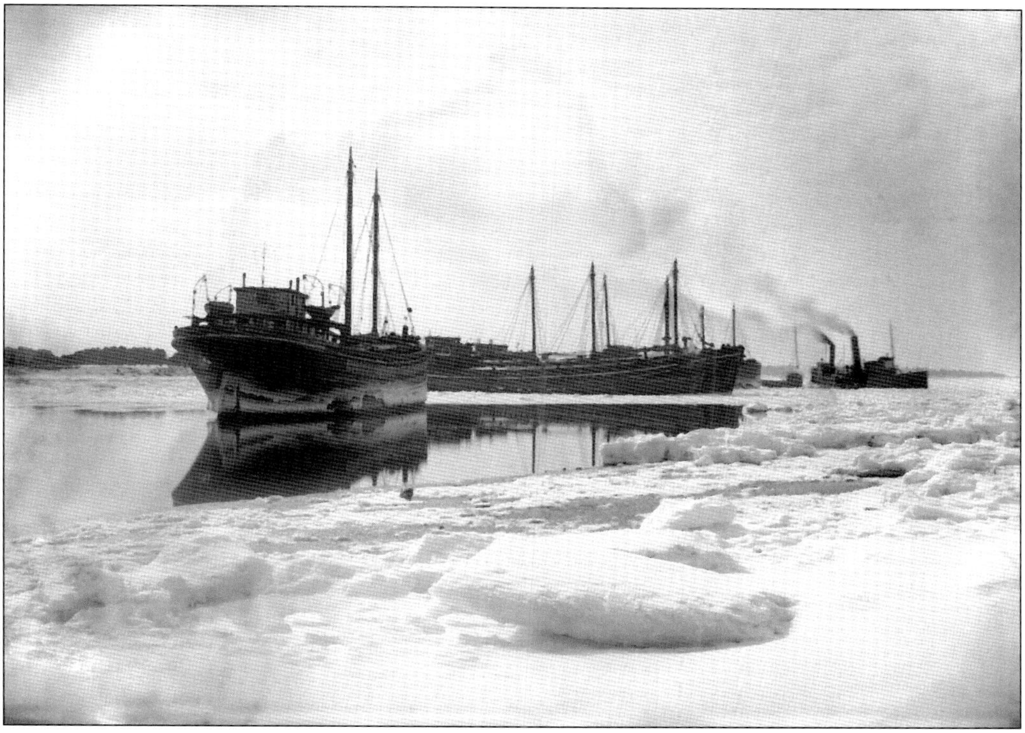

Ships are encrusted with ice as they sit in the waters of Buzzards Bay around 1925. The waters of Buzzards Bay have always been fraught with danger in the winter, when it gets cold enough for the ice to build up and surround ships.

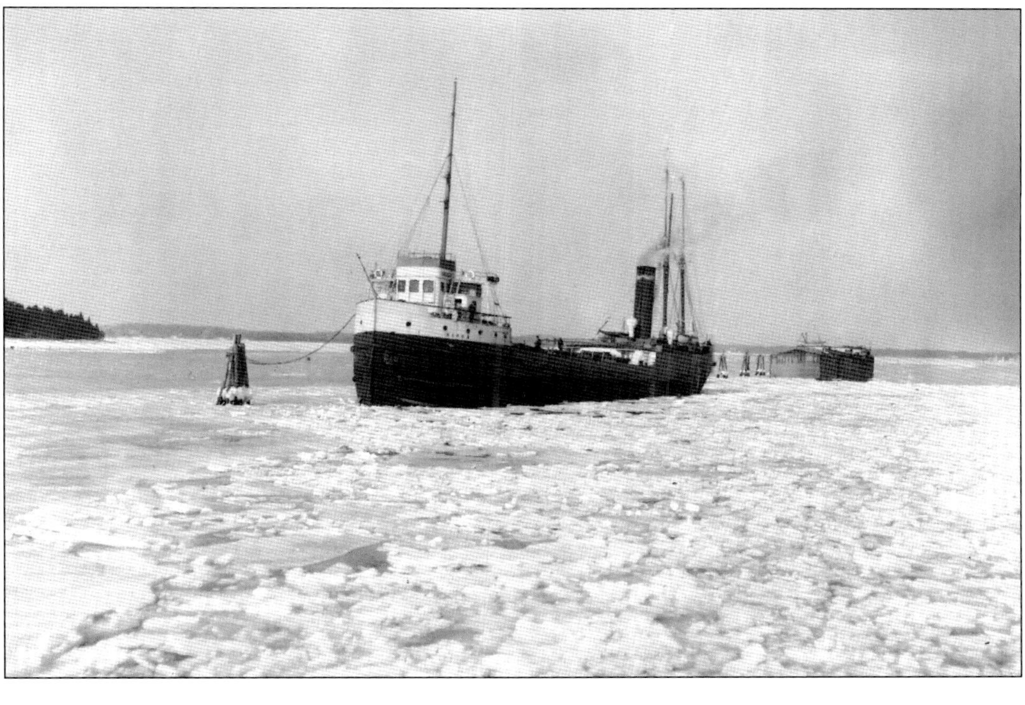

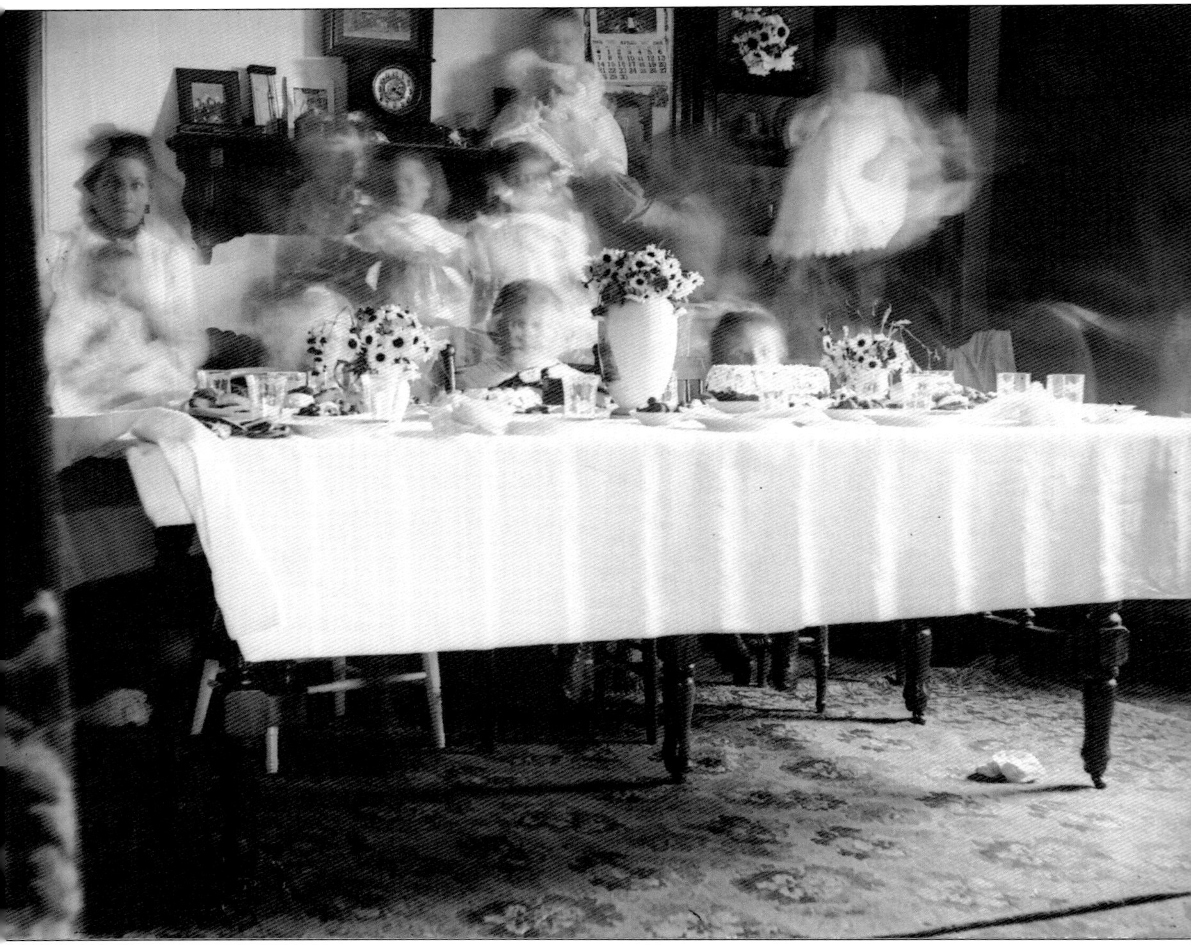

Oops! This group of women and children cannot sit still long enough for the photographer to record anything but the table decorations at this tea party around 1912. Getting children to sit for the long exposures necessary for photographers in the past to record their faces was a monumental and sometimes unsuccessful task.

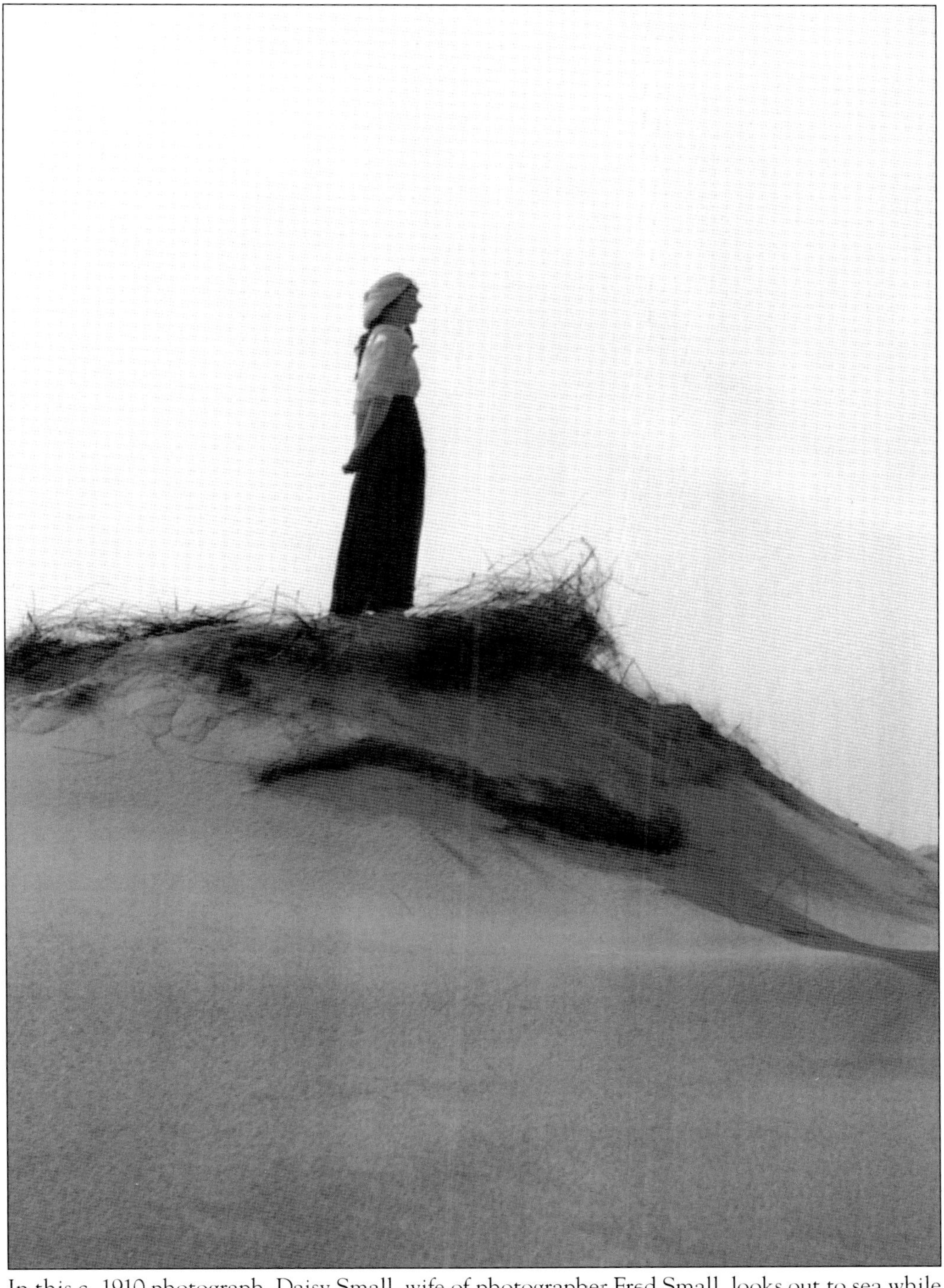

In this c. 1910 photograph, Daisy Small, wife of photographer Fred Small, looks out to sea while dressed in the style of the times. The wistful photograph evokes the spirit of the people who live here and the spirit of visitors as well.